MEDITATIONS FOR WOMEN

Meditations for Women

By

 EDITH LOVEJOY PIERCE
HELEN C. WHITE
RUTH SWANBERG ROHLFS
ROSE TERLIN
MAUDE ROYDEN SHAW
BLANCHE H. DOW

ELIZABETH WRAY TAYLOR
SUE BAILEY THURMAN
JEAN BEAVEN ABERNETHY
JOSEPHINE W. JOHNSON
BONARO W. OVERSTREET
LOUISE DUDLEY

Edited by

JEAN BEAVEN ABERNETHY

With an Introduction by

DOROTHY CANFIELD FISHER

ABINGDON PRESS
New York • Nashville

MEDITATIONS FOR WOMEN

Copyright MCMXLVII by Stone & Pierce

Library of Congress Catalog Card Number: 48-286

PRINTED AND BOUND AT NASHVILLE,
TENNESSEE, UNITED STATES OF AMERICA

INTRODUCTION

Dorothy Canfield Fisher

If ever anybody needed to look up from the magnified importance of details and glance at the horizons of life, mid-twentieth-century American women need to. We are survivors of two vast wars, which have left our hemisphere unscratched while tearing lives, homes, and families to pieces by many millions in Europe and Asia. So far away from this mass of pain and hardship are we that we can scarcely realize any more than a child could, for a fleeting troubled minute, that it exists. But the closer framework, the nationally general one that surrounds us, we know intimately and well. Its most noticeable characteristic is that wherever we are—in home, office, factory, schoolroom; in library, laboratory, kitchen, or salesroom—we are surrounded by machinery for speeding faster our everyday activities.

Take the homemaker. Alone in the house or apartment much of the time, yet with hardly a daytime hour free for uninterrupted thought, she finds her life at once, you might say, lonely and cluttered. Most of the vital physical activities of the great undertaking for which she has, time out of mind, been responsible—carrying on the home and bringing up children—have been taken out of her hands and put in those of professional specialists. If husband, child, or elderly relative falls ill, his care is taken from her at once, and given to nurse, doctor, and hospital. Everybody knows that they can do for the sick far better than she can. To her, the amateur, are left the trifling ailments, the colds and digestive upsets. "Book-learning" used to be acquired by children "at their mother's knee"— a phrase that sounds like the spinning wheel and the old oaken bucket! With such primary teaching, nowadays, no child could hold his own for an hour in a twentieth-century school. Great deep-freeze plants and canneries, alongside vast truck gardens and orchards, supply preserved foods superior in vitamin values to most home-canned ones. They diminish the mother's once-inspiring need to garden and to cook.

All these processes of scooping the old home responsibilities out of the home have not yet given the home-maker much consecutive free time. She still must, to a large extent, be on hand to perform those small but responsible fragments left her out of what used to be the greatest functions of mother and wife. In spite of a constant flow of new machines for saving her time and labor, her outside activities, personal and public—which are often numerous—must still be carried on with odds and ends of time, punctuated by interruptions.

Probably we shall emerge from this particular period— which, like all periods of history, is transitional—with more sensible, imaginative, flexible arrangements for utilizing part-time work. Society will call into play the potential activities of people now excluded from modern usefulness because they are too old, too young, too infirm, or with too many personal cares, to fit into our outmoded nine-

6

teenth-century fetish, "Eight hours a day or nothing!"

But children can't wait for another period! They keep on growing up, a day's worth every day. And as a grandmother, past the responsibilities for growing children, I am lost in admiration for the splendid younger American homemakers, sturdily and devotedly filling in the gaps, flinging heart, mind, and soul into the nerve-racking many-sidedness they are responsible for, and still trying to keep their hearts, minds, and souls alive and growing.

They need to reflect. The disconnected snippets of time and authority left them are like small change—plenty in numbers, but much less in value than one big bill. They need to catch, through the constant blinding flicker of small details, some glimpse of the steady glory of the undertaking to which they are dedicated.

So do those multitudes of women, married and unmarried, whose home life is only a precious margin around their daily work—a loved interlude, left early in the morning and returned to late in the afternoon.

One great group of these are teachers, nurses, and social workers, who sometimes find in their work the deep delight and responsibility of creative contacts with youth. I think teachers, after mothers themselves, come closest to children, have happiest relations with them, and find their memories most enriched, far into old age, by friendships, often lifelong, with their former pupils. To give out so much cheer and creativeness these women need to replenish their sources of inspiration. It is no news to them that they need to think and meditate! They will be among the most appreciative readers of such books as this.

How about women who work in industrial plants?

Or who concentrate their powers, along with fellow specialists, in research? How about restaurant workers? saleswomen? labor union organizers? household helpers, on whole or part time? hostesses and secretaries? and a hundred other callings? Most of these have chances not a few to develop loyalties, comradeships, social concern. Among workers organized in labor's fellowships, the sense of solidarity is deeply cultivated. Many women feel, from the inherent motherhood in their natures, strong concerns for individual fellow workers; they provide one another, many a time, with little helps and ready sympathy; some have the delicacy to counsel acceptably the headstrong and and irritable, and to soothe the asperities that rise between the hotheads from time to time. They too, in their everyday contacts, feel the vast importance of the human touch. Some of them develop great personal influence for good.

This bloom, which appears occasionally in so many women's lives, can be fertilized—sometimes by the quickening presence and spoken words of others; sometimes by music; best of all, most universally, I think, by books.

Sisters under our skins as we are, we all need to reflect, and to catch some glimpse of the potential steady glory of life itself. We need to meditate, for meditation brings that calm continuity of spiritual and mental effort without which few can have the heart-satisfying sense of understanding.

In George Eliot's novel The Mill on the Floss a parcel of shabby little secondhand books is given to the heroine by an ignorant peddler. One of them, The Imitation of

Christ by Thomas à Kempis, has been marked here and there by an unknown reader. She reads what "the quiet hand points to," and by this anonymous finger are opened to her the floodgates of understanding of her life and its boundless worth.

To reflect and meditate we need help in the form of reminders of the wholeness of which we, and our families, are parts. Such a reminder and such a help is this book, written sensitively and beautifully by twelve different women, who themselves meditate, and whose hope it is that there are other women who, in the reading of this book, may care to take time each day to do so too.

There have been, in the past few years, many attempts to word the whole realm of daily meditation and prayer in modern terms. The ever-increasing number of pamphlets, booklets, and books designed to this end testifies to the need people feel for this type of help. There is, of course, the vast treasure house of the classics: Augustine, Thomas à Kempis, John Woolman, to mention only a few. But many of us like the insights of these great devotional writers, as well as of the Bible itself, illuminated by some contemporary thinking. This book is such an attempt. Here are meditations written by today's women—women in the midst of today's routine and work—housework, children, jobs. Here is what they think and pray about when they take "time out" every day.

Most modern devotional material has been written by men professionally trained in the church, and it has tended to follow one set pattern—namely, a Bible verse, an exposition or illustration of that verse, and a closing prayer. This book, it will be immediately apparent, does not follow any such set pattern—perhaps because it is a book written by women for women, and women do not think sermonically. At any rate, we have felt there is room for some new departures in the field of personal meditation. The very qualities which have brought women, in the last few years, into their own in the field of fiction—a willingness to experiment with traditionally accepted forms, a breadth and warmth of human detail, and the authentic touch of autobiography—these characteristics are to be found in this book as well.

But this book is not fiction. It is a record of the personal thinking and the spiritual pilgrimage of twelve women who feel there are God-given resources available to make each day a richer experience, and who themselves are trying to tap them. When you open this book, it is something like your inviting these women to come into your home, sitting down informally to share with them some of their thinking. You will have, you'll discover as you read, a wide range of guests. Some of the women are younger, some older; they come from all parts of our country, one from England, and from any number of backgrounds. And as in any good conversation, so in this book —the insights will be varied, unpredictable, original. Each month, written by a different woman, is a new experience, a new way of putting things, a new personality to become acquainted with through whose eyes one looks at the general theme of living.

But with all our different ways of saying it, we have the important things in common—all twelve of us are sensitive to the same values, seek the same Source for the meaning of life, feel strongly the need for daily meditation, and write not so much in terms of achievement as of attempt. In our best moments—in our own periods of meditation—here is what we see life, and our part in it, to be. Here is what we believe God intended for us, as we try to master the disciplines necessary for measuring up to it.

12

With the hope that the stimulus of daily meditation, and the interplay of your thinking with ours, will serve to make the everyday more meaningful we invite you to read this book.

JEAN BEAVEN ABERNETHY

CONTENTS

15

CONTENTS

On Opening Things

EDITH LOVEJOY PIERCE

1   **SNOW-BLIND**

We will open the book. Its pages are blank. We are going to put words on them ourselves. The book is called *Opportunity*, and its first chapter is New Year's Day.

Yes, let us write that kind letter we have hesitated over so long, greet that wayfarer we pass by in the street, invite that stranger in to dinner. "Thereby some have entertained angels unawares."

Let us open the door. See, outside snow has fallen, altering the landscape, obliterating the known ways. Let us go out and walk in the snow, making our own path. There is no longer any boundary between our garden and our neighbor's garden, no exact geographical line where we could raise a fence if we wanted to. Under the white benediction all distinctions are erased—of creed, of color, of class.

"Prepare ye the way of the Lord, make straight in the desert a highway for our God. Every valley shall be exalted, and every mountain and hill shall be made low: and the

17

crooked shall be made straight, and the rough places plain: and the glory of the Lord shall be revealed."

Over our world snow has fallen, silent and soft. Let us go out and walk in the snow.

2   ART, LIKE SUNLIGHT

There are two attitudes the lover of beauty can take. Let us call them the "open" and the "shut." The "open" admirer wants to share the treasure, wants to have others admire it too. He rejoices in it for itself alone, not because the beautiful object happens to be his.

The "shut" admirer, on the other hand, wants only to hoard. While others must admire, it is not the treasure they are supposed to be impressed with, but his ownership. He has the private-collector mind, not the public-museum mind.

If sharing a picture or a landscape reduced its charm, this attitude would be understandable. One could sympathize; one might even approve. But works of art acquire even more meaning when they have been loved by multitudes and have served as inspiration for many. So the hoarder has no excuse for his selfishness. He is even a thief if he seeks to deprive others of their common inheritance. Art, like sunlight, is the birthright of all men.

3   NOT GIVEN, BUT LENT

This open and shut mentality has other, more subtle manifestations. There is the man who loves dogs, and the man who loves wild birds. The dog lover looks for a response from his pet. The dog must come when he calls, follow, obey, show affection to him. If it shows affection to him alone he is prouder still of his "one-man" dog.

But the bird lover looks for no recognition or response from the objects of his interest. The birds may call, but they don't call him. They may sing, but they don't sing to him. He isn't personally offended if he steps too near the tree and they fly away.

The dog lover magnifies himself through the dog. The bird lover loses himself in the birds.

And how many of us mothers are like this with our children? How hard it is to avoid "shut" feelings when thinking of them! It requires perhaps more than is humanly possible for a parent to see in a son or a daughter *that* individual, *that* child of God, instead of *my* John or *my* Mary, whose prowess at school or on the athletic field or in the ballroom reflects due credit on *me*.

4   THIS LITTLE BREAK

Grace before meals may not mean very much at times. It's not as though the food on the table were being handed to us on a silver platter. We've worked to earn it, perhaps; we've stood in a grocery store to buy it; we've labored over the kitchen stove to cook it.

Still, it is good to relax and get one's balance again before swallowing food, after the whirl and bustle of serving and getting the family all collected around the table. One's dignity is restored, and one's composure. This little break divides the charming hostess from the harried servant.

And it is good to be quiet for a few moments before eating, as we remember that there are many in the world who couldn't obtain this much food at any price, or at the cost of any amount of effort. It is good to offer a brief prayer for them.

5   ON WORK AND REST

It seems as though more of the world's work is accomplished through relaxation than through effort. I always do better if I rest *before* a piece of work instead of after it. The day the kitchen floor has to be scrubbed I take a deep and restful nap, awake refreshed, pull on my oldest dress and shoes, and slop around over the linoleum with a will.

The stiff and false idea that one should not leave dishes in the sink or beds unmade until the middle of the day, that it's demoralizing to go back to sleep for an hour after one's husband has left for work and the children for school—all this fails to impress me.

There was some awfully poor housekeeping in the gospel story. Mary of Bethany neglected the dishes to sit at the feet of the Master. The woman of Samaria, who had come to draw water in the heat of the day, ran off without her pitcher. The housewife who found the lost coin, and invited her neighbors in to rejoice with her, probably spent more on refreshments than the coin was worth!

We should occasionally give place to an extra Sunday in the midst of the week, without too much fear of losing time from our work.

20

6   THE ONE THING NEEDFUL

Everywhere in the Gospel is this almost studied carelessness, as though Jesus were trying to break people away from convention and jolt them out of a rut. "Take no thought for your life, what ye shall eat, or what ye shall drink. . . . Behold the fowls of the air. . . . Consider the lilies of the field." Not that we should altogether neglect the business of living and cast our helpless selves as an unwanted burden on others, but simply that the kingdom of God should come first in our scale of values. Sweeping, cooking, and marketing are important, but it is more important to leave the kettle on the stove and run out into the street, waving palm branches and shouting hosanna, if the King of heaven should happen to be passing our way.

Yet the thinking of Jesus transcends rather than ignores the mechanics of daily living. How observant he was in small matters! How clear was his judgment in household affairs, as well as in affairs of the soul. We may profit by his most casual illustrations.

Is this dress too worn to patch? "No man . . . seweth a piece of new cloth on an old garment." Should I wash out these clothes, late at night as it is? "Is not . . . the body [more] than raiment?" My rest is more important.

No, we do not discover disorder in following him, but a better order. Nothing could be worse than turning one's house into a well-kept tomb, and one's living body into an untimely corpse.

21

7   CONCERNING WORRY

In the eyes of Jesus worry takes on almost the status of a sin. We are definitely forbidden to worry. How hard it is to comply!

But if we must worry, the great art is to entertain only one worry at a time. The worry next in line, not the one that properly belongs to tomorrow, or maybe next week. One trouble at a time can usually be borne; it's the whole tangled confusion of troubles that is so overwhelming.

Take this matter of crossing bridges before we come to them. It's not so much crossing them in advance—it's crossing twenty at a time, that's so nerve-racking. Then there are occasions when the magnificent bridges we march over do not span raging rivers at all. Halfway along we look down and find our bridge built upon perfectly dry land that we might just as well be crossing on the ground.

Every time I go for a routine check-up at the doctor's I prepare mentally for the discovery of some dread and hidden disease. I face all the possibilities. In imagination I take leave of my near and dear and set my affairs in order. But it's always the same story. "Heart—normal. Lungs—normal. Blood pressure—normal. Good-by. See you next year." Suddenly everything falls delightfully flat.

8   THAT BOMB AGAIN

"I'm tired of the atomic bomb," whispered the plump lady sitting next to me at the meeting. I too am tired of the bomb. Sometimes I feel I would almost rather be destroyed by it than hear it mentioned once more by some earnest speaker on the lecture platform.

Granted we shouldn't plunge our ostrich heads into the sand. Granted we should be forever ashamed—so I believe, at least—of the role our country played with this engine of torture and destruction. But there is a certain glibness about much of our talk concerning the bomb; there is almost an immoral element in the way we lean on it. It has become the new hell fire and damnation of the twentieth century.

Must the world unite? Must we live like brothers? Yes! Not because brotherhood is intrinsically good, but because, if we don't co-operate, the bomb will get us. True, it will get us if we don't learn brotherly love, but our emphasis should be on the right-doing rather than on the punishment for failure. "Whatsoever things are true, . . . whatsoever things are lovely, . . . think on these things."

9   THE JEW ON OUR STREET

"They're tight and they're crooked; they'll skin you out of everything you own." Vainly one tries to argue back. The Jews are no more crooked than anybody else. There are just as many crooked Gentiles. Unconvinced, they retort that they would never do business with Jews.

The furrier who stored my winter coat proved so un satisfactory that I took it to the little Jewish firm on Central Street. The atmosphere inside this store was different—quiet, polite, efficient. One of the clerks, obviously the son of the house, had such a gentle, noble bearing that it was not hard to imagine in him something of the Hebrew prophets of old. I stored my coat there twice, and had it repaired very competently.

But the young man never reappeared. It was only by accident that I learned what had happened while I was out of town for the summer. He had gone boating on the lake with some friends. The boat had capsized, and he had lost his life saving a woman from drowning. "Greater love hath no man than this . . ."

Next time they start talking about the "business Jew" I must tell them the story of the young tailor on Central Street.

10   THE TALLEST SPIRE

I sat on the lawn in front of Salisbury Cathedral one sunny afternoon when I was last in England. I just sat there staring at the satisfying beauty before me—the broad, flat, green approaches leading to the yellow-gray stone monument with the tallest spire in the country. How could the thirteenth century, without machinery, without power, without our modern science, produce this great work?

Then it suddenly seemed to me that we are going backward in time. It is the twentieth century that is unable to create masterpieces! We have all the tools but we lack the inspiration. Our skyscrapers are high without giving the impression of elevation. Our railroad stations are big but give no feeling of vastness. Perhaps it is because we are all huddled together without any space around our beauty. We lack the appropriate frame for the picture. But this is not the whole answer. The miracle was not the construction itself but the thought behind the work.

Is our generation unable to think cathedrals and imagine spires? Is man less human than he used to be? More machinelike, and less human?

11   HEART AND TREASURE

Salisbury Cathedral is not the product of any one nation. We cannot say: "Here is the flowering of the English genius." It was built before the days of the nation-state, and similar great structures are scattered all over Europe: Cologne, Rouen, Milan.

It was not this or that country; it was Christendom that built the cathedrals! It was the "one world" of the Middle Ages. What does our fragmented modern world build? Camouflaged airplane factories, floating docks for invasions. Yes, I saw these also on my postwar visit to England. Everywhere in the cathedrals were little boxes begging shillings for the upkeep of the treasures of the past, while pounds were being spent on the implements of modern warfare.

The question arises: Can we ever really have one world until we start building cathedrals together? Houses of God set within spacious parks and made the focal points of our cities, instead of bomber factories hidden away in the fields by camouflage paint. "Everyone that doeth evil hateth the light."

12   NOT MADE WITH HANDS

But you and I build neither cathedrals nor guns, at least not directly. We do contribute to their building through the influence of our thoughts, words, and votes, and the use we make of our money. We all tend toward either guns or cathedrals. Without our collective will neither could be produced. Still, we often feel as though the big showy structures were not of our making. Others wrest them out of our hands, for good or for ill. What private churches of our own can we build?

The woman of Samaria went out into the desert to draw water. When she came to the well, she found the Master sitting upon it. Here was the opportunity to settle an old quarrel between the Jews and the Samaritans. Which was the real holy place: the historic mountain or the temple in Jerusalem? And Jesus showed her that it was neither the one nor the other. That well in the desert was the genuine temple. The one sitting upon it gave the water of life. It is a temple not made with hands that we should be seeking. Such temples we ourselves can build.

13   ON GROWING OLD

Where does the dividing line fall between growing up and growing old? It is a very movable boundary, which has nothing to do with the calendar. We all know that. Some people start to grow old on leaving college. Others, in their seventies, have not yet embarked on the fatal descent.

The summer when I returned to my native England,

after an absence of twelve years, I found my parents more unchanged than the intervening war led me to fear. The only change was a change of perspective. Photographs of my brother, killed in action, were all over the house. In the family circle there was constant reference to our childhood. We visited the village where I was brought up, the beach where I played as a child during World War I. I was taken to see my grandmother's grave. My parents were always looking backward. They had grown old. That boundary line is nothing more or less than a shift in one's mental direction.

Some of us younger people grow old prematurely when we hark back to the babyhood of our children, remembering nostalgically how cute they were at the age of two or three. We must be content to let their infancy go, realizing that growth is a constant death and resurrection.

14   ON GROWING UP

When I first came to the United States as a bride, leaving all my past behind me, I felt like a flower head cut off from its stem. My husband could reminisce about the old days with his mother and sister, while nobody could tell a single story about my own infantile sayings and doings. If I'd had sufficient ingenuity, I could have provided myself with a really glorious past. As it was, I used to think about it all in silence.

But after that visit to England, when the old familiar places looked a bit dull and tarnished in comparison with the shiny New World, I was content to drop my past once and for all, erase it from the blackboard like a lesson well learned, and get on to the next piece of business in this matter of growing up.

When mature men and women, at what should be the height of their powers, look back on their childhood or college years as the happiest days of their life, we know they have grown old. Life should become ever more significant and satisfying—not one flaming burst of scintillating fun, then ashes of drudgery, a long-drawn-out anticlimax.

But the committed Christian never really grows old. How can he? The kingdom is always ahead. All the looking back to the time when our Lord was on the earth does not age us, for somehow that time is with us still. If Jesus ever left us, he has returned, as the constantly recurring cycle of the Christian year reminds us. Christmas is not as dated as yesterday's newspaper. Easter will be fresh and young when all the politics, pacts, and wars of our time are forgotten.

15   THIS NATION, UNDER GOD

People wrung shocked hands over the behavior of American soldiers in occupied countries. "Why, oh why?" they asked. What has failed—home, school, church, or the army itself? The answer was not far to seek: The average American has no respect for authority. Authority! Sounds old-fashioned, doesn't it? And didn't all the woes of Nazi Germany stem from too much respect for authority? Yes, but there is more than one kind of authority—there is human and there is divine.

We Americans are so carried away with being equal that

28

we forget our inalienable rights are a gift of our Creator! Democracy does not, or should not, mean that our own little ego is the final court of appeals. The founding fathers feared God and built a nation. The Nazi yes men feared the gauleiter and built a tyranny. But we who fear neither God nor a gauleiter succeed only in being irresponsible adolescents bent on perpetual Halloween pranks.

Remember: "This nation, under God . . ."

16   ON SELF-DISCIPLINE

Perhaps we parents fail to provide the spiritual roughage that our children's systems require. True, all too many children are intimately connected with misery, and neglect is by no means confined to poverty-stricken homes. No child should be neglected, abused, or subjected to avoidable trouble. But neither is it necessary to upholster our children's lives to quite the extent that we do. A greater self-discipline in regard to sodas and candy, gum and cigarettes, might result in greater self-control in the matter of loot on foreign soil. More promptness in meeting school requirements, fewer dances and movies, services around the home cheerfully performed, appropriate punishments when needed—such little things, but perhaps enough to tip the scales between an army of boors and an army of gentlemen.

Of course it goes without saying that parents should discipline themselves to the same extent. We can hardly frown on sodas and candy for the young if we ourselves munch, chew, suck, and puff on various commercial offerings day and night. Time spent on the daily paper should also be rationed for young and old alike. One half hour of such mediocrity is all the human brain can stand without turning to jelly. As for the comics, words fail me. It's not the extent of our national literacy that should concern us, but what we read, once we've learned how.

17   WOE BECAUSE OF OFFENSES!

I think we forget that children take on the protective coloring, not of their homes alone, but of society in general. In a law-abiding world less parental discipline would be required. But you can't have hate-filled newspapers, crime-soaked movies, and corrupting advertising without a tremendous counteraction within home and church, if you are going to avoid juvenile delinquency.

Cutthroat trade practices, international juggling for oil in the Near East, stolen automobiles on Main Street, immigration quotas based on race, name-calling and fist fights in the back alley, Hiroshima, Nagasaki, shootings in the local tavern—it's all part of the warp and woof of society. Reform should start in the government and end in the slum.

18   WHO IS MY NEIGHBOR?

Our modern American children should know about, and learn to feel imaginatively, the sorrow and misery in other parts of the world. That other, less fortunate, children are hungry, homeless, lost, should be brought home to those able to bear it. How are we fitting them for the world if they don't know what goes on in the world? Then let their pity immediately be directed into constructive channels of help.

Again, we should take pains to show our children that if crime and tyranny exist, they are only one side of the picture. For every act of cruelty there is a corresponding act of kindness; for every act of cowardice, an act of courage. Heroism, unselfishness, and mutual aid in trouble are all part of an otherwise desperate scene, and a very important part. Modern history is full of saints and martyrs, inside the church and out. Especially inside, perhaps. The Niemöllers, the Berggravs, the Verniers should not be strangers to our young people. Gandhi and Kagawa should be as well known to them as Hitler and Goering. They should realize that there is a side of the angels to be on. We might be surprised at how readily they would align themselves on that side.

19   FIRST FLIGHT

As we flew over the Newfoundland wilderness, the setting sun stepped on pool after pool, touching each one with gold, then leaving it in shadow. No roads, no houses— this was indeed a lost world on the edge of the north. We landed at an outpost, then took off again for the transatlantic flight. Night had fallen. The single street down below looked like a disjointed gold snake. Fires were burning on the coast. We must have been over the water already, but nothing could be seen—only veils of dark haze and a great red moon balancing like a balloon at our wing tip.

When I awoke, I looked out at the white dawn and

thought the ocean must be rough. But those indentations on the horizon were not water at all; they were clouds. The sun rose, and we were in a clean, clear no man's land. Below us might have been polar regions—snowy fields, hills, cliffs, icebergs of white cloud, only lacking the blue shadows of snow and ice. Instead, the landscape was white with light gray shadows, high-lighted by pale gold or pink where the sun caressed it. Clouds floated beneath us. Some were bare wisps, a mere breath through which one could catch sight of the surface of the ocean with its tiny whitecaps that budded and bloomed and withered.

This was a high, exalted region. One felt happy up here. There were no problems up here. Escapism? Why the slur on the word? Is escape into beauty a crime?

20   OVER THE ATLANTIC

"Weren't you afraid?" asked everybody. Calmly and dispassionately I considered the matter. Was I afraid? No, I don't think so. It was very beautiful, and one felt reckless. Since we were so far removed from the earth, it didn't seem likely that we would come into sudden and violent contact with it. There is much less friction in a plane than in a train, even if you rock about a bit. Nothing but air is offering resistance. Neither do you yourself resist. There are times when you're not quite sure where the world is, but it really doesn't matter very much. You have your own private stamping ground. You are lighthearted and happy; you have no problems.

In a few hours it will all be over. In a few hours you will land and be confronted with problems once again—

people to deal with, difficulties to solve. You don't have to fly the plane; there are absolutely no problems for you in the sky. Provided you stay where you are, there is no danger. All the danger emanates from the earth. All the rocket bombs and horrible things that seem to come out of the sky really come out of the earth.

21   HAPPY LANDING

To the east a hazy coast line, surf on rock, then green, green fields. Ireland! The Old World. A different continent, a different hemisphere from the one you were in nine hours ago. Tiny stone farmhouses and fences, tiny roads with toy horses and carts creeping slowly along them. Miniature painted wooden cows lying in fields. Pinpoint chickens. Gray capes and inlets, amorphous pieces of geography, then the faint outlines of the airfield, and slowly you start to spiral down. Nearer, clearer, more and more earthbound, till a rabbit startles at your approach, a skylark takes wing, the wind from your propellers swishes the grasses. A sudden little bump and you're running on land. The interlude is over; you have flown the Atlantic.

"How did you dare?" ask some timid souls. "Weren't you taking a chance?" Well, what do they mean? How can one live in absolute and utter security? If one is afraid of a dull humdrum existence, nothing could be more dangerous than avoiding adventure. Life is not kind to the cautious.

The trouble with security is that it's not merely an illusion, a harmless pretty bubble it does our hearts good to blow. Security, as it is generally thought of, is a desperately dangerous fallacy. In the name of security we pile up armaments and make our world ever more insecure. Each nation is bent on committing suicide while trying to prolong its days.

There is nothing safe any more but the long chance, nothing secure but the gamble on faith. Take a chance? There's nothing else left to take. "Whosoever will save his life shall lose it."

22   THE MAILBOX

The mailbox by the front door. What a fascinating object it can be! This gaping little case of wood or metal, so forlorn when it is empty. But what a large part of life passes into it and out again! Words of love or sorrow, words of comfort or elation. All the comings and goings of friends, and the thoughts of friends who never come and go because they are in the far corners of the earth. Perhaps one has never seen their faces, but the mailbox has brought their spirits near.

How a day can be changed by the brief buzz of the mailman's bell! An unexpected announcement of joy or, conversely, everything else but the letter one was hoping for. Bills, magazines, circulars, appeals—one would gladly toss all this imposing bulk of worthless paper into the wastebasket. All one asked for was one little letter, just a few lines if need be. Why, why doesn't he or she write?

Has it ever occurred to us that perhaps somebody is asking the same question about us? Running hopefully to the mailbox, feeling into its dark empty depths and turning away disappointed, thinking, "There is another delivery this afternoon. Perhaps then . . ." If we realized this, we would all seize our pens and do our duty by our near and dear. Or more likely our far and dear, for how often our dearest ones are far away.

23 ON MAKING POEMS AND OTHER THINGS

Often people ask: "How do you write a poem? Do you sit down at your desk for two hours every morning, or does inspiration just come?"

It's hard to describe what happens. When you construct a machine or sew a dress, you have to know exactly what you are doing at every turn. Each operation produces a certain result which contributes to the success of the whole. But in writing a poem, somehow, the less you know about how it originates the better. You can't sit down at your desk and make it come. Conceivably you might get words set down metrically. And the result? A perfectly constructed failure.

No, the only way to write a poem is to get very stirred up over something. Then words start to come, like steam through a safety valve. Perhaps only a line or two, and immediately one may get frightened: "This is too hard for me; I can't finish it!" Then it is necessary to pray to God for help. After this one may relax, calm one's fear of failure, and allow oneself to believe: "This poem is really important. I must write it. I can, with God's help." Nothing is so utterly devastating as any modest feeling, such as: "Why try? Shakespeare did better than this!"

I suppose there isn't a worker alive who could move a finger if he let himself think: "This is just a silly old

machine. The world would be a lot better off if the
technological era had never dawned." And what woman
could bring a child into the world if she let herself think:
"This is just one more nondescript member of the human
race, and not the most wonderful baby ever born"?

24   EXCEPT THE LORD BUILD THE HOUSE

In nothing is one less the master of one's fate than in
this matter of writing. It sounds grand to say that God
helps one write poetry. "Thus saith the Lord." Shades of
the prophets! But the counterpart of this is also true and
to be reckoned with. If God *doesn't* help, one can't write.
And sometimes he doesn't, and one can't.

Editors may clamor, but to no avail. Perhaps one has
acquired a sympathetic public; magazines would publish
this or that. A few lines here or there, on some subject of
current interest, would be very effective and have good
publicity value. One must keep before the public eye; the
public is fickle and forgets. Anything published now would
give a boost to the new book which is soon due to appear.
But the heavens are shut. God remains silent. The brilliant
opportunity passes by unfulfilled. Not a word can one
write!

Of course it is possible that one's time has not been
altogether wasted. It is just possible that one has been
taught a much needed lesson in humility. The world has
not been saved by a sonnet, but that minute portion of the
world which consists of one's own soul has been cleansed
and made more receptive to the coming of the kingdom.

25   JOURNEY INTO A FAR COUNTRY

To watch one's children make mistakes and get punished
for their weakness is heartbreaking. Why can't they understand plain English words? How often with family or
friends, or even with government officials, does one long to
"knock a little sense into their heads." But sense, apparently, will not be knocked into anyone's head.

The church told the State Department that the Morgenthau Plan to punish Germany wouldn't work. Did the
State Department believe the church? No. What did the
church know about such things? So the Morgenthau Plan
stood, and brought chaos, inefficiency, defeat of end in
view. Ignominiously the government had to change its
mind, but not until after vast damage had been done.

Why can't human beings be rational? Why do they
have to be warped by prejudice, vanity, hate, greed, even
to their own detriment? It may be necessary to burn one's
fingers before discovering that fire is hot. But why do we
have to burn them twice and three times before we stop
poking them into the fire?

"I know why," hisses a voice that sounds very like the
serpent in the Garden of Eden. "I know why."

Surely God feels about us the way we feel about our
own children when we see them go astray. And the meaning
of the Cross becomes plainer to us when, from personal
experience, we grasp some faint measure of the Father's
sorrowing love.

26   STAGE AND PULPIT

I heard Martin Niemöller preach at the Chicago Civic
Opera. The hall had to be large enough to hold the crowds.
But whoever was in charge of arrangements had in mind
stage drama rather than the drama of real life. There was
a backdrop of the vaulted arches and stained-glass windows
of a cathedral; there were floodlights which fell on the
stage, while the auditorium was darkened. But as soon as
the great German churchman, "Hitler's personal prisoner,"
was on his feet, he asked to have the floodlights turned off
and the house lighted up. "I want to see your faces," he
said to his audience.

This request seemed to me to symbolize the difference
between the stage and the pulpit. The actor on the stage
wants to be seen. He doesn't care about seeing anybody
else. He speaks his piece into a darkened hall, and the
reaction he gets is a mass reaction coming from no one in
particular. But the preacher in the pulpit is used to watching his hearers, noting the expressions on their faces,
feeling in friendly contact with them. He and they are all
alike children of God, servants of the Most High. The
actor all too often is a little god in himself, handing down
his art to the groveling masses beneath him.

Where art is a servant of God it is greater than where it
is a master in its own right.

27   A DIFFERENT KIND OF ACTOR

After hearing Niemöller preach at the opera house, I
thought to myself, "Nothing so grandly dramatic has ever

taken place on this stage before." All the tawdry props mistakenly designed to enhance the effect were thrown down like so many defeated flags.

These boards had been trodden by glamorous tenors and sopranos in gorgeous costumes and seductive make-up. Their glowing voices had thrilled their audiences, but once the enjoyable evening was over it was definitely past. One did not go on remembering, as one did after hearing Martin Niemöller, the ex-prisoner of Dachau.

For here was a different kind of actor on a different kind of stage. This was a world stage; this heartfelt voice had been heard around the globe, in protest against tyranny and paganism; this unspectacular little man, in a plain suit with no trappings, was in reality an important actor in a great historical drama. A great cosmic drama, even—the war of the unbound word of God against the satanic powers.

There is a time in one's youth when nothing seems so important as fiction, but as one grows older, nothing seems nearly so exciting as real life.

28   THE CLOUD OF WITNESSES

We thought of Europe as being dead and decaying. Out of pity and kindness of heart we despatched food and clothing to the destitute of that war-ravaged continent. And so we should have done. But there was something we either forgot or didn't know. Europe had a spiritual gift to offer us! Yes, out of this caldron of hatreds and wars something very precious was distilled. God makes the wrath of man to praise him.

I think of Martin Niemöller and his depth of Christian faith. I think of Roland de Pury, a Swiss pastor in France when the Nazis imprisoned him. His *Journal from My Cell* is a pilgrim's progress into great spiritual glory. I think of Philippe Vernier in his parish in the mining region of Belgium. This modern Francis of Assisi, who has known months of imprisonment and solitary confinement for his stand as a pacifist, shares the living conditions of his poorest parishioners, whom he serves night and day in the joy of the Lord.

Nor are these men alone. Men and women everywhere have stood out against corruption. Well might we envy them the intensity of their faith, the clarity of their joy, and their utter trust in the Lord.

We have never been in a situation where, stripped of everything, we had to trust or go under. We may wish never to be in such a situation. But until we are, we will never know at first hand all that these others know about the great trustworthiness of God.

29   EUROPEAN INCIDENT

I once gave a dime to a beggar. I remember it still. It was a scorching hot July day in Vienna. The city was not yet back on its feet after the war. The fountain in the square was empty, dry, and dusty; dirty papers had been tossed into it by passers-by. Inflation was rife; beggars were everywhere.

I went with my mother and sister to a delicatessen to buy something for supper. This small, dark shop also did duty as a makeshift soda fountain. On a table against the wall someone had left half a dish of melted ice cream. My mother and sister were at the counter, but I sat by myself, resting. An old woman tottered in. She had bright eyes like a hawk scouring the countryside for prey. Seeing the leftover ice cream, she rushed at it and drank it without a word.

Suddenly I felt very uncomfortable. I opened my purse. In it were two thousand kronen, perhaps the equivalent of a dime, perhaps of a quarter—I forget. When one gave hundred-kronen bills to beggars, they dropped them with Olympian scorn; but still it would be considered scandalous to hand out two thousand kronen, just like that. (Perhaps a dime, perhaps a quarter!) I gave it to the woman surreptitiously, in silence. Surprise, then gratitude overwhelmed her; she seized my hand and kissed it—the softest, tenderest kiss I have ever known. Not a word passed between us. Nobody saw.

This was after World War I. She was an old woman then and must be dead by now. But her grandchildren—what about them?

30   THIRTY PIECES OF SILVER

I attended a conference in Chicago on "The Unsegregated Church." Yes, believe it or not, two thousand years after Christianity came into the world it still seems necessary to hold such a conference!

St. Paul, what did you have to say on this subject? "Ye are all the children of God by faith in Christ Jesus. . . . There is neither Jew nor Greek, there is neither bond nor free, there is neither male nor female: for ye are all one in

Christ Jesus." Have we forgotten, or didn't we hear you? Say it again, St. Paul.

As a matter of fact those who truly are "in Christ" are always one in him who breaks down barriers of race and caste. The cleavage is not between brothers in Christ, not really. One felt the unity among those present at this inter-racial gathering. There is a cleavage, however, but the split is in another direction.

I walked out onto Michigan Avenue. I had been among a group of dedicated people; then I walked out into the world. Two men were passing a store featuring elegant men's apparel. "See those socks," said one to the other admiringly; "this is a very exclusive shop." That word "exclusive" struck me. All day long we had been emphasizing the necessity for an *inclusive* church, and here was someone commending an *exclusive* shop. (There are also exclusive schools and exclusive hotels, which of course no Negro ever enters!) In the thinking of the world exclusiveness is a badge of honor. In the thinking of the Christian brotherhood it is a curse.

It seems that race prejudice, fundamentally, has an economic background, or at least an economic origin. So there you have the great chasm, as the inclusive church faces the exclusive shop, and the genuine Christian finds it impossible to serve both God and mammon.

31   THE HALF-SEEN

I love to walk past lighted windows. Each house reveals its own story, or rather a fragment of its story, and you guess the rest. Like Alice through the looking glass, you can't see every corner. You only get an abstract through that lighted square.

There is the family portrait hanging over the mantel; there are bookcases filled with books to the ceiling on either side. Perhaps a little girl is coming down the stairs. A worried-looking woman sits at a desk, conversing heatedly with a man in the background. Or the family sits at supper, or there are guests and they play cards. Plain ordinary people are made suddenly fascinating by being seen through the frame of a window.

How beautiful also are gardens framed by archways, or seen between narrow walls! The lavender of lilacs peering beyond the gray stone! There are gardens all around us, to which we pay little attention, but let us walk past an open gate and catch a glimpse of something half hidden, and we are immediately enthralled.

It seems as though delimitation, framework, is a necessary part of the joy of life. And when we talk of the "resurrection of the body," surely we mean that the very principle of framework will endure; that heaven will not be a great amorphous mass of timelessness and spacelessness, but that there will be times and places, and people—very definite people. There will be doors and windows, of that we may be sure. Open doors and lighted windows. And we shall no more pass by. We shall go in.

Not Without Sentiment

ELIZABETH WRAY TAYLOR

1   ON BEING AFRAID OF SENTIMENT

Fear of sentimentality has been too deeply bred in most of us. Even to begin meditations on domesticity may make us cringe in the spirit. Suppose someone should discover that we are sentimental about our life? We haven't minded *being* sentimental, but to be caught at it—there's the rub!

Being afraid to show our feelings has caused a certain brittleness in women. What is this "sentiment" that we fear? "A refined sensitivity on subjects affecting the heart," says the dictionary. Surely this is a woman's art. Let us take a new pride in it.

Old Chinese scholars roll walnuts in their calloused palms to retain the sensitivity of their fingers. No muscular movements will exercise the sensitivity of the heart. There is only the practice of making oneself available. Only the unlatched door and a warmth of welcome in the heart.

44

"Which is the greater lie, to be sentimental, or to be paralyzed by the fear of sentimentality?" [1]

2   WITH NO STRINGS ATTACHED

Attaching strings is a frailty of human nature. We want a return from our investments which will be guaranteed in advance. And most of all, we want an assurance that the biggest investment of ourselves, in our children, will not fail.

So we bind our young to us with strings of our own weaving. Perhaps they are made of silk, and we make believe that they are only fancy tokens. Perhaps they are made of rope, and we fool ourselves that their generous length will never need uncoiling.

But as long as there are strings, they will be pulled, and the tautness will rub against the flesh and bruise the spirit.

Why are we so afraid to let go? Haven't we yet learned that fellowship is only achieved by setting free, in advance?

Strings are obligations that we tie around the child's heart, in order to guarantee a return.

Strings are duties that we tie around the child's conscience, in order to ensure his loving.

But love never asks for a return. It carries its own insurance. It is given with no strings attached.

Freely have we received. Let us freely give.

[1] Charles Morgan, *The Voyage* (The Macmillan Co.).

3   WINGS FOR THE ASKING

In the post office a sign has appeared recently, advertising the reduction of air-mail postage. It reads, "Now, wings for a nickel."

What a bargain price for wings!

Lovers smile at the message. The pedestrian mind is content with the slower rhythm of the weekly letter home, but speed is a miracle for those who hold communion of the heart. Words written by the hand of a beloved friend have the power to move and to excite, far beyond the limits of the spoken word.

What is distance? Is it the length of miles the airplane travels? Is it the hours that the sun takes to span the horizons of the sky? Is it a substance which is the fabrication of the heart?

Distance dissolves for those who live in the romance of wings.

But there is one remoteness which no communication can penetrate. When the heavy fogs of misunderstanding ground two minds at variance with each other, wings are not available.

It is the will that sets the mileage limits.
It is the heart that spans the skies.

4   "THE WRAPTURED SOLE"

This is not a misspelling of some careless copy writer. This is a deliberate trick of the advertiser to draw attention to his wares.

The advertisement read: "Wraptured Sole. A brand-new kind of sorcery for your orchidaceous hours of ease.—The rhapsodical sandal, new and revolutionary, beautiful and soft as sentiment."

Sentiment? Mr. Advertiser, what do you know about a refined sensitivity on subjects affecting the heart? But you wouldn't know. You are not interested in souls. You only want to bind the soul as you bind the feet of those who buy your wares.

Who gave you the right to drag spiritual values into advertising? Are there no standards of integrity in your trade? Make no mistake about this. The soul pays a fine price for its rapture. It is never induced by languid hours of ease. It is never bribed by a new kind of sorcery. The soul pays for its rapture with tears and heartbreak.

Take your buying and selling out of the temple. Change your money elsewhere. Do not mock the rapture that has cost the few so dearly.

5   THE HEDGE

What makes the grass look so much greener on the other side of the hedge? Is it the hedge that is resented or the limits of our own confinement?

Housework is a solitary job. It has to be done without the benefit of friends. It is an easy trick of the lonely mind to feel that other neighbors have there wherewithal to manage happier lives: the second car, the maid by the hour, the foursome of congenial friends. The envious bleaching of the mind fades all the colors in our own

47

domain, and our lives look poor and streaked by the acid of its contrast.

Though circumscribed, we do not need to lead these lives that seem deprived. There is always a way of being friendly. There is always a way of cutting a gate through our own hedge to meet the friendship of the neighbors. And when we step out on their grass, we do not even remember that once we thought it was greener than our own.

"For all the law is fulfilled in one word, even in this; Thou shalt love thy neighbour as thyself."

6   THE COURAGE OF FAILURE

There is an ominous atmosphere in the household when the report cards come home. Are we parents anxious because our children may fail? Or are we anxious because our children may not know how to accept failure?

There is a standard of success that we want our children to reach. But there is a discipline that comes from learning to fail that may be more important than all the success in the world.

It takes courage to face failure. Perhaps it means that a subject in school must be repeated. Does this new effort leave us open to shame?

The individual who is not willing to fail must fight only on minor battlefields. He concerns himself with details in his own back yard because he dares not risk failure in greater adventures.

Success is not a state of achievement in which we must come out on top of the heap. Success is a direction which

the individual takes as he accepts more and more responsibility for himself.

When we transfer our efforts to major battlefields,
where significant things are done, individual success or
failure becomes relatively insignificant. We learn to carry
responsibility for our share of the total adventure.

7   THE THERMOSTAT

For years past, parental love was lauded by the poets
and held up at the altar as a great virtue. In this sunshine
of praise, we basked.

Twenty-five years ago a school of psychologists began
to frown upon too much show of loving. We brought up
our children by "the book" and put away the rocking chair
and the fondling. In this frustration we became detached.

Now our experts are saying that there cannot be too
much love between the parent and the child, but it has
to be the right kind of love. In this confusion we have
become anxious.

But anxious love has no steady control. It blows hot or
cold by some fictitious standard. Real loving is a natural
grace, and it is never tepid.

We can find release from these artificial thermometers
by being our whole, genuine selves. If we accept ourselves,
we will take refuge neither in rules nor in fashions. We
can then set the thermostatic control in our households
by the steady temperature of our own natural affections.

8   DISHPAN DRUDGERY

There isn't any way to avoid the kitchen sink. Three times a day it demands its toll of time, of energy, of red and soapy hands.

There is no escape from its monotonous repetition, but there is a way to accept its drudgery without enslavement of the mind. The dishpan does not have to be resented; resentment makes us slaves to the very things from which we would be free.

Graceful acceptance of the inevitable is not a sign of the lack of a desire for domestic emancipation. But it removes the dishpan from the battleground, and there are other battles more worth the fighting.

Let us not confuse acceptance with the mood or resignation. To be resigned is to be tight-lipped though still indignant. To accept is to pass through the drudgery and to be untouched by its indignity.

There is a patience of the mind that is willing to do the job of the cluttered present so that the future hours, released from disorder, can attain the freedom of the spirit.

9   BELLWETHER

We who manage households are so apt to manage everybody but ourselves. It becomes a fever in the nerves. Superintendent of the clothes; overseer of the neck washings; inspector of finger nails; foreman of the homework; manager of the meals; controller of the budget; bellwether of the family.

Are we the only ones who are appointed to wear the

bell? If only we could see orselves in the ludicrous position of file leader, regulating precisely the movements of the flock.

Why not stop ringing the bell? Why not slacken the pace, moderate the pattern, curb the slavish demand for perfection?

Good sheep must also have a shepherd. Once there was a Shepherd who took the weary lambs in his arms and carried them in his bosom.

Let us wear the bell, if we must. Only let us muffle the clapper and swing the bell gently.

10   THE WHOLE PERSON

How simple life would be if we could deal only with integers. Alas, fractions seem to be a part of growing up! The tutoring father produces the apple from the fruit basket and explains again the relation of the parts to the whole. But the quartered apple is no longer beautiful.

Wholeness is a quality of beauty. It need not be perfect as to features, but it must be sincere as to purpose. It need not be absolute as to design, but it must be honest as to motivation.

Integrity is a word that comes from integer, or the whole number, the complete entity. The whole person is an integrated person. Integrity has no counterfeit. It makes an affirmation of the whole self and permits other people to be themselves. It says, "I am what I am," without boasting and without smugness.

Jesus once explained, "They that are whole have no need of the physician." Blessed are the whole people.

They are saved already. And they contribute to the re-demption of society through the preservation of their own integrity.

11   HOUSEHOLD CEMENT

There is usually a tube of household cement on the pantry shelf. It works well with a broken plate, less well with a cup handle, and hardly at all when it is someone else's treasures that are broken.

It is hard to graft the cracked branches of the neighbor's favorite boxwood when our children are involved. It is hard to putty the shattered windowpane when our children are on the baseball team. It is hard to bandage the scalp wounds of the boy across the street when our children are included in the stone throwing.

Household cement can mend the pieces, but it cannot mend the feelings.

These are soldered together, less by the reparations of the pocketbook than by the mending power of the spoken word. And the apology must pinch the heart as it is made, or the cement won't close the cracks in the neighbors' relationship.

"The sacrifices of God are a broken spirit: a broken and a contrite heart, O God, thou wilt not despise."

12   D.V.

To the one who delights in planning, interruptions are a source of much annoyance. Measles break out and quarantine the family; fog grounds the plane on which we were planning to travel. Somehow we didn't count on anything happening to our own plans.

Our grandparents knew that anything might happen. Their plans for the future were marked with the initials "D.V."—Deo volente, or God willing. Do we smile at its quaintness? This was no mere empty form. It acknowledged their belief that every action is subject to the willingness of God.

We ignore the initials today. And why? Perhaps we think that our control is so far advanced that we no longer need to calculate on an unknown factor. Perhaps we have substituted a code of manners that tells us how to behave when we are confronted with "acts of God."

Are interruptions accepted with better humor because we obey a moral code of good sportsmanship? Are accidents received with better grace because we call life a game of chance wherein the victim's "number" comes up in the cards?

But Deo volente produced a rare humility.

Perhaps we shall believe again in the words we so often repeat.

"Thy will be done in earth, as it is in heaven."

13   THE MEASURING CUP

In most of our homes there is a doorway against which are penciled the inches of the children as a record of birthday growth. This height we measure with a yardstick. But where is the cup that will measure what is inside the child?

Parents take an unforgivable pride in the "bigness" of

their children. Our vocabulary is full of such phrases as, "Be a big boy," or "When you are big, you will know the answer." Is there anything good about being simply big? Do all the answers come with bigness?

Littleness must learn to live in relation to bigness, without fear and without favor.

Strength must learn to resist in relation to greater strength, without condescension and without resentment.

To hold up one's cup to life, to rise to heights of joy and to know deep sorrow, to go on far adventures in spite of loneliness, to catch lofty ideals and to carry them into action—these are the fullness of the stature.

There are no marks of gradation on the cup.

Out of the fullness of life we cry with the psalmist, "My cup runneth over."

14   SWATCHING

Swatching is a synthetic word—the slurred derivation of "sample" and "match." It can be a length of thread, a shred of wallpaper, the selvage of material. "Swatching" is the process of the matching over the counter. Sometimes we swatch material things; sometimes we swatch the attainments of our children!

Does our child measure up to the standard? Does he speak all the words that he is supposed to speak at his age? How does he compare with other children? What are his marks in school?

Compare him. Grade him. Measure him. Plot him on the curve of the average. And when we know where he stands, do we keep it as a secret understanding? Though pride may lash or praise its offspring, love is not concerned with placement.

Let us remember this. The swatch is less than the whole cloth. The curve is less than the whole child.

Though the world may appraise by measurement, the parent appreciates the whole by affection.

15   THE COMFORT STANDARD

Recently there appeared in a magazine a picture of what the editors assumed was the American woman's dream. It included the mink coat and the diamond necklace and the sable wrap. Is this dream of comfort the measure of the American woman?

Modern women have accepted the freedom that goes with money and comfort. What about the responsibility that also goes with leisure? What do we do with our leisure time?

Leisure is a privilege, and every privilege carries an obligation, a responsibility of leadership of the mind and heart.

There is a world of need, crying for the service that women's hands can bring to it.

There is a world of government, crying for the participation of its women as thinking citizens.

There is a world of beauty, crying for expression through the intuition and sensitivity of women.

There is a world of human relations, crying desperately for the sympathy and understanding of women.

Is the comfort standard the measure of our sense of responsibility as well as the measure of our demands?

16   THIS DAY

"Don't bother me now, dear. Can't you see I'm busy?"
This is a pat phrase among parents. It may be softened by
the tone of the voice, but it still means that we think our
busyness is more important.

There is no past or future for the little child. It is only
the now which is important. The past cannot be lost. But
the present moment may be lost.

There is something inexorable about the choices that
we make when our children implore our attention.

Perhaps it is only a bright-colored bird on the fence. If
we do not come now, the moment of beauty to be shared
is gone.

Perhaps it is only a dead mouse that the cat killed. The
words about life and death will not wait for the evening
armchair.

The dishes can wait without damage.

The telephone conversation can be interrupted without
misunderstanding.

But the moment with our child will not wait. Nor can
we count on its returning with the same overtones of
emotion.

Parents do not decide to have certain relations with
their children. Nor do they decide to relate their children
to the world in this way or that. We ourselves are the
relation.

"Look you well, therefore, to this day."

17   DIVIDING WHAT'S LEFT

Perhaps if there had never been a story about the wise
and foolish virgins, we could do a lot more borrowing
among our neighbors with an easy conscience. The five
virgins refused to share their oil with their less provident
sisters. "Peradventure," they said, "there will not be
enough for us and you."

Whatever the truth about the teaching in its entirety,
there has come down through the Puritan tradition the
keen sense that those who get down to the bottom of the
oil can are somehow the foolish ones. "Against the rainy
day," our fathers warned.

But rainy day borrowing among the neighbors is one
of the lovely arts of life. To borrow from someone next
door, and to share with joy, restores a sense of inter-
dependence to all-but-too independent neighbors.

This simplicity of fellowship is worth so much more
than outright giving because it involves a sharing of ourselves.

When we give, we usually give out of our abundance.

When we share, we usually divide what's left in the
oil can.

18   WINDOWPANES

Who has never wondered why there are two sides to a
pane of glass has never had to wash his own windows!
Oh, the backbreaking job of scrubbing the outside sash
only to find that the smudge is still between us and the
view. And usually it is the inside dirt that is hardest of all
to polish.

No need to argue about whether the outside or the inside is the more important. Both must be attended to. But to be obsessed with outside appearances is to have little thought for that which must only come from the inside.

We cannot choose between doing the necessary things and living the contemplative life. But we must take time to look up through the clear window at the fathomless sky, and at the drift of clouds, and at the shimmer of moonlight.

If both the inside and the outside of the window are clean, the vision will be there for the seeing.

19   FITTING THE HARNESS

Our modern U.S.A. living is a soft life for our young and offers few disciplines. There used to be household chores that carried their own restraints. There used to be family tasks that were shared as a part of the harness of living. Sensitive parents now feel that their children are ill prepared to meet the pain and work of life.

Has our protection turned out to be a matter of defense? Those who live their lives protected against hardships may be defended from grief, but the glory also passes them by.

There are things that are right for enjoyment, in simple appreciation.

There are things which can only be achieved by hard, dull work.

There are things which we must endure, not grimly but triumphantly.

Men extract from their work a strength for greater living so that joys can be taken away, not without grief, but without ruin.

It was a man acquainted with grief who said, "My Father worketh hitherto, and I work." By his work and the work of men like him, the world is clothed and put in its right mind.

20   BELONGING

The child loves to stretch his address from the number on the house to the street; from the street to the city; from the city to the state; from the state to the United States. Finally he stretches his imagination to the ultimate; the continent of North America, western hemisphere, the world, the universe, God.

We begin by belonging to one spot of real estate, and we end by belonging to all that there is. It sounds so simple, like the concentric circles on the water's surface when the pebble is dropped into the pool, ever widening to lap the farthest shore.

But somewhere in the growing-up process the circles begin to freeze into rigid circumferences.

We can feel that we belong to a family, and to a community. But when do we begin to feel that we belong to the human race?

Belonging likes to know exclusion in order to feel the security of being included. We freeze the circles because we lack the warmth of imagination and love to let the circumference flow to the outmost edge.

Few are the giants of the soul who actually feel that the human race is their family circle.

They have stretched their hearts because they know God as the Father.

21   THE ELECTRIC MINUTE

The newest substitute for the pendulum is a dial-less clock which drops a number every minute. To watch this noiseless marker of time's progress is to feel a frenzied competition in the race against the numbered minutes.

So against the electric hour let everything be pressed. So many minutes to wash the dishes. So many minutes to make the beds. So many minutes to hang out the clothes. Hurry! Hurry! Hurry!

But wait. Is it really the electric minute that gives us time?

Twice a day the nation's clocks are checked against the evidence of the stars. The stars give us the length of our minutes. Why do we set our pace against an electric number that stops when we pull out the plug?

When we check against the evidence of the stars, we are tempered by the knowledge of God's time that extends through the sweep of centuries.

22   PLEASE FORWARD

The children of this generation have learned to accommodate themselves to the moving van without heartbreak. This makes for a certain flexibility and freedom from too close an emotional tie with things.

For the older members of the family, moving is still a poignant experience. Never again the same trees from the window. Never again the same dear friends as neighbors. Does the heart falter?

Handle gently the lares and penates and place them on the new mantelpiece. Dig up the scoopsful of dirt around the rose bushes and carry them carefully to the new garden spot.

Once the ark of the covenant moved a people to a new home through the wilderness. They went out to a land that was only promised. We go out to a new address.

They couldn't say to the Egyptian postmaster, "Please forward." They could leave no forwarding address. For they themselves were the ones who went forward.

23   RESTRICTIONS

Women have often spoken out against the restrictions which seem to be imposed upon them by the life of domesticity. Such a voice has cried out recently against "the isolated, undernourished, haphazard life within the family."

Housewives often fear that if they were to accept the compensations that go with family living, they would crave to be poured into the mold of the Pollyanna that exalts a sterile goodness. In this mood restrictions seem like bars that imprison and trap and suffocate.

Many are persuaded that against these bars they must beat their heads so that they may finally either make their escape or destroy the restrictions entirely.

But there is another way within the reach of all of us.

There is the power to wonder, to imagine, to listen, and to create.

These are the universal approaches to the spirit. These are the ways of renewal for the mind and heart. Through increasing the powers of our imagination we can walk through our restrictions instead of planning an assault against them.

24   THE MORNING WATCH

"And yet a great while before it was day . . ."

The saints of the ages have attested to the power of vision that comes to the early riser who watches the morning break.

Perhaps we kneel at the open window. Perhaps we stand with bowed heart. But here, for a brief space of time, is absolute detachment and solitude—a supreme awareness of beauty.

In the hush of the morning all nature stands on tiptoe, expectant. Gradually color returns to the earth. The trees take on shadow again. The birds burst forth into rapturous music.

The miracle of the revolving universe sheds its shaft of sunlight on the window ledge. We lift up our heads to greet the dawn, feeling the miracle work inside us, absolved of guilt and worthy of life again.

Swiftly we pass into the necessities of the old regime, but the world for us has been made afresh. In this refreshment we perceive the members of our family with deeper appreciation, loving them afresh and starting them off on the day with a light heart and a light touch.

25 THE DESIGN

Prepare thy distaff and thy spindle,
And the Lord will send the flax.

This is a curious proverb from the days of long ago. But the women of this generation appreciate its hidden meaning.

Whether we wind the spindle, ready for the weaving; or sharpen the pencil, ready for the design; or thread the machine, ready for the sewing—we are preparing with the hands for the inspiration that can come only through the mind and the heart.

Our great-grandmothers found the patterns for their treasured coverlets in the shape of snowflakes, in the twisted honeysuckle vine, in the slithering snail's trail, in the cluster of the stars. They took their colors from the walnut shells and from the root of the madder plant and from the berry of the elder bush.

Our heritage is great. When we sew threads into new patterns or arrange colors into new harmonies of delight, we are finding a way of renewal of the spirit which has its roots in the long, long past.

What matters is not that we should make a crude design; nor that we should fashion a rough garment. What matters is that we should feel the impulse to create and be willing to try our wings.

26 THE TUNING FORK

The piano tuner carries a magic instrument in his black bag of tools. With the simple twang of the tuning fork, he vibrates all the piano strings into harmony again.

But suppose there are no hands to make the music available to us? Now through the miracle of the record player will come the harmony of the greatest symphonies.

Though some of us may never create our own music, we can learn to appreciate. We can learn to listen.

The art of listening is not a passive acceptance of tonality. It is a participation of the mind and soul. With the records of great symphonies we can repeat the melody over and over again until we learn to know it and to anticipate it. In anticipation we become active participants.

What is this strange power to move us?

To be moved through appreciation is to learn a new kind of intercourse that sings with the rhythm of the universe.

If we would turn our souls into tuning forks, there is one demand that the master makes of the listener. Thoreau has put it into words, "Music says, 'You must believe what I know before I can tell you.' "

27   **THE INVITATION**

When the poet writes a poem, he issues an invitation to his friends to come and share with him the enjoyment of his experience.

Some people discourteously avoid the invitation by being out of town.

Some people politely regret the invitation, fearing boredom.

Some people rudely ignore the invitation, as though it had never been sent to them.

Without the power to imagine through the words of

the poet, we sentence ourselves to the world of the prosaic. There are inspirations to be had from contemporary novels, but they demand a lot of precious time. There are truths to be had from some of the current magazines, but they ask for a lot of searching. There are swift renewals of the spirit that can be deliberately chosen by accepting the invitation of the poet.

Here is something trying to be said with a minimum of words. Here is beauty set to music, and truth that has a strange power to fascinate. The reader, when he experiences the truth, is transported from the world of the immediate to the timeless world of the permanent.

This is the invitation of the poet—to share with him the wonder of man's deepest experience.

28   THE SPADE

The gardeners of all the years have testified to the renewal of the spirit that comes from close association with the soil.

The gardener has a receptive state of mind. He knows that he cannot push, that he cannot hurry the fulfillment of his work. Though he co-operates with pruning knife and fertilizer to bring the bud, he knows that the fruit will come only in its season.

It takes faith to believe that the planted seed will burst its shell in the dark earth and push its green reach toward the sunshine.

It takes great faith to believe that the miracle will happen again.

Man at his greatest stature has always been a gardener—

spading, weeding, pruning. He never despairs and is always hopeful because he rests upon the assurance of the seasons.

He knows well the parable of the barren fig tree and pleads for another chance to help it bring forth its fruit.

"Lord, let it alone this year also, till I shall dig about it, and dung it: and if it bear fruit, well: and if not, then after that thou shalt cut it down."

The gardener, like the parent, goes down on his knees to intercede, not that justice be denied, but that mercy will be persuaded to offer another chance.

29   REPRIEVE

Once in every four years our astronomy gives us an extra day. Oh, joyous reprieve!

The dictionary calls this an intercalary day, a day to make the civil year correspond with the astronomical year. But the twenty-ninth of February is a compliment from the stars, an extension of time to every mortal.

Does this day have to be inserted into the calendar? Couldn't it be an extra day, a holiday, without a weekday title?

Think of what we could do with twenty-four hours that are a compliment to the joy of living, with reprieve from suffering, from debt, from guilt—aware that we are angels.

But the angels know that it wouldn't do for mortals to taste immortality. Who would go back to ordinary living on the first of March!

Yes, better to have it a day of the week.

But let us return the compliment of the stars by the quality of our mortal living:

Without reprieve from suffering, but through its transfiguration. Without reprieve from debt, but through its repayment. Without reprieve from guilt, but through its absolution. And let us have just a little awareness that we are angels!

Reaching Up

HELEN C. WHITE

1 A COURAGE SO DEEP

Not long ago I sat with a young mother who was watching her little children at play. "They're such fun at this age!" she said. "But I'm afraid—sometimes I'm terrified! What is going to become of them? No real peace yet! Half the world starving, freezing, in turmoil! That horrible atom bomb! I suppose the only answer is courage; but it's surely hard to manage in times like these!"

Yes, the times call for courage—courage that is more than dogged grit and more than merely the ability to "keep a brave front," valuable as both these types are. The courage the world needs now, the courage we need personally, must spring clear and shining from a sort of inner stability and poise, a source of power and serenity. Looking at the frightened young mother, I wondered. Can we, just ordinary women, not great heroines or great saints, hope to attain a courage like this, and to give it to our children?

Then I remembered a letter I had received from a young

French friend of mine recently, a girl who was "just an ordinary woman" when I knew her years ago. Her husband died in a German prison early in 1945, and she is struggling unaided to care for their three young children. She wrote, "Times are hard, very hard. We are sometimes hungry, often cold. But the children are nearly always merry, and what you call 'good sports.' For myself, I do not know how people who lack a sure faith in a loving God preserve their sanity. Perhaps I feel nearer Him because Pierre is with Him, and Pierre seems so close to me, but it is a fact that though my mind is often perturbed (for how could it be otherwise?) my heart is calm and even gay."

Recalling these words, I knew, with a sudden thrill, that because she had known where to go for it, this French girl had been able to find and to give to her children a security so deep that it was not at the mercy of outward circumstances—a courage that rested on, and in, God himself.

2   CUI BONO?

Long ago a philosopher of ancient Rome asked in weary cynicism, *"Cui bono?"* The question was an old one when he posed it, and men have been asking it ever since, but never more urgently perhaps than now. *Cui bono?* For what good? Has life any ultimate meaning, any lasting values?

A certain elderly woman remarked to me rather drearily not long ago that she supposed this query was one "you can successfully dodge as long as you're lucky." She added, lifting a wry shoulder, "But sooner or later life takes everything away from you! Grief, illness, old age, one thing or another, strip you of every joy—unless you die first. And that's when you need an answer, the right answer, and need it terribly!"

She seemed to be implying that one does not really "need" that "right answer" as long as he's "lucky." He only needs it as a sort of insurance against future woes, something to fall back on when things begin to go wrong. This I take to be a fallacy. It is true that the right answer does constitute this sort of insurance, and it is true also that when trouble strikes we do need it quite desperately. But I feel very sure that we need it at all other times too. The happiest and most fortunate lives present ample opportunity for the use of qualities like wisdom, courage, strength, serenity—or for the sad display of their opposites!

The Christian answer, at once simple and profound, is that every life is vastly important because every individual is a child of God; and that every life has ultimate value because God's children are immortal. To one who accepts this answer, and lives by it, poised and serene living is possible in the most confusing of circumstances. Nor can such a one ever be stripped of every joy. For I have known Christians whom death could not separate from their loved ones, and I have known shut-ins whose days of purposeful activity were supposedly over, yet from whose rooms radiated activity and influence so purposeful that it has seemed to me the entire community was affected by it.

3   **FAITH PLUS REASON**

"I grant everything you say!" a restless-eyed young woman said to me a few days ago. "Of course I have sense
enough to realize what the Christian answer would mean
to me, but I can't believe it just because I'd like to, can I?
The question I want to ask is, Have I got a right to an
intelligent conviction that there is any answer to the riddle of life? Maybe Omar was right, and the universe is the
whim of an irresponsible creator! Maybe the materialists
are right, and there isn't any creator, just a big, impersonal
force! How do I know? What grounds have I got?"

I told her truthfully that it was my conviction that the
final reply lay in a faculty higher than reason; but that I
also believed that reason supported this faculty. It is clear
that we live in a universe constructed with beautiful order
and logic—"God is the great Mathematician," a famous
scientist has said—and that here on earth only man, of all
living creatures, is able to see and appreciate this order, is
able to acquire understanding and, to some extent, mastery
of natural laws. It seems therefore that the proposition
that man is the high point of creation is not open to argument. And this makes the materialistic position an absurdity. Can one possibly believe that a world in which the
highest value is personality is the result of an impersonal
force? Machines produce robots.

So then, if I conclude that I have a rational right to my
belief in a creator who possesses personality, and if I must
also grant the mathematical perfection of utter, logical
consistency with which he has planned his world, must I
suppose that he became inconsistent and illogical only

in regard to man, his highest creation of all? It seems to me a far less rational and intelligent conclusion than the one faith reaches, "I cannot see nor understand his plan, but I know he has one, and I trust it."

4   WHAT OF MAN'S LONGING?

I have always felt that there was a certain bleak nobility in the Stoic's attitude, which declares that even though there is no kindly God, and the end of all human hope and endeavor is just a heap of ashes, still man should conduct himself with dignity and courage during his brief stay here. But it leaves the human heart hungry and shivering.

Man wants an answer to this question of *Cui bono?* He wants it with his whole being. And I find that one part of my belief that there is one lies in just this very passionate need and longing for it. I observe that for every other need man has there is a corresponding gratification; food for his nourishment, shelter for his protection, sleep for his rest, friends for his gregarious instinct, love for his heart's cry—all his deepest needs can be met. Then why should I conclude that his spiritual nature alone is to be starved and denied? Man has longed for God and immortality persistently down through the ages. As persistently, one might say, as he has longed for life, because it is life itself for which he longs when he yearns for God and immortality. Can it be that it is only this great need which is answered by silence, emptiness, darkness? If I am justified in assuming that the creator of personalities possesses personality, as I believe I am, then surely it must be that this deep, age-

less, universal longing of man for him is in response to his
love for man; and if he loves us, then for this need also we
may be certain there is satisfaction.

5   BY ANY OTHER NAME

I spoke earlier of "a faculty higher than reason." It is this
faculty—hard to name explicitly—by which man is en-
abled to feel the vivid, living presence of God; it is this
faculty through which he can respond to God's guidance;
it is this faculty by means of which he can fling his
imagination boldly out into the unseen and apprehend
truth. I wish that a new adjective, almost any serviceable
one, could be found to describe this ability of man's! The
one most often used is "mystical," and that has come to
have unfortunate connotations. You may take as many
pages as you like to explain that all religions are by their
very nature and essence "mystical," since they rely wholly
on faith in the unseen; you may successfully argue that
nothing more "mystical" than the splitting of the atom can
be imagined, for the very scientists who worked on it have
described it as this exact bold flinging out of the imagination to seize truth and have called it an artistic, an intui-
tive, an imaginative, even a spiritual achievement. Nevertheless, the term continues to suggest to the average
individual something queer, fanatical, fantastic, by which
he, as a practical person, is instinctively repelled. So
I wish we might discard it, or else redefine it, when
talking about this particular faculty of man's. For about
the gift itself there is nothing whatsoever fantastic. It is a
part of man's standard equipment. He can lose it, of

73

course, just as he can lose hearing or sight or any of the physical senses, by injury or neglect. But he is by nature and ability as truly a spiritual being as he is a physical, and thus as truly the possessor of a spiritual sense as he is of physical senses.

6   USE MAKES PERFECT

If it is true that man is as much a spiritual being as he is a physical one, it must follow that he is just as maladjusted, just as warped and stunted and one-sided, when this spiritual part of him is denied and starved and mistreated as he is when the physical side is denied and starved and mistreated. It also follows naturally that the use of this spiritual faculty is a matter of intense practical value to him in his everyday living and activities. For if he has been given it, it is for a purpose—and that purpose can only be its use for his needs. So we may say that if it is practical to travel armed when crossing a jungle where tigers lurk; if it is practical to provide oneself with a light in darkness; if it is practical to make a fire against the cold; if any realization of, and provision for, vital needs is practical; then the recognition and the cultivation of this faculty is practical. For it gives man armor for danger, light for darkness, warmth for cold, and help for all his needs.

7   THE FIRST STEP

It is a help, when one seeks to cultivate this sensitive awareness of God, to have the solid conviction that God is there and will respond. To start a conversation with a person when you are not at all sure whether he is really present or not is definitely a handicap to fellowship! But the one fundamental prerequisite, I am sure, is to want it. I do not mean to want it in a mild, lukewarm way as something that would be rather nice and comforting to have. No, I mean to want it passionately, with all your heart, because you feel the need of God so greatly; because you realize that even the happiest environment is powerless to bring lasting satisfaction without him; because you know that the only answer to the whole riddle of *Cui bono?* is to be found in him. This urgent desire is the first step—and the most fundamental.

8   GOING AHEAD WITHOUT IT

Rather oddly there are people who do feel the need of God, and do want him, almost desperately, but find the emotional conviction of his reality extremely difficult to attain. Perhaps early influences have given them a "set" they cannot overcome; at any rate, for whatever reason, there is an emotional block there which often proves a barrier. Must they, therefore, be forever bound to a tormented quest for him? No, oh, no! Not unless they pursue that quest by means of a way alien to him, one which can never lead to him. If they seek him through Christ—"I am the Way"—and through honest, constructive prayer, they will discover a new meaning in the words, "Knock and it shall be opened."

"I knew I needed God," a highly intelligent college girl said once. "I knew there ought to be a God. But I just couldn't get hold of the feeling that there was one, or that Anything listened when I spoke. And then—it was almost like a miracle to me, really, and I hardly know how to tell it—I discovered that you don't even have to believe in him to find him, if you just want him and keep trying. The belief comes; the sure knowledge that he's there comes; but you can go ahead without it—and be sure of getting it! It's almost as if he were so anxious to respond to you, so eager, that if you just make the smallest sincere gesture toward him, he pours out his answering love. That's what I meant when I said that it was a miracle."

9   GOD HAS TO WAIT

Remembering what this lovely girl had said, I found myself thinking back to a time in my own life when heartbreak that seemed intolerable had driven me to a frantic search for comfort. I recalled the nights when I'd paced up and down the library floor, crying reproachfully to God, "Why did you let it happen? Why can't you help me now? I beg you and beg you—but you never answer! Don't you care? Do something for me! Oh, why must you make it so hard to reach you?"

Once when one of our boys was a baby of less than three, he had a severe attack of poison ivy. He'd wake in the night, hysterical and half out of his head with the unbearable itching, flinging his hot little body from one side of the bed to the other, "Mommy! Mommy! I want Muzzer! Mommy! *Mommy!*"

I was right there, kneeling beside the bed, trying to hold him in my arms, trying to quiet his hysteria, saying

over and over, "Darling, Mother's here. She's right here!
Listen, listen—sweet—this is Mother!" But distracted with
pain and fear, he could neither see nor hear me. It was
not until he had grown quieter, not until he had stopped
the frantic screaming and threshing from side to side,
that he knew I was beside him, loving him, wanting to
help him.

So it must have been with God while I hurled reproaches
at him, never stopping my frantic thoughts to listen, able
to hear no voice at all but my own! Why, God might
have shouted at me, and I'd never have known it then! I
wonder if perhaps he tossed my question right back at me—
"Oh, why must you make it so hard to reach you, child?"

10   KEEPING CONTACT

Meditation and prayer are a vital necessity in this reaching for God. We gain the contact with him that way, and
we keep it that way. For our fellowship with him, and
our ability to be guided by him, will only be maintained,
like freedom, at the cost of vigilance. The strains of life
are going to be constantly jerking loose our spiritual connection; and while a lamp may be perfectly constructed,
with a good bulb and a strong cord, if that cord is not
plugged in to the source from whence power flows, the
lamp will give no light. The quiet times when we think
about God, read about him, talk to him, listen to him,
are our most effective and vital methods of staying plugged
in, of keeping our current flowing and our light burning.
The old gospel hymn my grandmother sang said it another
way:

O, what peace we often forfeit,
 O, what needless pain we bear,
All because we do not carry
 Ev'rything to God in pray'r!

11   THE TEST OF QUIET

Yet here it must be said that if we withdraw for these
periods of quiet as Jesus did, it is only that we may come
back again to serve more fully, as Jesus always came back
to serve. If they do not make us able to deal with life and
human situations more wisely, kindly, efficiently, and un-
selfishly, then depend on it, something has been wrong
about them. Another common meaning attached to that
word "mystical" which I dislike is the idea of turning
one's back on the world, a complete withdrawal in favor
of self-induced hypnotic rapture. There have been "mys-
tics" like that, but I cannot believe that their inspiration
came from God. Any authentic contact with the spiritual
world must involve an individual more vividly and more
fully than ever before in living and serving, must make him
not less eager about participation in life but more eager.

12   TUNING IN

Years ago I witnessed an illustration, which I have never
forgotten, of what deliberate, trained, "plugging in" to
spiritual contact may mean. I was sitting, with several
dozen others, on the platform with a noted Christian
leader who was to address a huge throng that was rapidly
filling all the seats in the auditorium before us. I was two

seats away from the speaker, and I noted with concern that
he looked white and tired, really exhausted. At that instant
he turned to the gentleman next to him and spoke—I
heard his voice clearly, and his tone was simple and matter-
of-fact.

"I find I am more tired than I had realized. I shall step
to the wings a moment. Can you see that no one speaks to
me for that little time?"

He took hardly more than a dozen steps—just enough
to get out of sight of the great audience. Then he bent
his head and stood there, his back toward us. His arms
hung loose; the pose of the whole figure suggested relaxation. Noise was buzzing all around him, but he seemed not
to hear. It was not more than ten minutes, perhaps less,
that he stood, quiet and relaxed and withdrawn. Then
he came back to his seat. And I stared in something like
awe. For during that brief space the weary lines in his
face had smoothed out; the "drained" look was gone. In
just that short time he had visited a country I did not
know; he had received a message I could not hear; he had
gained strength from a source mysterious to me. I understood only vaguely that he had tuned in to Something.
But one thing I did know; whatever his secret, I wanted to
find it out! He had withdrawn—yes; but as I listened to
that ringing, enthusiastic address which so stirred and
moved his hearers, one thing was beautifully clear to me—
those few moments of withdrawal had given him infinitely
more to give to us.

13   ADVENTURE FOR THE ASKING

Naturally I realized that the missionary leader whom I watched that day must be praying as he stood there with bent head. But I knew so little about that kind of prayer! My own formula was simple. You thanked God; you asked his blessing on your loved ones; you requested help and strength; a little timidly and doubtfully you put in a plea for the things you most wanted; and you closed with the Lord's Prayer. I went through this routine dutifully once a day. There was nothing wrong with it except that it had small vitality! The words were all right. But no words mean more than the feeling behind them. I was not really reaching for God. I was going through a sort of patter. Even so, I think it helped and soothed me. It was a tenuous contact, but it was better than nothing. The point was that I knew nothing whatsoever about the sort of prayer that is a direct, living, tingling connection with God—a direct plugging in of the spiritual cord, so that power and strength flow through to the individual. It was the late Gilbert K. Chesterton who insisted that the Christian's life has a romantic and adventurous quality that the non-Christian's lacks. What I had seen that day was adventure of the most thrilling type, romance of the highest order; and the best part about it, though it took me a long time to find that out, was that it was the sort of adventure that anybody who wants it with his whole heart may have—as simple, as direct as sunlight, and with the same quality of health-giving warmth and light.

This kind of tuning in at a time of emergency is, naturally, trained prayer; it means that many hours have been spent in companionship with God in the past. To this great and good man God was never far away, and the connection was therefore possible at a moment's notice. He had only to stretch out one finger and touch the hem of his garment to be made whole. This sensation of the nearness of God is a vital factor in prayer like this. Sometimes I feel that some of our metaphors have done spiritual sensitiveness—no doubt because we insist on translating them into literal terms—actual harm. There is, for instance, that widespread, almost universal, picture of heaven as located somewhere in our actual skies, with God residing there! Naturally we know it isn't true. Astronomy would tell us this if common sense didn't. But the idea is so deep-rooted, and the picture has taken such hold on our imaginations by years of repetition, that I doubt if we realize ourselves quite how much influence it has had. He is "up there" somewhere; he "reaches down" to us; our voices "ascend" to him. All the time we are talking to him our imaginations are struggling with this vision of a being a million light-years and more away. By some magic we can speak to him, as if over a celestial long distance telephone; but how faint and far away must our words be by the time they reach him! Also by some equally mysterious magic he sees us; but oh, how far removed from all our troubles he is, enthroned up there and gazing telescopically down!

But suppose that is all wrong. Suppose, after all, he is

right here. Suppose he lives among us; moves at our elbows; catches the faintest, most incomplete gesture we make toward him; hears us if we so much as whisper his name in our hearts. Ah, that makes it different. We can speak quickly to a God like that. We can reach out and put our hand in his in a second. Let us give up this vision of a heaven with a definite location in space. Fortunately our space presents no barrier to God.

15   SPACE AND DISTANCE

The same sort of muddled imagination, trying to see heaven in terms of earth and putting our finite limitations upon infinity, makes grief very much more painful when death snatches those we love from us for a while. Thinking again of our own sort of space, we immediately picture the loved ones as having been removed to an incredible physical distance. They gleam in our heartsick fancy as beautiful, as bright, and as heartbreakingly inaccessible as the stars. Our yearning thoughts, our aching love, may humbly follow them, but mostly we accept it as a sad, hard fact that no current of love and thought flows back to us from them. I wonder why! When they were here in the flesh, distance was no ban to thought and love. They might have been far away from us, even in spots from whence letters came only rarely, but we could go about our work contentedly, in the main, sure we were still a vital part of their lives as they were of ours, not feeling cut off. Yet now that they are all spirit, we do not believe that their love can reach us any longer!

Once two friends stood gazing at a brilliantly starry sky.

Said one, pointing to two small bright stars huddled close together and speaking with a break in her voice, "Somehow I always think of those two as Mother and Dad!" Looking at the tiny, glittering pin points of light, unbelievably remote, the other shivered a little. And then, quite suddenly, there swept over her the lovely sensation of her own mother's love. Warm, tender, close, it wrapped her like a shining garment; it comforted her and made her glad in every corner of her being. True, she had seen nothing; she had heard nothing; she had felt nothing tangible. But she found that she had stopped shivering. For she knew, with a deep conviction, that her mother's love was not gleaming coldly down at her from an unimaginable distance; it was there beside her.

16   CALL IT WHAT YOU WILL

When we speak of imagination, we usually mean fancy or daydreaming, spinning tales for the fun of it, perhaps. But the word has a deeper meaning than this. It is the meaning that the physicists give it when they say that the splitting of the atom is an imaginative feat. Some weeks ago I heard a brilliant physicist who had taken part in this achievement discussing it. "You see," he explained, "we were working in an incommensurable substance. I mean, it was immaterial, by any of our old definitions of matter. It follows that a very important element in our calculations was something you might call intuition. Or maybe you'd rather call it imagination. Anyway, time after time we struck places where all we could do was fling this sixth sense boldly out into space and try to seize the truth. One of my colleagues has pointed out in print that the queer part of it all was that when we were most daring we were most likely to be right. It was as if—" he paused. "Don't think I'm fantastic," he said half apologetically, "but it was as if this intuition, imagination, whatever it is, was our bridge between the known and the unknown."

Whatever it is! What else can it be, except that unnamed and unnamable faculty "higher than reason" which we were talking about a few days ago? And then I found myself thinking suddenly, "Paul called it faith," and recalling certain deeply moving words: "Now faith is the substance of things hoped for, the evidence of things not seen."

17   CONSTRUCTING THE BRIDGE

It is by this sort of imaginative faith that man is helped to understand the love of God, and to preserve unbroken his contact with God. It is when we picture God as a parent, though tenderer and more understanding than any human parent could be, that we begin emotionally to realize his love. Proceeding from what we do know, the love of a mother or a father, we use this imaginative faith to—in the words of my scientist friend—construct a bridge between the known and the unknown; and thus we learn, so far as mortal man may learn a thing so transcendent, how God loves us. It takes little imaginative faith to realize his might and our helplessness; that is a fact which slaps us in the face. Without the corresponding realization of his love, it is a fact which may well slap us down, as well. Yet the fact of his love is a greater, deeper truth than any

other truth which we are at all likely to comprehend about
him. It is the truth which fills all our needs; it is the thing
hoped for and not seen which faith makes a substance.

18   IN HIS IMAGE

If God is our Father, we are his children; and children
resemble parents. So we take another imaginative leap
of faith, and the words "made in his own image" become
true for us.

"Am I like the great creator of the universe?" contemp-
tuously asked a bitter-looking woman, referring to this
phrase. "If there is one, my mental processes are about as
much like his as an amoeba's are like mine!"

"I think your simile is wrong," said a quiet, slim girl,
almost hesitantly. "Yours are about as much like his as a
baby's are like yours."

No simile is perfect, and none can be carried too far.
The baby will grow up to have the powers of an adult, and
we can never grow to the stature of God. Yet this young
friend of mine had a point. We are, she was trying to say,
the same *kind* of being God is. We are embryo; and he has
infinitely more of everything than we, as well as many
qualities for which we do not even possess the possibility
of development. Nevertheless, the vital fact remains that
on a very different scale we are beings like unto him. He
is an immortal spirit; so are we immortal spirits. I once
heard somebody object to this statement with a worried
frown. "We *will* be immortal spirits," she corrected. Then,
as she saw the absurdity of her remark, as the logical,
inescapable conclusion that if we are immortal, we are

born immortal, that it is not a gift for the future but a present condition—as this realization swept over her, her face assumed an almost dazed look. "Why, then," she stammered, "it's *true!* We were made in his image, and we were meant to be like him, weren't we?"

19   FURTHER SUPPORT

In this thrilling realization that we are actually like God we find many of the prominent modern scientists of the day—those to whom the mechanistic, materialistic theory is now dead and "dated"—coming to our support. It is a heartening thing, this alliance of science and religion, so long pictured in the popular fancy as irreconcilable. To find science discovering a scientific foundation for the truths which religion has long known by revelation is a happy sign. For the materialistic conception has influenced our age so deeply in the past that even those of us who have rejected it have still not utterly escaped its taint. Things we could not see, or touch, or measure, or compute, did not seem quite "real." And now here come the physicists telling us that our five senses are quite insufficient to reveal to us the "real" universe! One great scientist has publicly stated recently that he finds his deepest conviction of the reality of a Creator in this very realization of our own likeness to him; for as he learns more about the laws that govern the universe, he realizes that his mind is actually reconstructing what God's mind planned. This must mean, he argues, that to some extent and degree his mind is patterned on God's; and he himself is a sharer of God's thoughts.

20   ENJOYMENT OF BEAUTY

Said a character in a mountain story, "God must love
pretty things. He made so many of them."

We, God's children, made in his image, have implanted
deep within us, a vital part of us, this love of beauty too.
We may bury it so deep under a multitude of other preoccupations that most of the time we forget it; we may
remain stupidly blind to the loveliness around us day
after day; but in very few of us is this aching joy in beauty
completely atrophied. Walking or riding along, absorbed
in our thoughts, our minds, perhaps, going like a squirrel
in a cage, completely tied up inside ourselves, we suddenly
see a church spire outlined against a rose-gold, azure-
edged, sunset sky—and we stop, and our restless thoughts
halt as, with a little gasp, our whole hearts go out to the
lovely spectacle. For that short instant we step clear outside of ourselves, and into fairyland. Almost, for a moment,
as if we had been vouchsafed a sort of foreglimpse of
poignant beauty, we seem to tremble on the verge of
knowing and understanding something very big. Inevitably
the vision fades, but the glow lingers; and even as our
thoughts turn back to the things that preoccupy them, we
are conscious of a sense of added peace and mastery.

21   OUTSIDE ONESELF

Many men and women have testified to this increased peace and mastery which wholehearted, outgoing
appreciation of beauty has brought to them. Poets have
been singing it for ages. But the ordinary man who doesn't
write poetry means exactly the same thing when he says,

"I didn't know how I could live through it, and then I chanced to look out my window; and I saw the crab apple tree in bloom, and got a whiff of its fragrance, and heard a bird singing in one of its branches, and all of a sudden things looked better, and I felt I could go on!"

What is it that has happened? For that instant he has fully come into his heritage as the beauty-loving child of a beauty-loving God. He has shared an emotion—joy in beauty—with God. And in giving his heart even for only a moment to loveliness, he has left the prison of self and walked in a wider space, breathed a different air. So he returns from this brief journey to another country, refreshed and renewed. Whether he knows it or not, he has been in contact with God.

22   THE PILOT'S CROSS

Even an occasional and spasmodic contact with beauty can do much for us. A young airman, later killed in combat in World War II, wrote his mother while he was in training, "Did you ever hear of the Pilot's Cross? It's a familiar phenomenon, but I'd never happened to see it till the other day. You know we must fly above or below the cloud banks. I was flying quite high, and beneath me there was a thunderstorm going on. Then the sun began to shine, and suddenly there below me I saw something that took my breath away. It was a cross—the shadow of my plane—entirely enclosed and encircled by a rainbow. I begin now to understand why flyers so often grow mystical. Alone up there, with so much loveliness around you and beneath you, you know you're drawing close to Something great. I can't describe it, but there's a sense of something wonderful just around the corner, and a feeling that one of these days you're sure to find it! Your blood begins to race exultantly, and you want to laugh out loud—oh well, I'm saying it poorly, but it makes living a very great adventure! I don't know—perhaps I'm trying to express something too big for me—but just for a little you feel as if you know, dimly, what the whole darn business is about, and as if dying is going to be a very great adventure too."

23   BEAUTY FOR THE TAKING

If even the occasional and spasmodic contact with beauty can mean so much, it is clear that the conscious training of oneself to see it, and hear it, and feel it, could mean much more. We do not, most of the time, realize how much beauty has to teach us; and so, tragically, we neglect this source of strength and poise. It is Bernard Shaw who has one of his characters in a play remark, "A picture gallery is a dull place for a blind man!" So this world may become a dull and commonplace affair for one who walks through it unseeing. But once you open your eyes and your ears and your heart to beauty, see what happens! It becomes a magic place, fresh and sparkling; and always with that "something wonderful just around the corner," always with that zestful sense of ever-springing adventure which usually we think of as belonging just to youth. You live on a more vivid plane; that is really what happens; there is all the difference that there is between a pen-and-ink sketch and a water color. You step into a new world, a world of color and of glow. And you recognize it for your very own, your native air, the real world God meant you to see and enjoy, not the pale shadow your lack of perception has hitherto presented to you.

24   GREAT ART

Especially does beauty bring one this new vividness in living if one learns to feel God behind it, and in it. This is true not only of the beauty of nature; it is true also of the beauty that men make. Dr. Fosdick has said that the greatest artists have always felt not so much that they were doing something, but that something was being done through them. The same young airman quoted above wrote shortly before his death, after hearing a great pianist, "What he does with a piano is beyond belief! You can talk about his wonderful singing tone, his lack of percussive effect, his marvelous technique, and it's all true enough. But it leaves out the biggest thing of all. It leaves out that deep tenderness, that spiritual glow, that glimpse into infinite beauty, which could only come from a great mind and heart which is, in turn, in touch with some power more than human. Do I sound gushy? Well, truly, in the presence of art like this what can one do but pray? I never listen to great music without becoming keenly aware that it stems from a power much bigger than the man who is performing it—and even bigger than the man who composed it."

25   GRADUAL GROWTH

Of course it is only a truism to say that our mountaintop moments cannot last forever. They come—and go. Those instants when we seem to feel "as if we know, dimly, what the whole darn business is about" are not a steady pouring out of light, but a flash which illumines the whole landscape for a moment. It is a very great mistake, when the scene grows dim once more, to feel discouraged and let down. Rather, let us hold fast to the memory of that second when we saw clearly and know that it will come again and again, brighter and plainer to the view each time; unless, indeed, we let the strains and preoccupations of life make us forget and deny the vision. It is so much easier to catch that vision than to hold it! But if only we keep our faith in it, and we believe that it was at that instant that we saw truth, then we can be sure it will return. And each return will leave the way brighter, our ultimate goal clearer, until real discouragement at last becomes impossible—because the road is never again totally dark.

26   DISCOURAGE DISCOURAGEMENT

There is no greater or more insidious foe to growth, achievement, and spiritual contact than discouragement. There is a quaint little story to the effect that the devil once offered to sell at auction all his tools save one— discouragement. "For," said he, "if I have that, I can get along very well without the others."

A veteran who had been half blinded in combat and had lost one arm and leg as well, replied when asked whether he did not often feel greatly discouraged, "Can't afford to! I've got too many other handicaps to add discouragement to the rest." There was not only great courage in that remark; there was also very great good sense. The paralyzing effect of discouragement, the utter fatigue and inertia that accompany it, make it a luxury no one can afford. It not only bars vital achievement; it even makes constructive thought or planning all but impossible in the fog of distress and weariness it induces.

27   THE EASIER WAY

"But," perhaps one protests, "I can't just wave a magic wand and banish discouragement! When everything goes wrong, how can one help but be discouraged?"

We might, in the first place, make very sure that a secret part of us does not welcome discouragement and use it as an excuse! If we can really become convinced that everything has gone against us, and we might as well give up the struggle, it saves a lot of strain and effort, you know. One modern writer has pointed out that while the rewards of success—she is not speaking merely of worldly success here—are well known, the rewards of failure are not so clearly recognized. Failure is so much easier! It is so much easier to dream than to do; so much easier to resort to cheap bitterness because of handicaps than to work hard at surmounting them; so much easier to take refuge in cynicism and agnosticism than it is to build up and keep a constructive faith. So let us examine ourselves very closely to make certain that we are not using discouragement as an escape from the necessity for courageous hard effort.

28   **CREEP CLOSE**

Sometimes it is a wise thing simply to walk away from discouragement instead of fighting it. Crowd it out, instead of attempting to uproot it. Replace that emotion with other emotions. This is good psychology, and it often works. We tackle a problem with renewed vigor because of having left it for a time and interested ourselves in other matters. But if things have reached a point where that seems impossible—if we are so weary and sad and frightened that we do not seem able even to pray constructively or re-establish our spiritual contact—then there is still something left to do. The old hymn put it very clearly and very simply: "Cast thy burden on the Lord." It is not at all impossible. Men and women have been doing it successfully for a very long time. They have said, "It's too much for me, God. You take it! Only show me where to go and what to do!"—and have risen from their knees with fresh courage and insight and strength. In effect, they have crept close to the heart of God and let his strength flow into them.

29   **IT IS WORTH WHILE**

A friend asked me doubtfully not long ago, "Do you really think that a few quiet moments spent regularly at some time every day in prayer, or meditation, can help as much as the devotional books tell us? I'm always meaning to do it—and always forgetting. Would it really make a difference?"

Genuine prayer, genuine contact with God, even for

just ten moments a day, can revitalize a life. We simply must learn that spirituality is no cloudy, unsubstantial thing, but the best possible practical basis for living. However, it isn't a free gift just handed to us. It is something we earn. And that plugging-in process of which we spoke a while back is a conscious and deliberate process, and one which must be maintained with courageous persistence if it is to become habitual.

So the answer to my friend's question is Yes. If poise instead of fretfulness makes a difference, if control of jangling nerves helps, if a sureness of faith and a clear judgment and a quiet heart and a courage to meet anything life brings are worth the trying to attain—then it is worth while to make these moments of prayer and meditation a regular part of every twenty-four hours.

30   UNLOCK THAT POWER

Psychologists and psychiatrists alike agree that most men and women go through life using only a very small percentage of their native abilities. The subconscious—which in the popular mind has become, since Freud, a repository for all unwanted thoughts and feelings, a sort of closed chamber of horrors—is much more than this, according to them. It is also the seat of a very great deal of unused energy and ability. If that is true, there must be a way to unlock that power. But how? A noted New York psychiatrist and a noted New York pastor have lately agreed in print that the answer is spiritual contact. In companionship with God, in the power and the peace that flow to us and through us from him, we can begin to realize all our abili-

ties instead of only a part of them. "So," asked a girl
wonderingly, "when I call on God for help in some knotty
problem, I'm really calling on myself? I mean, that part of
me I don't usually use, my reserves?" No, not exactly.
You are calling on God—consciously, deliberately, asking
him—to help you make available all the strength, all the
energy, all the talent which lies stored up within yourself.
"Does God actually *speak* to you when you pray?" I once
heard someone inquire curiously of a man of great spiritual power, great personal magnetism, great energy and
efficiency. The great man hesitated. Then he answered, "In
words—no. But contact with him so stimulates and height-
ens and intensifies my thinking that words come to me."
After a moment he added, "Communion with him means
peace and poise and strength—but it means power, too."

31   ONLY ONE AIM

Yet it should perhaps be said that all of these desirable
and happy results that spring from a vital association with
God and a vivid sense of life as a great spiritual adventure
are, in one aspect, by-products. They are tremendously
worth while in and of themselves. But they are not, nor
should they become, our main objectives in seeking him.
There is even a certain danger inherent in their becoming
so. People who seek spiritual contact for "joy" or "power"
or "escape" are likely to be those who go off into the unwholesome queernesses of cranks, cults, and systems. Deep
down and fundamentally there is only one aim, only one
motive which constitutes the most direct pathway toward
the high country of the spirit to which we want to travel:

to seek God for his own sake. I once heard a noted psychiatrist remark with self-conscious broad-mindedness that
he knew many of his colleagues would disagree with him,
but that he often sent his patients to church! "I don't
believe in any religion myself," he explained, "but I've
found that it's the best stabilizing influence a man can
have, and very conducive to both health and happiness."
What a crazy quilt of a world takes shape for us with
those words! That the best thing a man can possibly get
hold of is something that isn't true! That security and
health and happiness find their firmest foundation on
falsehoods! If that were true, we would live in a universe
that makes no sense; and it is abundantly clear we don't.
Seek ye the kingdom of God—and all these things shall
be added. But the kingdom comes first. So we turn to God
as the flower toward the sun—because to deny him and
look away from him is to thwart the deepest instincts of
our natures; because until we have found him there must
forever be, whether we are conscious of its cause or not, a
fierce hunger unappeased, a burning thirst unslaked; because only in him can we truly find fulfillment, and lacking
him we are creatures incomplete and unfulfilled; because
he is God, and we are his.

Personalities of Springtime

SUE BAILEY THURMAN

1   APRIL CHILDREN

It must have been in the mind of the gracious Creator of men, of places, and of seasons, to make his rarest offerings fall due in the spring. With the return of the "high tide of each year" we offer gratitude for his gift of men, particularly the gift of April children—Juliette Derricotte and Thomas Jefferson—and for Rabindranath Tagore, three shining ones, who in their several distinctive ways, gave such vast illumination to their time. During this spring month we shall be considering these three personalities and their contributions to the art of living.

Any modern spring is an occasion to offer a special paean for Juliette Derricotte, magnificent brown American, who in her thirty-four brief years demonstrated so vividly one vital truth to men. She might be called the perfect revelation of the lofty, tragic sense of values in life—shared by considerable numbers in all countries today—that the true lover of God must ever be challenged and impelled by the impossible. And in the transcendent, delicate realm of relationships involving men with fellow men, one may pay with physical death for the ultimate triumph of some heroic dream to which he has given the whole of life.

2   ALL MAY BE ONE

Juliette Derricotte was for some years a leader in student movements around the world, and she labored with kindred minds of other countries to help lay the subsoil of permanent peace. Her efforts were distinguished by insistence that the basis of understanding which they sought must be broadened to include a knowledge of all men. Times, occasions, and events were never too difficult for her to give eager practice to this belief. It became the consuming passion of an amazing career.

She was appointed American delegate to the World Christian Student Federation Conference meeting in Mysore, India, in 1928. She sent a dispatch back to friends in her own country, pleading that they try to understand the intricacies of this problem in human relations and the common struggle which binds men together:

"How can I tell you that I am no longer free; that the wealth as well as the poverty of India haunts me, that I ache with actual physical pain when I remember the struggles of all India today—religious, economic, social, political? How can I tell you of the control which oil and rubber and jute have in the relation of East and West, or explain how back of these are the more fundamental and eternal puzzles of economics, race and religion? . . . But then I become aware that there is so much more for us to know than we are accustomed to knowing and so much more for us to love than we are accustomed to loving, and that somewhere ahead '*All May Be One.*' "

3 GHOSTS WILL DRIVE US ON

An extended ministry to the youth of the Americas, Europe, and the Orient was the ultimate achievement of this young woman whose life opened up avenues of friendship and understanding among many peoples of the world, transcending all differences of race, creed, or culture. But in the tragic sense her life was given in token for the dream. Juliette Derricotte returned to her homeland from the last long tour, only to meet death in an automobile accident after the hospital authorities of Dalton, Georgia, had refused her ambulance and hospital service because of her color.

Telegrams from five continents poured into Athens, her home, on the bright November afternoon of her funeral. Her friends of both races gathered at night to assess the overwhelming loss. "If her death can stab fellow Americans awake to the high cost of hatred, misunderstanding, and prejudice, she shall not have died in vain."

The challenge was repeated in services held in memory of her in communities, and on college and university campuses, from Seattle, Washington, to Daytona Beach, Florida, including an American Indian college in a remote corner of the Middle West.

The young minister who had been a warm friend and comrade in all of her labor through the years summarized the peculiar meaning of this sacrifice:

"There is work to be done, and ghosts will drive us on.

. . . This is an unfinished world; she has left an unfinished
task. Who will take it up? Driven by the power of her spirit
we dedicate ourselves anew to the continuance of the developing process which she had begun in an imperfect
world. To this we set our hands in our time."

4   LOVE MEANS KNOWLEDGE

Through the tribulation which has recently shattered our
world, we remember Juliette Derricotte. We remember
her amazing insight, which must become the religious
man's imperative: "I cannot say that I love my neighbor as
myself if indeed I do not *realize* and know my neighbor
as myself." Only the sensitive artist-at-living, the supreme
knower among us who has reduced the sense of differentiation between himself and his neighbor to a vanishing point,
can say that he has been able to make real the injunction,
"Love thy neighbor as thyself."

Too often the maudlin, sentimental, "I love you for
Christ's sake only" dictum of the western conscience is
offered as unworthy counterfeit for a genuine achievement.
Such an act of will is required to *know* one's neighbor as
oneself that often the discipline is refused. We deny our
spirits the challenge of so high a flight over hitherto uncon-
quered territory, and therefore, leaving the quest, we lose
the venture.

5   THINGS OF PEACE

It is springtime in Jerusalem, and the Son of man
broods over the Holy City; "If thou hadst known the

things which belong unto thy peace." "If thou hadst known"—the cumulative effect of an ever-recurring theme.

It is springtime in my street—an American street in which many interesting people live, people of varying hue and color, of diverse nationality and creedal origins. One neighbor, a native daughter of the street, is tight-lipped and strangely out of step with the rhythm of the scene. She scowls in the midst of laughter. She is careful that none of her branches shall hang over the fence. She has been grievously enslaved by the prejudice to which self-consideration alone can give full birth. She knows nothing of the things which belong unto her peace or to the greater peace of all mankind.

It is a call to one of the highest flights in religion for my spirit to attempt to deal creatively with my neighbor. I will not accept the easier way—simply to negate or ignore this "sneer of selfish men," this greeting "where no kindness is," so close at hand.

6   WHERE THE WORLD BEGINS

I would continue to breathe a prayer for the happy fulfillment and well-being of women and children in all parts of the world. But if I do, I must include the ill-bred, prejudiced neighbor. I can will to understand her rude disregard for the racial or creedal group which may differ from her own, as a distortion of spirit which springs from deep personal unhappiness or malcontent. But I would need a morning to seek a new creative energy for myself that I may appreciate the neighbor in my mind.

I find vitality for such creativeness in various ways. I sit in the pew of a beautiful church or cathedral so that the colors of its stained glass windows may fall flush in my face. I listen again and again to a rendition of the *First Symphony* of Brahms. I read the sonorous prose of a Hebrew prophet. Then I can breathe a wish that my neighbor may find a fresh abiding happiness, that some wonderful thing, as yet denied, may happen in her life. She has in return for prejudice what I may have of creative good will.

What my heart can wish for the neighbor on my street is one of the surest indicators of the quality of good will which I may have for people in faraway places—the Russians, the Senegalese, the French.

7   **GO TELL THEM**

We watched at the Golden Gate as four hundred missionaries sailed with a cargo of gifts for exchange in foreign fields. They will be, it is hoped, so much the embodiment of the finest culture of our Judaeo-Christian tradition that their veneration for the culture of the peoples to whom they go must needs be deep and instinctive. They should be creatures of such sensitive perception that God may be revealed through them as "the glory of order, beauty, and variety," that he is, "known to be active, loving, wise, and unweariable power"—a definition to be found in the language of any people.

They will have William Blake's interpretation of the meaning of their quest:

> Go tell them that worshipping God
> is honoring His gifts in other men.

The messenger who seeks the highest import and purport of this commission will become so identified with the people of the culture he has chosen that their dreams, hopes, visions, and achievements may be known and appreciated by him, in time, as the messenger knows and appreciates his own dreams, hopes, and visions.

8   EXCHANGE OF GIFTS

Those who take their gifts afar will find other rare gifts offered in exchange—the glory of beauty and variety in all the peoples of the East. It should become a commonplace for natives of an ancient oriental culture to hear the messenger declare on Sabbath morning, "You are a beautiful people, as beautiful of face as you are potentially beautiful within. You are the kingdom of heaven. It is within you, within your face, within your eyes, within your heart. . . . There is inherent beauty in your speech. I have learned the literature languages, Bengali, Tagalog, or Mandarin, not only to offer the English Bible to you in their media, but because they reveal to me the subtle and inclusive evidence of God in the 'other soul,' which is the the goal of all my questing in your midst." The messenger, the seeker, then comes to affirm the unity of all sons of God, as one who knows and realizes the human experience of which he is a part. And in this act he bears invariable witness that he has not been brought to a land alien to his feet.

103

In Washington, D.C., a poet-teacher adopted an unusual custom of taking friends on periodic journeys to the shrine of Thomas Jefferson. One evening under bright stars, in the memorable spring of 1944, she assembled a group of Jeffersonian devotees—with Meta Warrick Fuller, the sculptor of Farmingham among them—for moments of communion at the foot of the statue.

"Why do we come here so often rather than to some other shrine in the nation's capital?"

"Because we want to feel that we are one in the company of him who articulated for all our kind the great American dream."

"It is the constant search for this, our greatest heritage—the freedom of the mind—that draws us to this place."

"He was the greatest force for liberalism our country has ever known."

"The most accomplished American, and still he had the deepest faith in the worth and dignity of men."

Esther Popel, the poet-teacher, caught and held one of our moments at the shrine in her poem, "Jefferson Memorial at Midnight—An Impression."

I

Pale midnight floods the world!
Thin mists uncurl
About the Grecian pile,
In silhouette
Against the midnight sky.

II

The bald dome curved
Above the columned grace
Of gleaming marble,
Makes the stately shrine
A templed sepulchre
Exquisite, chaste
For him
Whose honored name it bears.

III

He stands within
In silent awesomeness,
A darkly towering figure
Keeping watch,
A calm and stately sentinel
On guard,
On guard and lonely,
In the quiet night.
And, as he watches,
Soft! the city sleeps.[1]

10   AN ELOQUENT TESTIMONY

Jefferson has much to teach us in this day as we search
for modern weapons to use in the struggle against the
formidable confusion which threatens to destroy us without and within. He gave to our world a certainty of belief
in the ultimate triumph of the forces of right. He was a
zealous disciple of the moral teachings of Jesus. He wrote
letters to John Adams and Benjamin Rush setting forth

[1] Used by permission of the author.

his theory in this regard. Under the date of April 21, 1803, to Doctor Rush, Jefferson wrote:

"To the corruptions of Christianity I am, indeed, opposed, but not to the genuine precepts of Jesus himself. . . . His moral doctrines, relating to kindred and friends, were more pure and perfect than those of the most correct of the philosophers, . . . and they went far beyond [them] . . . in inculcating universal philanthropy, not only to kindred and friends, to neighbours and countrymen, but to all mankind, gathering all into one family, under the bonds of love, charity, peace, common wants, and common aids. . . . He pushed his scrutinies into the heart of man; erected his tribunal in the region of his thoughts, and purified the waters at the fountain head."

11   IN THE NOBLE SUCCESSION

A distinguished Christian in the Jeffersonian tradition of those having deep and abiding faith in the dignity and worth of all men was Dean Edward Increase Bosworth of Oberlin. Through the years, generations of Oberlin students have left Finney Chapel trying to remember some exact phrase from one of his chapel talks.

"What was Dean Bosworth's definition of a Christian?"

"I didn't quite get it. I think Betty Rugh or Mickey Edgar might have it."

"Oh yes, it was this, 'A Christian is one who works together with God to bring about a race of men, honest, wise, and friendly.' "

We remember snow in deep winter at Oberlin, and against the background of that snow a scholarly gentleman walking a block out of his way to say, "Good morning," to a colored janitor who was clearing the snow from the walkways. There were many other expressions of his way of life—deeper, more significant perhaps, which provided our campus with a vigorous demonstration of the insights of Jefferson as they would appear in a specifically Christian frame of reference. So in this sense he was for us a constant presence calling attention to Jeffersonian philosophy in a Christian manifestation.

12   AMATEURS

There are other Christians—it would seem a manifold company—who offer no grace to the kingdom. They are so lacking in taste and tact in the area in which they wish most to succeed. They are the unforgivably rude individuals who pride themselves on being obvious, forthright, and blunt. They tread on pearls with cloven feet. They ignore the demands of the innumerable, delicate, and prolonged adjustments required of those who would work constantly with God "to bring about a race of men, honest, wise, and friendly."

They are often seen in woman's auxiliaries, in committee organizations, in conference and convention assemblies where all have gathered avowedly to help in building the kingdom of right-relations. But before united thought or action can be directed toward the ideals of this kingdom, often the entire corporate effort of the group must be devitalized in the struggle against the bad taste and bad manners of some of its members.

It is strange that many of this variety consider themselves numbered among the professionals of the artists-at-living—more especially among those who claim to take all their cues in the drama from the gracious Jesus of Nazareth, the greatest artist of them all. They should have the searching scrutiny of the personal presence of the master director looking on them always as they go through their acts. It would be a telling judgment. He would be ashamed of their amateurish performance.

13   MASTERING TECHNIQUES

There is another group, and they too are a host, whose minds and spirits have been tempered with that finer essence of forbearance without which there can be no refinement of being. We are grateful to encounter them in our daily lives. They are decisive personalities who give all of their skills to the re-creating of life about them, operating as sensitive observers of human need and feeling. They have mastered the broad techniques of form—the use of excellent methods in everything they do. They seek to create a better world, beginning where they live.

A Caucasian home owner, who belongs to an inter-cultural, interracial, intercreedal fellowship on the west coast, was eager to rent her second-floor apartment to tenants belonging to one of the minority groups—either Filipino, Japanese-American, Negro, or Chinese. She wanted her action to be intelligible to the long line of neighbors who lived on her "select" street. She had a rather unusual type of "at home," inviting all the neighbors, including many whom she had not known before. She explained what she was about to do, insisting that as she respected their intelligence, she hoped they would respect her philosophy of how human beings should live together. The minority-group family moved in. The street goes on apace with its quiet living. The neighbors have constant exposure to a superior-religious individual's way of life in action.

14   ARTISTS AT WORK

There have been other demonstrations of unusual form.

Residents on a special block of a beautiful street in a certain city had put their signatures on a restrictive covenant which had been circulating among them for some time. The mistress of one of the homes, a most creative and influential citizen, had refused to sign the papers. So that section of her street could not be covenanted. However, she was sure that her neighbors would profit by hearing a fine presentation of the intricate problem of intergroupal relationships in the city. She invited them to her elegant drawing room and gave them the rare experience of an evening of discussion with one of the country's most eminent scholars in the field of human affairs. The neighbors could only be impressed with the dignity of her choice. And they found even in that dignity, perhaps, the greatest challenge to their own position.

There is an artist in the use of form in Georgia. She has been teaching the youth of a quaint little town for almost half a century. She lives on one of the interesting streets found in practically every southern town or city, where colored and white neighbors have their dwellings side by side. Her neighbor resented being required to live next door to colored persons even if they were among the most cultured people in the town. So she moved her pig-pen up to the fence adjoining their house, as close to the colored family's door as she could place it. The school-teacher in turn planted finest cuttings of scented roses close to her side of the fence, so that their fragrance and color might be shared by those on the other side. Spring came, and with it a riot of rambling beauty which bore its silent tribute to a magnificent gesture of the spirit.

15   WHEN NO ONE SEES

"Love your enemies, bless them that curse you, do good to them that hate you, and pray for them which despitefully use you and persecute you; that ye may be the children of your Father which is in heaven; for he maketh his sun to rise on the evil and the good, and sendeth rain on the just and on the unjust."

In *The Great Hunger*, a novel by Bojer, the hero planted his enemy's field under cover of night, because there was no grain, drought had covered the land, and his enemy faced a winter of starvation. He wanted to plant the enemy's field with grain that God might be in the world. This was one of the greatest utterances of God in man imaginable.

To plant the enemy's field when the world is asleep; when no one, not even the enemy, can know who has done the deed; when there is no chance to "heap coals of fire on his head" and then stand by in self-righteousness and see it burn; when the coveted opportunity to win plaudits of the community has been forfeited because the act was accomplished when no man could see—this is a deed for the lover of unreachable heights. Others, with smaller concepts of the realm of God in man, would only dishonor the kingdom in any such attempt.

16   LAMPS AND LIGHT

Feminine grace expresses itself in a beautiful custom in India, which should find appreciation in all the households of the world. When the Hindu-Indian woman lights the lamps of her home at the approach of night, it is a ceremonial always performed with the singing of a chant appropriate to twilight hours. Music, the odor of flowers, and purifying incense fill the house and yard. She uses a stately brass lamp which holds a fragrant, bland coconut oil. This is an ancient Hindu custom which may not be observed by outsiders unless they are privileged to visit a Hindu home at this particular hour.

The worshipper indulges an act of quiet meditation. She may chant from the popular lamp-lighting song, "Light your lamps in honor of the great Creator." Or she may evoke the mood of worship in the Brihad-Aranyaka Upanishad,

> From the unreal lead me to the real!
> From darkness lead me to light!
> From death lead me to immortality!

Strangely, or perhaps not so strangely, the home seems suddenly purified with a diffusion of spirit. And the diffusion lingers as an "inner light."

17   BEFORE THE CARNIVAL OF LIGHTS

Rabindranath Tagore's maiden in one of the prose poems of his *Gitanjali* takes her lamp down to the river to offer it to the carnival of lights.

Maiden, where do you go shadowing your lamp with your mantle? My house is all dark and lonesome—lend me your light!

. . . I have come to the river, to float my lamp on the stream when the daylight wanes in the west.

. . . In the silence of gathering night I asked her,
Maiden, your lights are all lit—then where do you go with your lamp?

. . . I have come . . . to dedicate my lamp to the sky.
In the moonless gloom of midnight I asked,
Maiden, what is your quest holding the lamp near your heart?

. . . I have brought my lamp to join the carnival of lamps.[2]

We like to think that the maiden expressed the yearning of all men to dedicate their lamps to the sky, to the universal carnival of lights. But we would hope that the maiden paused long enough to have the lamp-lighting ceremonial in her home before taking her lamp down to the river. She would want to purify and illumine her own house first. Then, and then only, could its fragrance and light be offered to the larger stream of life.

[2]Rabindranath Tagore, *Gitanjali*. (The Macmillan Co.) Used by permission.

18   TAGORE—SPRING'S POET

A group of Americans on a pilgrimage of friendship to colleges and universities of India, Burma, and Ceylon were given a benediction of long, generous hours at Santineeketan with Tagore. The poet was gratified that at least an initial gesture had been accomplished in cementing friendships between the youth of East and West. Those were the closing years of his life and for some time he had been devoting all of his remarkable energies to bringing about warm understanding and fellowship between the peoples of the world.

It was a "feast of reason and a flow of soul" to hear one of the great poets of the century express his undying faith in the "remnant of the faithful" in every country, who will never leave off their seeing of visions and dreaming of dreams. His belief was that a sufficiency of spirit could be released by this "sensitive minority" to save the soul of any nation.

He was a being of such rare beauty, so elegant of form and face—so redolent of the world's great seers who reflect the glory of a lighted mind! We were grateful that earth had seen a person like him.

He read poetry to his class in the quiet of evening under the banyan trees. They heard his ode to the high cause of freedom, repeated in languages around the world:

Where the mind is without fear and the head is held high;
Where knowledge is free; . . .
Where the mind is led forward by thee into ever-widening
    thought and action—

113

Into that heaven of freedom, my Father, let my country
   awake.[8]

The generation of today—those multitudes who have
known the terror of walking in darkness—will find in Tagore a hand that can light the way, even for the solitary
pilgrim.

19   SLAVES

One tenet of Moslem worshipers should come highly
commended to their brethren of other faiths. It is the
democratic policy of Islam. It is a concept of brotherhood among themselves which is in practice very real. It
cuts across all lines of caste, class, color, or racial distinction. It is one of the first precepts taught by their leader,
Mohammed. Like a true prophet he dealt one by one with
the problems of his day, giving careful thought and attention to the ancient practice of slavery. He ordered the
freeing of all slaves who embraced the faith of Islam. He
counseled a humane attitude toward those slaves who
did not become his followers: "See that ye feed them with
such food as ye yourselves eat, and clothe them with the
stuff ye yourselves wear, for they are the servants of the
Lord, and are not to be tormented."
Furthermore, he ordered that no stigma be attached
to an emancipated slave. He was to be regarded and dealt
with as a brother. It is not surprising that Bilalibn Rabah,
Negro of compelling voice and presence, would be chosen

[8] Rabindranath Tagore, *Gitanjali*. (The Macmillan Co.) Used
by permission.

by Mohammed to be the first Moslem muezzin. His haunting cry calling the faithful to prayer has come down the centuries,

> Allah is most great.
> Come to prayer.
> Come to progress.
> I bear witness there is no God but God.

And one seventh of the world's population, men of all races and of all continents, hear the echo of this call and turn their faces toward Mecca.

A Moslem professor in a famous university of the East inquired of visitors from another country, with a sly twinkle in his eye, "What has been the tradition of the other great religions when the slave has embraced the religion of his master?"

20   WHETHER MOUNTAIN OR VALLEY

Two friends were spending some days in the region of Darjeeling. One of them had persuaded their companion-guide to go with him to the top of Tiger Hill, so that he might catch the vision of sunrise over the Himalayas. The plans were made; the hour set. They would start climbing at early morning in order to reach the summit for the one silver instant when Kinchinjunga would be flooded with rays of shimmering light.

The other friend remained in the valley. There were visits to make: A Buddhist priest in saffron robe would be sitting near a shop in the bazaar fingering his prayer wheel. Friendly street vendors would be peddling their wares of

shining brass decorated with semi-precious turquoise.
There would be salutations to the sunrise in a thousand
different languages. "I shall not climb Tiger Hill. The
valley is so pleasant. The object of my search is in the
valley."

The mountain climber might return from his heights
with an attitude of condescension toward the valley seeker,
not perceiving that the preferences of their choosing in-
dicated only the difference in their goals. Once the goal of
the quest of any individual is made clear, it is revealed
that whether he searches mountain or valley, he finds his
own "acre of diamonds" where he is.

21   A NEW BEGINNING

We had come home from the funeral of a friend. She
had been so vital, so contagious, so alive at the center
that we could hardly imagine that an occasion in memo-
riam of *her* could be filled with so much gloom. The
hymns were cheerless and taken out of their original context—"Lead Kindly Light," chant of all the living who
walk the earth with assurance and dignity, was sung as a
requiem; "Nearer My God to Thee," a prayer of those who
seek the everydayness of God, was droned as a dirge. Aging
flowers of dreary color and suffocating fragrance stifled the
air. The organ peeled forth with a "March of Death"
which some hapless nineteenth century composer had
written for just such an occasion. All in all it had seemed
a betrayal of the joyous person being celebrated as well as
of that radiant company of which she was still a part.

"Do you remember how much she liked the great hymns

of nature? "The Spacious Firmament on High," set to Haydn's music, or the majestic melody of Nicaea, with Gannett's words,

> Bring, O morn, thy music! bring, O night, thy silence!
> Ocean, chant the rapture to the storm-wind coursing free!
> Sun and stars are singing,—Thou art our Creator,
> Who wert and art and evermore shalt be.

"And she would have liked a reading from the Sermon on the Mount, and from the ode of David,

> The Eternal's law is a sound law,
>   reviving life;
> The Eternal's is a trusty witness,
>   that instructs the open minded;
> The Eternal's orders are just,
>   a joy to the heart;
> The Eternal's command is clear,
>   a light to the mind.[4]

"She would have wanted some of the poems of adventure—Yeats's 'I will arise and go now, and go to Innisfree.' It should have ended with a deep favorite, 'The Lord's Prayer,' with the music of Malotte."

Hymns of praise and adoration, scripture of exultant mood, poems of adventure—these only can acclaim that life in the highlands, here, is the climax to life in a new beginning.

[4] Psalm 19:1-8. From *The Bible: A New Translation* by James Moffatt. Used by permission of Harper & Brothers.

The lives of some people are of such quality that they merit having great music selected to interpret them in the end. Franz Liszt in the tone poem *Les Preludes* has written such a summary of a heroic man's life. I know of certain characters who should have no other ceremony than the playing of *Les Preludes* at their death. Liszt based his theme on the poetic meditation of Lamartine:

"What is our life but a series of preludes to that unknown symphony whose initial solemn chord is intoned by death. The enchanted dawn of every life is love; but where is the destiny on whose first delicious joys some storm does not break?—a storm whose deadly blast disperses youth's illusion, whose fatal bolt consumes its altar? . . . But when the trumpet gives the signal man hastens to danger's post whatever be the fight which draws him to its lists, that in the struggle he may once more regain full knowledge of himself and all his strength."

Perhaps the inspiring service of tribute to the life of the dead, through music, should take place only in the privacy of a drawing room with an intimate circle of friends. There should be chrysanthemums, roses, camellias, and light from a setting sun.

If it were an occasion for me, I would like nothing better than to merit the "Triumphal March" from *Sigurd Jorsalfar* by Edvard Grieg, with a resonant voice reading an Oswald McCall's offering from "The Hand of God."

23   THE WAY OF THE POETS

A group was sitting around the fire at Fellowship House, social meeting place of the Church for the Fellowship of All Peoples, in San Francisco. It was an interesting gathering of friends—homemakers, social workers, business administrators, teachers, and artists—who had achieved through the months an amazing unity of spirit. They met often in this way to think together about many things. This night they were discussing the various stairways men have used to reach the altar of God. Some had found him in the Book alone, others through the arts, others through nature or through participation in the affairs of men.

A university student observed that a large group of people whom he represented made their primary approach to God by way of the poets. "The poets are the perfect see-ers and realizers of experience," he said. . . . "I am always thinking of how accurately Tennyson expresses one of the greatest frustrations in life, through the anguish he gives King Arthur, in *The Idyls of the King*:

> I found Him in the shining of the stars,
> I marked Him in the flowering of His fields,
> But in His ways with men I find Him not.

That is the realm in which we wish so desperately to find Him."

There was more discussion—more observations about the poets. Yes, they could put their fingers on the core of the frustration. Matthew Arnold, especially. He had certainly summed it up for the world of the twentieth century. Growing numbers everywhere who would stress

the pre-eminence of human relations were remembering
with grim realism his lines from "Dover Beach": *"Let
us be true to one another!"* Groups in other places, no
doubt at that very moment, were gazing into other fire-
lights, attempting to draw closer together, sensing the immediate peril to their very young dream of brotherhood,
inasmuch as they were

> on a darkling plain
> Swept with confused alarms of struggle and flight,
> Where ignorant armies clash by night.

24   LIKE THY GLORY, TITAN

But there were other poets too. The fellowship group
felt that if Shelley were living today, perhaps he might be
called to their very ranks, to say nothing of Blake. "Shelley would render our cause an inspiriting service. Did he
not believe fiercely that love is God, and that love will
win ultimately in the struggle against force?" *Prometheus
Unbound* had spoken directly to their day, they thought.
It was the story of the old, old conflict. Jove was force;
Prometheus was love. As always love had to challenge the
impossible in order to win the fire. Shelley believed with
equal fervor that justice was the light of love, and so had
spent all of his brief, turbulent years in the "high cause of
Love's magnificence," fighting the forces of darkness which
threatened to destroy his world. For him this would be
the only stairway to the altar. Like one previsioning the
future, he left to the generation that the fellowship group
represented a precious thing—an age-old faith, with a new
and daring commitment:

To suffer woes which Hope thinks infinite;
To forgive wrongs darker than death or night;
To defy Power, which seems omnipotent;
To love, and bear; to hope till Hope creates
From its own wreck the thing it contemplates;
Neither to change, nor falter, nor repent;
This, like thy glory, Titan, is to be
Good, great and joyous, beautiful and free;
This is alone Life, Joy, Empire, and Victory.

25　　　　　WITHIN

Shelley thought of Jesus as the "sublimest and most holy poet." Perhaps because to him Jesus was a revelation of the highest function of the poet—"to be a pathfinder between ourselves and Reality." Jesus aroused the depth of our dignity and pride as human beings in announcing the good news that we had so long waited for, "The kingdom of heaven is within you."

And then, poetry of poetry! "The kingdom of heaven is like a grain of mustard seed, which a man took, and sowed in his field . . ."

"It is like unto leaven which a woman took, and hid in three measures of meal . . ."

"The kingdom of heaven is like unto treasure hid in a field; the which when a man hath found, he hideth, and for joy thereof goeth and selleth all that he hath, and buyeth that field."

"It is like unto a merchant man, seeking goodly pearls: who when he had found one pearl of great price, went and sold all that he had and bought it."

And then like an echo or second-sight, "The kingdom of heaven is *within* you."

Thus wherever we move, the kingdom of heaven moves with us. By such a breath-taking revelation we are stirred to new creative energies; we are fired with an inexhaustible imagination; we discover a new enthusiasm for eternity by knowing that we can never outdistance the kingdom of God.

26   FOR GRACIOUSNESS

Lord of life, love, and beauty, accept this prayer of thanks for gracious things—for the graciousness we find in so many unexpected places, for rare kindliness and grace in creature beings.

For little children of starry eyes in Arizona and New Mexico who stop in their play to smile and wave at unknown friends on passing trains.

For the humility and tender kindness of one of the greatest of all scientists, who, without ever revealing his famous name, helped a small, stranger-girl do her "difficult sums" in arithmetic on the occasion of his frequent walks in the park.

For the vision of the widowed mother in Arkansas who for thirty years has contributed most of her meager substance to the support of schools in the southland, in Africa, and in China, in order to keep alive, in far-away children, the dream of a brilliant son who died rendering distinguished service to his country during World War I.

For the graciousness of the writer of a well-known children's prayer book—the busy hostess on a university campus in Connecticut—who dedicated her book to her devoted colored helper because the maid had relieved her of domestic duty that she might have the time and leisure required to write the book. Highly exalted personalities would have considered it a distinctive honor to have had the book dedicated to them. For its prayers, originals of the writer's own children, are repeated in American homes throughout the land, and author and helper working together have given new wings to children's prayers.

27   FURTHER GRATITUDE

God of all grace, we offer gratitude for the inward loneliness which draws all men together; for the hands of friends, touching ours in the darkness, giving assurance that we will never walk alone; for the one who writes so compellingly, "Say Yes to the Light," the Congregational minister of Southern California, who is like "a noontide in their twilight," and whose "shadow is a light upon their faces."

For the gracious conductor on the Southern Railway train, *The Memphis Special*, who took the hand of a little brown girl and showed her the mysteries of a cloud of steam escaping from a big green engine; for his wisdom and patience in meeting the bright curiosity of a nine-year-old, pointing out the different shades of autumn gold in the trees of the Shenandoah Valley; for his belief in tomorrow, for his words to her, "When my people and your people really get to know each other, we shall all be friends."

It brings to mind an earlier faith that "there is so much

more for us to know than we are accustomed to knowing,
and so much more for us to love than we are accustomed to
loving, that somewhere ahead, '*All May Be One.*' "

28   FOR KINDLY CITIES

We are grateful, too, for the gift of gracious cities—
for the surface indications of human spirit in them, so
important in the lives of people. One may have greater
faith in the human race and faith in the God above it if
the city in which he lives has the heart of a kindly city.

Rochester, New York, at Christmas—sales clerks in large
department stores handling thousands of pushing, shoving,
pressing, crowding shoppers. Five o'clock, on the twenty-
fourth day—nearing the closing hour. The clerks are too
exhausted to stay on their feet much longer. But the
patrons are beginning to file out of the store.

"Was it really true that I heard a 'Merry Christmas,'
from the weary sales girls when they gave me these last
packages? It will mean more to my memory than the singing of Christmas carols."

Yes, all men can be brothers. It was intended so—even
for a complex, sophisticated, urban community.

The bus driver on one of the long traffic arteries
through the city, reminds all passengers to "Watch your
step," with occasionally a pleasant "Good night." He
seemed to care genuinely about the safety of other human
beings. A very simple thing, perhaps, but it is wonderful-
ly heartening to know that kindness even on a carrier still
exists. I would breathe a prayer of thanksgiving for the
graciousness of Rochester.

29   A NEW NATION

San Francisco—10.45 Sunday morning.

Bells are ringing, calling the people to Saint Dominic's, to the First Church of Christ, Scientist, to Temple Eman-u-El—for the Sunday school—to the Buddhist Temple. Each a short distance from the other. Sixty differing nationality and racial groups will pass each other on the way, en route to prayers. There is courtesy among them, and tolerance. "It can be done," we think. "Men can be brothers!" But it happens only in such a city which has been tolerant to the world.

"Will you be special guests at the Coffee Hour following the service of our congregation next Sunday? We want you to explain to us the meaning of your beautiful Chanukkah—'Feast of Lights.' We are grateful forever to the seed of Israel, for the gift of monotheistic religion—your gift alone, without which we might be worshiping 365 gods of stone. Your lights and our lights shall stream from tall windows together."

George Washington, father of our country, envisioned the kindly, gracious American city in his great dream for the future of a brave new world—where all men shall contribute richly of their several gifts, where "they shall sit every man under his vine and under his fig tree; and none shall make him afraid."

30   BENEDICTION FOR SPRING

It is given to the lover of God to soar into the impossible and win his own Promethian fire. But he is able to soar only if he realizes the kingdom within and if from his own depths he calls to the kingdom in others. He seeks for God in everything. He finds him everywhere. To him, God becomes the all-pervading presence that disturbs men

> with the joy
> Of elevated thoughts; a sense sublime
> Of something far more deeply interfused,
> Whose dwelling is the light of setting suns,
> And the round ocean and the living air,
> And the blue sky, and in the mind of man.[5]

For him there will be inestimable gifts—light, freedom, beauty—and the peace of God. Marion Cuthbert in writing of the manifestations of this peace in her volume, *April Grasses* says:

> The peace of God . . .
>   Flowers at the foot of a tree.
>   The light of stars in the fields.
>   A child asleep where it knelt
>   To pray. No sails on a sea.
>
> That passeth all understanding . . .
>   Dawn! Flowers from earth.
>   The hurt of music. Dreams.
>   The myriad leaves in a wood.
>   Tears at laughter's birth.

[5] William Wordsworth, "Lines Composed a Few Miles Above Tintern Abbey."

Keep your hearts . . .
  Wide eyes outwatching night.
  Tall candles on an altar.
  Vows, unworded prayers.
  Jewels falling in light.

In the knowledge . . .
  Sapphires! Eden worlds!

And love . . .
  Rubies! Gethsemane's blood.
  Thorn drops where He passed.

Of God . . .
  Pearls! Pearls! Pearls! [6]

[6] Reprinted with the permission of The Woman's Press.

Together We Grow

RUTH SWANBERG ROHLFS

1   MEMBERS OF ONE BODY

Growth is a funny thing—it's so uneven. And it's unevenness causes so many of our problems. At one age all growth seems to go into legs, and in spite of hems and tucks and facings, garments are outgrown in a flash. Then again growth concentrates around the waistline, and wistfully we awaken to the realization that we're not as young as we once were. There are the seemingly endless years of growth of necessary academic knowledge. At varying times in different lives comes the—sometimes feverish, sometimes subtle—efforts to grow in prestige. Through this book of meditations we are endeavoring to grow in spirit. During the current month we would accent growth of understanding of women who walk through life on other paths than those we follow. Our desire is to recognize our likenesses, comprehend our differences, and experience our oneness.

We human beings stem from a common source, are endowed with similar faculties, experience emotions, needs, fears and desires very much akin. We are members of one

world, so bound together that—whether we will it or not
—the insecurity of one makes us all less secure. Our security can come only as we are willing to clear our eyes
and see our inseparable oneness with God and our inseparable oneness with each other.

"If the foot were to say, 'Because I am not the hand I do
not belong to the body,' that would not make it any less a
part of the body. . . . Now you are one body—the body of
Christ, and you individually are members of it. . . . If one
member suffers, all members suffer with it. If one member
is honored, all members share its honor." (I Cor. 12:15,
26, 27 Kent.)

Growth of oneness with God and our fellow men would
mean the peace which through the ages we have tried to
capture by using all weapons except those of love and
understanding.

As we approach the altar of God, let us see also the
other women who kneel there, share their thoughts, their
problems, and aspirations. Then we may begin our prayer
with the familiar "Our Father."

2   TO A STUDENT

Dear Jane,

The house has been ringing with emptiness this morning, now that you have left for school. Last night when
Dad and I stood on the station platform waving our last
good-by as the train carried you away, we were nearly
bursting with pride in this lovely young lady whom we are
so fortunate to have as a daughter.

These years at college are mighty important, my dear,

129

so use them well. Be diligent in your quest for truth, for the truth will make you a whole person. You must weigh all information—even at college—for as facts are sieved out to you through other people's minds, even there there may be conscious or unconscious selection or distortion.

I doubt that I need to remind you that if a *demonstrated* fact conflicts with your concept of God, by all means don't try to throw away God! Recognize that you have a wrong concept or idea about God which needs to be altered or discarded. God is truth. Remember how Dr. James interprets Jesus' words as "I am the Way and the Truth *about* Life?"

The doorbell rings! More anon.

In haste—
Your loving Mother.

3.   TO A STUDENT (Continued)

Late Evening

Dearest Jane,

Mrs. Graham and the postman arrived almost simultaneously this morning to interrupt my writing to you, and knowing I would not again be free until after the southbound mail left, I sealed your letter and sent it on its way. But before I close my eyes for the night, I want to complete the thoughts I had on my mind.

Superflous reminders they are, and yet they need to be enunciated from time to time so that the rushing excitement of the new adventure ahead will never want for a frame of reference.

No matter how often your courses change, there is one

textbook which is the constant and greatest source book of Christian teaching—the Bible. Covering at least fifteen hundred years, accumulated slowly over centuries, and originally written in many languages and in many forms, it is a record of those who experienced God and then desired to share that wonderful experience with others.

The spiritual truth of the Bible, plus all the other truth you will absorb, ought to clarify for you the laws of the universe—God's laws. Learn them well, that you may live in harmony with them.

Good night, dear. I know that the Big Dipper I see in tonight's clear sky is also looking down on you and that our dear Lord is close beside each of us while we are absent one from the other.

With much love,
Mother

P. S. Dad is writing tomorrow.

4   AN INDUSTRIAL WORKER DREAMS

"Mildred!" came the sharp voice of the laundry supervisor directly behind her. Guiltily her foot pressed the lever of the mangle with such haste her fingers were unable to escape the searing heat of the descending metal.

As the company nurse dressed the burns, Mildred half sobbed—as much from self-reproach and rebellion as from pain. "What's the matter with me—dreaming—just when Hatchet-face had to come along! Me, who can produce more finished work in a day than anyone else on the floor." Continuing, she became more thoughtful. "You want to know what I was dreaming about, Miss Adams? Sounds crazy, but I'm pretty good in art work, and I've been going to night school for almost a year now studying drafting. I was dreaming I got a drafting job and could do what I love to do *all day long*." And then ruefully, "Guess this'll teach me not to dream."

The nurse put the final smoothing touch to the last piece of adhesive and looked up with warm understanding in her friendly eyes. "I don't need to caution you against dreaming again with your foot on the mangle pedal. But Mildred, don't stop dreaming dreams! Dream—about the work you'd love to do, about the person you want to be, about the security you and your fellow workers need, about the kind of a world you want to live in! Dream dreams, my dear, because all things start from dreams. Dream, for out of dreams come the ideas from which reality is born."

5   A HOUSEHOLD WORKER'S MEDITATION

Dear Lord, as the carpenter of Galilee you know what it's like to stand all day and work with your hands. You said, "Come unto me, all ye that labor and are heavy laden and I will give you rest." I was included when you said that. I come to you for the peace and objectivity and strength which awaits me.

O Christ, help me to be one of many who dignify this task which so often is belittled. I have been hired to minister to the needs of the home because I am able and skilled in performing these common tasks which tradition seems to allocate to women. Often it is what I do—*I*, the household employee—which transforms the impersonal shell of a house into a warm, friendly home.

132

It is not only an occupation of the hands, but also one of the heart and mind. Give me wisdom as I share with the mother the responsibility for the care, discipline, and love the children need. Let me ever be mindful that I too am shaping their lives.

May I be slow to anger, quick to forgive, a calm defender of justice—whether it is my employer's, the children's, or my own rights which are at stake.

I pray that I may demonstrate a spirit which will stimulate respect and understanding to grow between all of us who dwell together beneath this roof.

6   A BUSINESS GIRL'S LETTER

"I know I sound baffled and dismayed, and I am. One tries to work for a better social order in her own small way and is always blundering and making mistakes—stumbling along. I'm sorry we all can't say we're doing it for the glory of God. It's not that clear to all of us. We're only trying to help mankind a little and ourselves in doing it—working for our own salvation and that of civilization because of some vague inner urge that we cannot dissect or understand. Is it religion? Our dynamic purpose? Is God a cheerer on the sidelines, urging the team into making a goal, rather than the ultimate shoulder to cry on? Do we know the meaning of life? Is it comedy or tragedy? Life is merely existence unless it has a particular meaning for the individual. Perhaps religion is a meaning we read into life, like a child investing a doll with human characteristics—a figment of our imagination. How can we know? But does it matter as long as it has meaning for us? Then our problem is, perhaps, not to question whether there is a God, a heaven, or a meaning to life, but merely to assume that religion is the meaning to life and make it real enough so that girls can put their teeth in it.

"I am, perhaps, merely being expedient in this, because I believe that . . . religion . . . infers action in working toward a better social order and that is one of the parts of workers' education. . . . I'm not clear as to why I do it, you know, but only clear that I have to keep on trying because I can't help myself. So how about some clarification on religion? When it comes to that, I'm rank and file, and the saints-on-earth talk way over my head with their vague theisms—their personal relations with God. Can we bring religion down to earth?" [1]

As you read over this young woman's letter, what would be your most helpful "down to earth" answer?

7   FORMULAS AND FAITH

Driving through the cold wind and rain, Dr. Allison reviewed the emergency call just made. The lateness of the hour and the storm outside had accentuated the hushed terror which vibrated through the household. The little girl was seriously ill without a doubt. Even before her examination, Dr. Allison had tentatively diagnosed the cause of the labored breathing and flushed cheeks. When she had left, the child was sleeping, and the mother had relaxed as though confidence in the treatment, the informa-

[1] From a letter written to the author and used by Marie Russ in *The Religion of a Growing Person*. Reprinted with the permission of The Woman's Press.

tion, and the instructions given her were tangible props
which would hold her up. The father had taken her to
the door gratefully, assuring her that she was the finest
pediatrician in town even if she was a woman.

How important to know what to do and when! Certainly there would have been little time to test or experiment, to consult texts or another doctor tonight. She had
needed the right injection immediately, and was able to
act promptly because she had been prepared in advance for
just such emergencies.

Only last night she had urged her young brother to work
toward clarifying his basic religious beliefs and standards.
As a pre-med student, Jim would search for the truth in
any field, it seemed, except religion, and toward that his
attitude failed to be scientific. It was as though a working
knowledge of chemistry could be gained by an occasional
glance at an old textbook, or by discussing it with someone
whose knowledge was but a partial and prejudiced memory, rather than by the research, reason, and faith he used
in any scientific effort.

Tonight's experience had been but one more example to
add proof to the theory that the time for decision is not the
time for preparation. If the measuring rod of Christian
standards was to be used in all of life's decisions, it needed
to be constructed carefully in advance of the moment of
judgment.

8   TRAVELERS THREE

Only three women remained in the dining car as the
train sped across the plains in the gathering dusk. Each

one sat at a table alone. All three were gazing out of their windows.

The first one noted with pleasure that the lamps just lit within caused her image to be quite clearly reflected on the heavy plate glass. And it was very satisfying. She liked what she saw and lingered, appreciating the sense of luxury and well-being this personable mirrored companion brought her.

The second woman peered through the twilight at the occasional dust-colored frame houses standing alone in the bleak flat fields. "What a barren, dismal existence," she thought. "They haven't the imagination and initiative to get away and live."

The third woman too was concentrating upon the swift-moving countryside. However, in her mind the simple houses were homes, the origin of some of the country's finest leadership, past and future. There leaders had learned frugality, the discipline of hard work, the importance of simplicity and faith. As the lights twinkled on, she could imagine the fragrant odors of dinner emanating from busy kitchens—how thrilling that electrical power had marched across the plains to lighten the tasks of these isolated families as they endlessly coaxed the nation's crops from the soil. The waiter brought her change, and she took one last look before returning to her car. The clear starlit sky seemed amazingly near. God must seem close at hand to these farm people, for no one in such a setting could help but be conscious of the beauty, the order and the creativity exemplified by the good earth and the fruits thereof, the seasons and the twinkling firmament.

To be mature is to see clearly and wholly.

9   TEACHING ADOLESCENTS

O thou great Teacher, I know thou art with me in this task, and at times that assurance alone keeps me at it. For teaching a class of adolescent girls has its baffling and fruitless moments.

Keep me from being pious and ponderous that I may teach *girls*, not lessons. Because they are restless, adventuresome, and independent, let me be creative in interpreting the challenge of Christ's teachings and ever be mindful of the tragedy of not asking onough of our young people. This is the age which needs to discover and become committed to the vital purposes of life, and the unfinished business of Christianity. Let the decisions be joint decisions, and not mine alone.

O God, I pray that I may not become impatient with their constant effort to be beautiful, independent, and casual. Guide me in channeling this natural longing for popularity into a realization of what it takes to be acceptable, constructive members of society, widening their horizons from a small individual circle until the world and its welfare are included.

There seems to be a fundamental urge in adolescents to be unlike the expectations of tradition and adulthood, and yet to be stereotyped in dress, actions, and thinking within their own group. As we observe this need to assert their own maturing personalities without a feeling of dictation, grant to us who are teachers and parents the wisdom of lifting by degrees—rather than tightening—our restraining hands, preparing them for the self-discipline they must accept with each added liberty.

Dear Father, help me to be a growing person that I may become more and more adequate to pilot this wonderful age—which races across the crests and depths of emotions in its starry-eyed haste to become familiar with the amazing wonders of life.

10   SISTERS

"Aunt Katherine, you're a peach to pal around with me the way you do." Penny's eyes traveled appreciatively around the dining room of the exclusive hotel where her aunt had invited her to lunch. Do you know, I feel like a different person when I'm out with you."

"You act like it," Katherine commented with quiet amusement.

Penny flushed. "I don't know why I'm so quick-tempered at home—unless it's because I'm such a superflous creature around the house. Ann gathers boy friends like a pot of honey gathers bees, but none of them seem to notice me. And mother's so worried she's going to have a sour spinster on her hands that she hovers near with far-from-subtle suggestions about improving my personality and appearance!"

"There's nothing wrong with your appearance, Penny. At least nothing that can't be easily remedied."

Penny nodded miserably. "I know. I'm fat."

Katherine leaned forward, and in her sternness it was easy to see she could hold her own as a business executive. "Penny, stop that. You're not *fat*. Do you realize that your refusal to watch your diet is simply another way of attempting to assert your rebellion? And it will get you no-

138

where at all. How do you think I'd look if I ate chocolate parfaits every afternoon?"

"Go on, Aunt Katherine, from you I can take it and like it."

"All right, Penny, here goes. Your personality is entirely different from Ann's, and yet—maybe subconsciously—you seem to think that success means being modeled after her. In the first place, since we're on the subject, your figure is different. Trim it down a little and start wearing tailored casuals. Then concentrate on the things you enjoy doing and in which you have some talent. Take a class or two at night school or University Extension, start singing in the church choir, join the Photography Club at the "Y," go on outings with the Mountaineers—there are any number of opportunities to choose from where you can have fun, learn something, make new contacts, become a purposeful person, gain spiritual serenity, and build a life of your own in your leisure time. Bend your efforts on accenting the positive, and automatically it will eliminate the negative in the minds of your family and friends—as well as in your own. Disregard the anxiety about pinning down boy friends, or you'll find yourself marrying the first serious prospect, and he might be the last one on earth capable of making you happy. Make yourself interesting enough so that you can enjoy your own company, and others will do likewise if you give them a chance. Be yourself, Penny, and like it!"

"It's all right for you to study what's wrong with the world," said the prominent industrialist to his wife, "but I warn you, I won't have you or your clubs fooling around trying to do anything about it."

Lao Tse, the great Chinese philosopher, once said that the peculiar thing about ideas is that they are no good unless you use them.

The Christian faith is a realistic combination or oneness of the personal and social religion—"Thou shalt love the Lord thy God with all thy heart, and with all thy soul, and with all thy mind, and with all thy strength, . . . and thy neighbor as thyself." As James declares, there must be a unity between our faith and our works, for "just as the body without the spirit is dead, faith is dead without good deeds" (Goodspeed translation). This unity is both difficult and stimulating, and we recognize that the Christian church and Christian individuals often want to overlook its necessity.

Jesus gave his opinion in his bitter denunciation of the Pharisees, for they adhered strictly to religious practices, but "devour widows houses" and "for pretense make long prayers." The prophets—Isaiah, Jeremiah, Micah, Amos— are equally strong in their censure of this attitude, which is one of the salient sins of all religions.

The seeking, growing person who arrives at a conviction cannot be wholly honest if that conviction is not accompanied by its twin, action. Action tests, perfects, and crystallizes the conviction; simultaneously it opens a new frontier of problematic thought—which again needs exploration, conviction, and action. It is like a long flight of stairs. Each step upward raises one's vision, and an additional need with its accompanying compulsion for action comes into view.

Sherwood Eddy expressed the demand for unity between our faith and works by defining that "faith is not something we believe in spite of the evidence; it is something we dare in spite of the consequences."

12   MEDITATION OF A NEGRO WOMAN

Our Father, with haste I seek thee. Again I was insulted, rejected as though I were something not quite human, as though I were a recognized notorious criminal —because through no effort of my own I was born with a dark skin. Only as I "steal away to Jesus" do I recover my calm, for in thy dear presence I regain my personal dignity and fortitude.

Let me remember *all* people of *all* tints and shades are occasionally subjected to rebuffs and disappointments. Restrain me from overestimating or emphasizing the significance of my own so that I make mountains out of molehills, dissipating the courage and energy needed to take advantage of truly progressive opportunities.

Keep me from becoming bitter, for bitterness quenches creativity and strength, turning our feet from the paths of effective action.

Let me not forget that there are a few who are color-blind when it comes to skin, whose understanding has "crossed the line." Make me aware of my share in the task of educating the white race to a fuller grasp of thy

141

concept of the brotherhood of man and the fatherhood of God.

I would know the achievements of leaders of my race and the winsomeness of my people. Help me to identify myself with the finest of their ideals and efforts and so to achieve a self-respect which will encourage me to proclaim my race with pride and reveal prejudice as lazy ignorance.

Dear Lord, keep me ever humble, mindful that I too have blind spots. I pray thee that the light of thy love will shine upon them that I may see and deal with them according to thy will.

13   AN IMPORTANT ASSIGNMENT

Kay Carlton   English I, Section 4
Theme: Democracy in the Church   May 13

A task facing Christians in the church today is that of transforming the belief of theoretical democracy into the practice of real democracy. In talking about real democracy there should be a differentiation of the dewy-eyed jingoistic brand from the kind that is expressed in the Bill of Rights, founded on the Christian principle of the sacredness of personality.

The only way to keep democracy healthy and wholesome in our homes, our churches, our organizations, and our government is by treating it like a child, insisting that it be vocal and active. Prohibiting participation in a major decision, or not expending the energy necessary to enable a project to be a co-operative one, turns people into puppets and drains democracy of its vitality and hope of survival.

Many are stifling democracy's power in the local church: the group of deacons who resent young fellows serving on the Board, or the youth who are unwilling to share in the tasks of the total church; the young men and women twenty-five and over who make little effort to train younger leaders and turn over to them the leadership of young people's activities; the Ladies' Aid, Presbytery, or Board of Trustees which repeatedly re-elects the same chairman because "no one else is so efficient"; the leaders or ministers who feel their suggestions should be final; the large contributors who use their contributions as a lever to swing decisions into line with their own opinions; any church group which is so satisfied with itself as it is that it fails to exert every effort to welcome the newcomer whose faith may be strengthened by this Christian fellowship. These procedures will increasingly dim out the purpose and message of the Christian church.

"The utility, the vitality, the fruitage of life does not come from the top to the bottom; it comes, like the natural growth of a great tree, from the soil, up through the trunk into the branches to the foliage and the fruit." [1]

14   YES, BUT NOT RIGHT NOW

When the moment is ripe, O Lord, I will act. I will pull together the full force of my finest thinking, my highest ideals, my scientific skills and enduring strength into

[1] Woodrow Wilson.

a combination to strike out for this better world for which
we yearn—of which we have so long dreamed. When we
can somehow see through this present confusion, and I
am freed to be creative and concentrate, then will I act.
When, you ask?

1916   Well, just now the war is in the way. The Kaiser
is on the march. Wait until he is out of the way
and liberty restored.

1918   Bolshevism must be stamped out.

1919   Of course we can't do much as long as the world is
gripped by this consuming post-war hatred and distrust. The Christian way cannot be clearly applied
at this point in history.

1921   And as soon as the chaotic ups and downs of our
speculative economy again become stabilized at a
normal tempo.

1933   O God, was anything ever more abnormal than this
depression? Millions upon millions are deprived of
work and livelihood. Youth and resources are
plowed under. Opportunity is dead.

1936   Totalitarianism is endangering democracy.

1939   The rumblings we hear—will this be another world
war?

1942   The entire world is in turmoil! We must all outdo
the dictators' evil methods of force if this conflict
is to be won; then the achievement of the good life
will be simple.

1945   The war is over! The war is won! But still the time
is not right. We are too confused to see which way
to turn.

1947   The world is gripped by consuming post-war distrust. Hatred, fear, and want paralyze the effort we would make.

Do I hear thee speak, O Lord? You say our waiting is in vain? We are losing by default?

My vision is clearing. The time is now—yesterday, to-day, tomorrow. Now is the moment for action, or tomorrow may be lost.

15   SECOND GENERATION CROSSROADS

I am at the crossroads of cultures. My parents were born in a foreign land where family life had different patterns, and social customs restricted a young woman's actions and opportunities.

Though my parents have been in America these many years, they still jealously guard their mother tongue, giving little effort to the learning or use of the language of their adopted country. One inadequate news weekly in the language my parents can read is the major source of their information and opinion while my wider resources and contacts are given little hearing. My parents question and criticize my friendships with schoolmates of other than my own nationality. "You will see," they warn darkly. "They will desert you when you need friends and are through school. Stay with your own people, my child." It is not easy to hold these friends now so dear to me. I hesitate to take them home lest they find it strange and crowded, and fail to see beyond Mama's and Papa's inability to converse in English, beyond their unfashionable working clothes, to the beauty behind their faces.

145

O God, I am torn and confused between these two patterns, both of which have such a tight hold upon me. I love and honor my parents and want to grow up a joy and source of comfort to them. And yet my whole being yearns to be a typical American, for I am proud to have been born a citizen of this country. I want the freedom of choice and the opportunities it offers; I want the fun and the beauty it holds within the reach of all. Dear Lord, can it be that upon me falls the task of rejecting or accepting the mores accumulated by my lineage over centuries of time? If I do not meet head on these problems of adjustment, my children, in their effort to do so, may make a far more drastic and painful break with the family. Humbly I beseech thee to grant me the judgment and courage to hold onto and carry forward the finest of my heritage, and to break away from those practices and attitudes which are obstructive and meaningless.

May I ever be conscious that I and the other second generation young people of my community form but a few of millions of various nationalities, each of whom in a distinct way is facing this same problem. We would join with those of the past and of the future whose opportunity and contribution in life has been and will be that of constructively harmonizing two cultures.

16   CAMPUS CHOICES

This is a time of decisions—my life in these moments I
  mold.
I'm deciding my future pattern, which values to choose and
  to hold.

Where shall I invest my vigor, do I dare speak my questions
out loud?
Can I bear to do that which is different and not be one of
the crowd?
"Everyone else always does it—you don't want to be a
bore!"
Then "Why don't you do it again—you know that you've
done it before."

"You're a Negro," "You're a maid," "You're a Jap," and
"You're a Jew."
Do I understand, befriend—or bend my weight to ex-
clude you?
What is my chief contribution, for what work shall I pre-
pare?
Is success prestige and money? Can it be to all folk fair?

Are the sciences, arts, and fellowship adequate fruits of my
years in college,
Or need I probe with equal zeal to gain mature religious
knowledge?
Is he the man to share my life, to make me partner, sweet-
heart, mother?
Can we agree upon our course and finer be due to each
other?

This is a time of decisions—my life in these moments I
mold.
Dear God, be near me and guide me lest my birthright be
foolishly sold.

17   OUR AMERICA

Kazuko was one of the many pre-war nisei—second generation Japanese—young people who had graduated from

high school with high scholastic honors. She had had
two years of college and now before completing her work
at the university was going to have the privilege of a visit
and six months study at a Christian college in her parents'
native land, Japan. One of Kazuko's classmates had spent
the previous year at her mother's alma mater in England and had come back aglow with accounts of relatives
visited and of actual acquaintanceship with places and
things first introduced to her by way of her mother's vivid
and fond memories. It was fortunate for Kazuko and the
other girls from her church group with whom she was
traveling that they lived on the Pacific Coast at one of the
jumping-off places for the Orient—because even at that
proximity, it was going to be no small strain on the family resources.

A year later when she looked back on her experiences
since that sunny day when, amidst serpentine and music,
the boat pulled away from the waving throngs on the
N. Y. K. dock, the intervening months became an unbe-
lievable dream.

In the first place the girls had been surprised to discover that in Japan they felt very much like strangers in
a strange land—not at home as they had expected. They
were taller, walked and dressed differently from the native
Japanese women. Regularly the secret police checked at
the college to ascertain what the "foreigners" would be
doing each day, as if they were under suspicion! They
saw the beauty of the country with warm appreciation and
made some lasting friendships, but going home to America was a joy far exceeding anything they had anticipated.

In a world boiling with wars and rumors of wars, it was

a relief to know that each throb of the ship's engines brought them nearer to that sanctuary of democracy and sanity which the United States alone seemed to typify. As the S. S. "Maru" sailed down the homeward stretch of the blue waters of Puget Sound, the snowcapped peaks seemed to carol with the salt breezes Thomas Paine's early paean to their native land:

"O! ye that love mankind! Ye that dare oppose, not only the tyranny, but the tyrant, stand forth! Every spot of the old world is overrun with oppression. Freedom hath been hunted round the globe. Asia and Africa have long expelled her. Europe regards her like a stranger, and England hath given her warning to depart. O receive the fugitive, and prepare in time an asylum for mankind."

18   OUR AMERICA NEVERTHELESS

The year of their return ended with Pearl Harbor and war! Most of the nisei girls who were working were told, "Sorry, I won't be able to use you any more." There was a fearful empty feeling that security was gone, that here too—in the land of their birth—they were looked upon as suspicious foreigners, people without a country.

The frustrating shock of proposed evacuation seemed almost more than endurance could bear. Leave the homes and businesses for which their families had labored so hard and long, the communities where they had spent their lives and invested their hopes, their churches where inspiration and fellowship had been so rich? Could it be reality?

The Sunday preceding the mass evacuation to hastily

constructed barracks on the muddy Puyallup fair grounds, Kazuko led the closing worship service of the college age church school class.

"Until now," she said, "we niseis must admit that our hard-working parents have made our lives very easy for us. Now it is up to us to work and help the older generation understand new situations as they arise. We must prove ourselves to be good American citizens. Some of our rights as American citizens have been temporarily taken away. Yet remember this is war. We will never be bitter. We will always remain loyal to the America we know and love. We must also prove ourselves to be strong Christians in whatever we must do, wherever we go."

And then she prayed, "Dear heavenly Father, we thank thee from the bottom of our hearts for the many friends who have rushed to our aid at this time, for the great love thou hast for us, and for the many blessings thou has given us. Dear Father, we accept thy great challenge with confidence and courage to prove ourselves to be leaders of the older generation, to be good American citizens, and to be strong Christians. O Father, we know that the days to come will be filled with trying heartaches, sorrows, and temptations, but with thee to help us at all times, at all places, we are not afraid. Amen."

19   WIDER HORIZONS

They had been married two years. It was a little perturbing, the way certain friends and relatives made jovial comments such as, "Well, the honeymoon is over now. Any star dust left?"

The star dust was far from gone—and never could be with Bill for a husband. And yet, Edith reflected, there were some differences they had not anticipated. They had thought all major issues were thoroughly discussed and settled. But living together "in holy matrimony" had given new depth to certain questions and left wanting some of the answers which they had previously arrived at with a sense of completion.

Edith was a Methodist. Born and brought up in the church, she sometimes said, and to her no other denomination seemed quite as much on the right track. Bill was a Friend, and although his fine Quaker attitude kept him from being critical, she sensed he found the Methodist church form of government difficult to accept and some of her personal religious concepts narrow. Because they had seemed deeply rooted in their respective churches, their premarital agreement had been to continue as before in attendance and responsibilities, each sharing whenever possible in the other's church fellowship. During these two years they had read together regularly some of the newer religious books, had attended several denominational and interdenominational conferences, and increasingly were a part of informal religious discussions with friends.

As Edith looked back, she was very conscious of the new vitality and commitment which had come into their lives. Long before they would have a family of church school age, she was certain their membership would be in one place—even though she could not now foresee where. For they were growing, growing closer to God and to each other.

151

20   **CREATION**

I am to be a mother. O God, thou are granting to me the peak experience in sharing with thee the task of creation. The very word is stirring and bold and awesome. Some would give it a prehistoric connotation, but to me each day brings new opportunities to participate in the creation of this world—oftentimes ploddingly, occasionally dramatically. This crowns them all.

Within me moves a human life, a being made in the image of God. Who knows what this child's destiny may be? Whatever it is, I shall have a major share in determining his physical strength by my care between now and the time of his birth. Whatever it is, we, his parents, will greatly influence his character, his spirit, his education, his reactions. Whatever it is, my prayer is that in some way he may aid in solving the problems of a world desperately in need of inspired leadership. Give me the courage to cleanse my life now of attitudes and habits out of keeping with my task. Dear Lord, when the common pressures of life irritate and crowd upon me during his childhood, let me be reminded of the beauty of these months of anticipation and preparation.

I would be an instrument in thy hand, O thou who art the Father and Maker of all mankind, for thou hast blessed me with the privilege of creating another son of God and of having a part in the creation of the future.

21   **SO BUSY**

"Peter, stop running round and round. You're getting dizzy."

"I *haf* to, Mommy."

"Why, dear? Who's making you?"

"Myself's making me."

Round and round we go. Early and late. Demands that never cease. Work that is never finished. That *must* be done today. This won't be cared for if left to others. Weariness, oversensitivity, conflict, and confusion.

O God, in restless living we lose our spirits' peace.
Calm our unwise confusion, bid Thou our clamor cease.
Let anxious hearts grow quiet like pools at evening still,
Till Thy reflected heavens all our spirits fill.

Teach us, beyond our striving, the rich rewards of rest.
Who does not live serenely is never deeply blest.
O tranquil, radiant Sunlight, bring Thou our lives to flower,
Less wearied with our effort, more aware of power.

Receptive make our spirits, our need is to be still;
As dawn fades flickering candle, so dim our anxious will.
Reveal Thy radiance through us, Thine ample strength release.
Not ours, but Thine the triumph, in the power of peace.

                                      . . . AMEN[2]

22   THE TEMPTATION TO WEAKEN

Two women shared the pleasant hospital room. Their progress through this antiseptic repairland was at diverse stages. The one by the window had come in the evening before for a thirty-six hour preparatory period and was to

---

[2] Harry Emerson Fosdick, "The Inner Life." Reprinted with the permission of The Woman's Press and of the author.

go to the surgery early the next day. The other occupant, Mrs. Wells, literally and figuratively was nearest the door. Two more days, the doctor smilingly had promised, was just about as long as they'd allow her to loll in this lazy luxury. She appreciated his jollying, for this had been the second in a series of three corrective hip operations, and the convalescence at home to which she was looking forward would be preliminary to what they all hoped could be the final one.

Two women shared the pleasant hospital room that day. And then there was one!

"I could see she was nervous," Mrs. Wells explained as the night nurse rubbed her back with alcohol, "and I tried first to assure her, and finally just endeavored to get her mind off herself. But I've never been so amazed as when she got up, took her clothing out of the closet and dressed! She said she'd rather have her goiter choke her to death than go to the surgery tomorrow morning. She was too afraid to go through with it!"

Courage always stands waiting but is snubbed constantly in favor of the seemingly easy way out. Progressively with each evasion the character is weakened when one is afraid to go through that which is unpleasant; afraid to admit having made a mistake; afraid to accept a penalty; avoiding the unpleasant task long past due; unwilling to exercise the discipline of self-control and temperance; indefinitely delaying breaking off an unwholesome relationship.

Every crisis situation carefully analyzed and prayerfully faced contains some pathway of creative betterment.

Probed with an open mind, sincerity, and courage, the way will be discovered.

"No temptation has overtaken you that is beyond man's power; but God is faithful, who will not let you be tempted beyond what you can bear, but will, with every temptation, provide the way of escape also, so that you may be able to withstand." (I Cor. 10:13 Montgomery translation.)

23   PHYSICAL PAIN

O God, only thou canst come within the iron curtain of pain which cuts me off from all others. Let my soul not cringe within me. Instead, make me ever aware that pain is for a purpose, when over easily forgotten, and that it is temporary.

Now is a time for evaluation, for the real values of life stand out in bold relief, while the unimportant fall rapidly away. Even my normal self is a being separate and apart—one upon whom I can look objectively and discerningly.

Can I ever again go thoughtlessly on my way, unaware of the many who are stifling moans in the cubicles and wards lining long hospital corridors, or the suffering who are filed away in the households of reluctant, impatient relatives? These latter bear not only the confining despair of invalidism, but also the far more intolerable pain of being a burden.

Can I ever climb a mountain path fragrant with the scent of pine needles on the leafy sod or hang my snowy washing on a joyously breezy spring day without a prayer of thanksgiving for the normal use of my arms, my mind, my eyes, and my ears? Dear Father, may those whose lives have great physical limitations be given compensating skills and satisfactions, and great strength of spirit.

May the isolation of pain create within me a lifelong desire to understand the causes of others' isolation and, in understanding it, help to rid the barrier. For all isolation is pain, whether it be caused by a feeling of inferiority; differences of complexion, habits, language, or belief; or the fear of being called upon to share one's wealth or self.

And deliver me from causing pain.

Dear Lord, help me to bear it bravely. Keep a hold on me—now and evermore.

24   THE HELPMATE EMANCIPATED

Mrs. Gay sat for some time in contemplation after her perusal of the church bulletin. Finally, as though her thoughts could no longer be kept to herself, she interrupted her husband's concentration on the evening paper. "You know, John, I have always credited the increasing emancipation of women to a growing awareness of the full meaning of the Christian concept of respect for all individuals."

Mr. Gay's eyes blinked impressively and then twinkled. "Meaning what, my dear?"

"Meaning, how can you be a member of a nominating committee in a day like this and turn out a slate like that?" With impatience she pushed the church news off her lap. "One woman candidate for the Board!" She waxed eloquent. "Who do most of the work in the church, get the dinners, see that it looks and feels like home, get the

156

families off to Sunday School, do most of the teaching, most of the missionary work, most of the calling, singing, and listening? The women, of course! And who determine policy and make the final decisions? The men! Sounds like the dark ages rather than the procedure of a supposedly progressive institution!"

"Edith, why didn't those of you who feel that way turn in names of some able women to the nominating committee? If the women suggested are prepared and willing to assume responsibility, I am sure fair consideration would be given them. But the women must do *their* part. You know, I've come to the conclusion that the feminine sex as a whole is not as conscious of the woman's status in the world in general and in her more immediate environment specifically as is the average man. The discerning man in the business world sees more of the inequalities and limitations of opportunity to which women are subjected than his wife will admit. Even so, so much progress has been made politically and economically in the United States that the right to vote, to hold an office, or to earn an adequate living wage is not recognized as the rare privilege it really is."

"What do you mean by 'rare privilege?' " interrupted his wife.

"Well, it is only within the last century and in but a *few* countries that these great strides toward independence of thought and action have been taken. Women of the Orient, Latin America, Europe, and Africa are just today being introduced to the thrill of freedom of expression and participation in community affairs, and some have even acquired the right to vote for the first time in the histories of their nations. They are venturing out from the seclusion of their homes and male domination to take their beginning steps on the steep climb toward equality with men. Naturally they are looking toward America for examples of what these privileges can accomplish. In my humble opinion the time has come for your women's groups to examine realistically how American women, particularly Christian women, can exert greater influence toward a better society through the social and legal freedom and political privileges granted them than so far has been accomplished."

25   THE HELPMATE EMANCIPATED (Continued)

Again Mrs. Gay was deep in thought. "You're in so many community activities, John—the Chest, the 'Y.' the community club. What would you say are the difficult hurdles when men and women try to work together on a completely equal plane of responsibility?"

Mr. Gay laughed. "Funny thing—Frank and I were discussing something of the sort today at the Community Chest office. Women have much more time it seems; at least it takes them three times as long to do a job. They're constantly calling exhaustive committee meetings for all hours of the day and don't come to a decision until everyone examines every detail and each subcommittee votes on it."

"Oh, but John, that's not entirely fair," interceded his wife. "Men in a group want to accomplish results with such dispatch that they sidetrack democratic practices and unload on the chairman, staff person, or minister by say-

ing 'You decide.' As a result the members are not stimu-
lated to grow through the process of assuming responsibility, the facts and wisdom of the total group are not
brought in to benefit a decision, and all the experience and
weariness, all the credit or blame, descends upon one person."

Before Mr. Gay could come to the defense of his sex,
she continued. "Somewhere in between lies the most
creative and efficient procedure. Certainly women need to
eliminate some of the belabored busy-work which clutters
their meetings and delays action, and men need to become
a little more patient with good group work procedure—
when it's really good. The world needs laboratories for ex-
perimentation with democracy on close-to-home problems,
with methods of dealing with controversial issues constructively, finding out how to draw in all kinds of people
of varying backgrounds, giving them dignity by recognition of their contributions. John, the church should be
such a laboratory! I wonder what immediate steps could
be taken to make it so."

26   THE HELPMATE EMANCIPATED (Continued)

"You know, Edith, I've thought of a couple more habits
women have when working with men which are seldom, if
ever, spoken of, but which are a subconscious source of
irritation."

"I'm listening, John."

"First, I wish women would do a better job of knowing
and remembering facts which are pertinent to a judgment
they are making. It makes no difference whether they're

discussing political candidates, labor, the neighbor's children, or somebody's operation, they shouldn't carry on a heated debate when their facts aren't accurate and their sources not quotable. Also their proof should be something more creditable than their husband's opinion or hearsay. Implying that judgment is based on information a person doesn't have, or exaggerating to make a statement effective, is not being honest."

"And what's the other one?"

"Well, not infrequently when men and women are working together on an equal basis, a difficult crisis seems to be the cue for the women to flutter their eyelashes and unload a bad situation on the men's strong shoulders. Oh, it's done nicely, and momentarily the men are complimented by the need for them; but before it's over, they're muttering in their beards that it's too bad the women can't see their problems through—particularly if it is a responsibility they have wanted to assume. A person or a group will grow in wisdom and skill, in spiritual strength, and in the esteem of their associates if they will work *through* their difficulties instead of getting out from under them."

27   HOW COULD IT HAPPEN!

Dear God, if ever I needed wisdom, it is now. Help me, I pray thee. What can I say to Emily—John, her only boy, convicted of embezzlement! She is asking why God is punishing her in this way when she worked and sacrificed that John might have education and opportunity.

I would remember James' admonishment; "When he is

being tempted let no one say 'It is God who tempts me,' for God cannot be tempted with evil, nor does he tempt any man. . . . Every good gift and every perfect gift is from above, and cometh down from the Father of lights, with whom is no variableness, neither shadow of turning" (Kent translation).

Whether it is a personal or a social sin, not only the sinners suffer, but many others who are innocent share that suffering—even as she and John's family are now suffering. Maybe we all should recognize our share in his guilt in a society which can so depress a man that in desperation he takes that which is not his own. Probably never in all his life has he known economic security.

O Father, forgive John for whatever he did. I pray that he has come to thee and can see thy will in what he must do. Let him go through this trial with his head up, strengthened because he faced it positively and courageously.

Dear Lord, help John's family see this entire episode in their lives objectively and be willing to search for that which is redeeming within it, assuring him of their continued faith in him, standing by to uphold him during his punishment—not adding to the rebuke. Together they have the choice of defeat or victory for the future. With thy help it can be victory.

28   NO SECOND CHANCE

There was a new fellowship which existed between mother and daughter now that daughter too had become a mother. They sat in the living room before the fireplace

161

cozily mending during the all-too-brief calm of the cherub's afternoon nap.

"Mother, do you ever look back and wish you could have a second chance at parts of your life?"

The older woman thoughtfully kept on with her darning awhile before answering. "When I look back and see how inextricably the joys and disappointments are woven into one another, it would be hard to lift out any one group of years in spite of my failures or inadequacies. Probably the times I neglected to speak words of encouragement or conviction cause me the greatest regret. When my father was taken to the hospital, deathly ill and never to return, I was too frightened to say the loving, appreciative, reassuring things I later thought of. When a bachelor uncle was ill, I failed to insist on an able specialist, and inadequate care cost his life. When I called on an elderly family friend who was ill, and he seriously wanted to talk to me of my religious beliefs about which he long had teased me, I put it off until later—which was too late. When I delayed inviting one of my Sunday school class boys to accept Christ and join the church, he was suddenly drafted into the Army and never came back. When I first saw a fine Negro refused service in a restaurant, I didn't have the courage to protest the discrimination to the management. Yes, it's the times I failed to testify which rise up to haunt me. I wish I could relive them and speak."

29   GRANDMOTHER LIVES WITH US

Dearest Mary,

How nice that your mother has come to live with you.

Believe me, I've been indulging in no small amount of introspection since receiving your letter. Your request for our "recipe for utopian congeniality" is flattery I know, and yet it leaves me humble and grateful that we have come thus far on our way—even though we have not arrived.

Each new addition to a family should mean added happiness. If a family doesn't want the new baby, doesn't plan for it, make room for it, and sacrifice for it, little of the great joy it could bring is realized. When an adult becomes a permanent member of the household—bringing attitudes, habits and possessions far less easy to fit in—all the more intelligent effort, self-discipline, and prayer is needed to create a satisfactory adjustment.

We made business-like agreements about finances, household chores, adequate privacy and clearance of dates. Where definite responsibilities are undertaken, we feel the grandmother should be a paid, rather than a paying, guest. We recognize her need to share in the busyness of the household—particularly in the kitchen—the right to entertain and be entertained, with us or without us, in our home and away from it. We appreciate that she has friends and interests of her own.

We present a united front on the children's discipline, respect for each other, and loyalty to one another inside and outside our home. I'm not sure we would have the right to attempt to live together if good will were not our primary motivation. It prevents sharp or subtle criticism, and it demands forgiveness unlimited. A willingness to sacrifice momentary satisfactions and conveniences for the long-range goal of increased love and understanding is another worth-while concession.

At least we have arrived at the place where we are passionately sorry for the home circle that doesn't have in it a grandmother.

With warm greetings to the family,

Jane

30   GRANDMOTHER

I have a job to do. Not what you might think. It is not "cramming for my finals," nor silently worrying far into the night about the infirmities of old age; it is not garrulous reminiscing into any courteous ear, nor continually deploring that which I have not in a degenerating desire for pity.

I have a job to do. Some say, "Have you retired at last?" And I answer with a proud smile, "No, I've graduated at last. My life to date has been preparation for the years ahead." For every year's experiences, every thoughtful decision, every healthful habit, every talent developed, every joyous friendship, every adventure evaluated, every cultivated interest has been a stair up which I've climbed to reach this point. From this vantage I now can see the struggles of life more clearly. The wasted effort, the tinsel that glitters like gold, the great joys too simple to attract, the real values too humble to gain common acclaim are now evident. I have the pleasure of reaping enjoyment from a life freed from many of the tiring and complex demands of younger years. I treasure this new leisure which permits unhurried exploration into new and old literature, music and art, which enables me to do the extra thought-

ful gesture or service for a relative, a friend, or neighbor.
My grandchildren, my church, my garden hold new wonders for me. I am gripped anew by the challenge to be
well informed and to help better the world. Senators and
congressmen who read their mail will soon recognize my
concerns.

I have a job to do. It is to live so abundantly that youth
around me will plan for old age with thoughtfulness and
appreciation, not dread. I would that the steps they now
are taking may lead them to later years of serenity and
purpose because they can witness the "vigorous faith, love,
and steadfastness" Paul urges those of advanced maturity
to exemplify.

31   IN REVIEW

                    All the world's a stage
              And all the men and women merely players,
said Shakespeare and then described his seven ages of man.

Each age has its functional importance, but the continuing theme of life is growth. Not growth in wisdom and
stature, then decadency. But throughout, a constant, conscious growth in the knowledge and love of God and the
practice of Jesus' teachings with relation to God and to
man. By ceaseless effort, life can be ever creative and at-
tractive.

The description "mewling, puking infant" seems unfair
to that delightful period of growing recognition when the
baby discovers his feet and fingers, perceives his mother
and smiles! He is learning who, what, when, and how
with amazing rapidity those first few years.

It is not as a "whining schoolboy" we view him during the next stage, but as a child who is finding out how to get along with his companions, becoming aware of cooperation and sharing, and the necessity of academic knowledge as a backdrop for his future contribution.

The exhilarating teen years are the introduction to adulthood, when independence from family is being asserted and contacts with the opposite sex are so very important while youth develops in the enjoyment and evaluation of others.

During the rich middle age the objectivity given by experience oils the machinery of everyday living, providing mature guidance to others and smoother, fuller pleasure to self.

Then comes the last "for which the first was made," furnishing the opportunity to explore some of the more time-consuming activities which the less-focused and more demanding years had crowded out. With judgment growing out of personal experience, the growth of Christian understanding, serenity, and faith crown the later years.

Larry, Dan, and Little Sister

JEAN BEAVEN ABERNETHY

1 BEGINNING THE DAY

She sat down to finish her breakfast. The family was gone. It was nice to relax from pressure and follow each one into his day. A sort of I-stay-here-but-I-have-sent-forth-and-I-will-be-here-when-they-return feeling.

When they return?

Of course they did not return all at once and in grand finale style. That was why she was around all day. They returned in stages. Judy, the youngest, every few minutes from the sand box in the front yard. The boys, at noon, from school, and again at supper time—with periodic afternoon invasions for cookies, the football, solace, and counsel; and Ross, on the six-fifteen bus, tired and hungry, ready to change from dictaphones and appointments, subway elbows and train smoke.

This was an ordinary day ahead of her, and, as she sat sipping her coffee, she faced it on three different levels. Besides her adult one, there would be the three-, the six-, and the nine-year-old way of looking at things. It was one of the more subtle parental assignments, she thought—

this spreading yourself out to cover several ages, and even while keeping your own figure. It was much more than wanting an extra hand or so. That would be arithmetic, if she could work it. This was chemistry and much more interesting. She was one. She was also three. A human trinity, no less. The thought made her stop a minute. Somehow, thinking of it that way gave new dimension to her task—the quite ordinary day just ahead of her.

O God, she thought, give me imagination in these next few hours, and courtesy, and, above all, understanding.

2   ENDING THE DAY

The end of her day began at five o'clock. Four-thirty was still afternoon and, if she was in the middle of something else, she could postpone matters a bit; but by five the end of the day was knocking at her door, and she rose to meet it with knives, forks, napkins, peeled potatoes, and warm water in the tub.

What else did she need to meet it with?

There was Judy who was fussy, the boys with their homework, questions, and the bathroom—clean this morning, but full of real dirt now and water, water everywhere—supper downstairs to keep going, and the telephone.

Dear God, she thought, this can be the most hectic time of the day—these next three hours when I'm tired and everyone else is too. Help me to remember that it's the family and not the routine that's important. Help me to take time out, even if it is the end of the day, to laugh and love and play with them. Otherwise, I'm hurrying with no place to go. Otherwise, I'm ending the day, but what's the fun in getting up tomorrow and beginning all over again?

She moved from here on very much as she moved in the morning, under pressure of events; but even though she moved under the pressure of events, even though everything went according to schedule, the end of the day was not hectic, nor hard on the digestion; as long as she remembered she could make of it something else. She could give it dignity and direction whenever she took enough time out to make sure of her own direction once more. She could make of it five people coming together, as the darkness fell, for warmth and light and food—a kind of sealing-in process to retain the juices and flavor of the day, five different days, really. In this way if one of them had just learned to ice skate, or whistle, or cut with a knife, or if Ross had had an interesting contact, or something had happened which reminded him of something, there was somewhere to put it, someone to tell—not just "how nice" or "uh huh"—but someone who cared, and who took it, whatever it was, and held it up to catch the light a bit, and made it a part of the family so that all of them grew a little before, together, they put it away.

3   BLACK AND WHITE

It was a game she had played as a child out on the sleeping porch after her mother had tucked her in—this roping off of life, this shoving into the closet every night what she hadn't liked about the day so that she could go to sleep with a neat and pleasant twelve-hour stretch in her mind. As a child it was the ride on the two-wheeler all the way to the corner, without the time the car had almost run her down; it was the soft fur of the cat, not the robin he had killed.

And now that she was grown up?

Of course, now she admitted accidents and death. An adult does. But in a way she was still playing her little game—dividing each day into black and white, putting the black away as less desirable, letting the white come to the top, like cream.

While memory, however, each night let her play this set of gymnastics, reality didn't. How adult, then, was she? That was what puzzled her. When she separated black from white, preferring the white, it wasn't escape, was it? She was not like the Puritans who took part of life and called it naughty, smothered it in petticoats, and acted as though it was something to be ashamed of. She was not trying to cover up the black. She said *all* of life existed— she admitted ugliness, monotony, and grief—it was just that she refused to "live" in these moments, that they were something to get over with in order to get on with the other.

But lately it had occurred to her—maybe because she was well into her thirties by now—that she didn't have as much time as all that, and that if she was going to live she would have to live *all* the time, not just in picked moments parenthetically inserted.

This much she knew—that God had given her all of life, black as well as white, and that she must not only learn to accept all of the gift, but, having accepted it, to be grateful for all of it. She must begin to see beauty "where

no beauty is"; to find meaning in places where she had
never found it before.

4   REMOVE THE COVERING

She remembered having bought a sheer wool once, a
French hand-knit original. It was so very trim that she had
rarely worn it—kept saving it for special occasions. Then,
one day, it was gone with the moths. And all the time she
had been afraid of wearing it she could have worn it, just
as all the many moments in her life when she had put off
living until they were over she could have been living.

That time when she was ill, and in genuine physical
pain, and all she had lived for was to get out of the hospital; that time when Ross had been gone on a long trip,
and she had merely marked time, waiting until his return
for the full chord in their family affection to be struck
again. In these moments—while Ross was gone, while
she was in pain—she could have been living?

But it was not only moments of pain and separation that
she must somehow learn to render, making clear their
value. It was the monotony of routine. For what made up
the bulk of life was not the climaxes, big and little, to
which one readily gave oneself, but the long, drawn-out
periods of getting ready for them: the hours and hours
spent in shopping for and preparing the food as well as the
finished meal; the time spent in getting ready for the guests
as well as the gracious moment of their arrival; the raking
and dumping of the leaves as well as the accomplished
clean yard; the long weary days of waiting as well as the
hour of the baby's birth. And it depended on her whether

she could learn to enjoy process as well as goal; the meager stretch as well as the more rounded moments.

"Life," said a sixteenth-century manuscript which hung over her desk, "is so generous a giver, but we, judging its gifts by their covering, cast them away as ugly or heavy or hard. Remove the covering and you will find beneath it a living splendour, woven of love, by wisdom, with power."

It would take infinite patience and insight to remove the covering, she knew, and courage too. But if she could find living splendor in place of what she had been calling routine, or pain, or grief, it would be worth all the discipline involved.

5   "YOU'RE NOT GOING TO DIE"

As she came up, she saw Dan putting on his pajamas and talking, falsetto voice, into the closet. "Who are you talking to, Dan?"

"To the little people."

"To the *little* people?" She asked it, smiling, since Dan was only six himself.

"Yes," said Dan, "they are my friends." He looked at her cautiously for a minute, trying to decide whether he would tell her more. Then, "They are the ones who live forever."

"They are! Why?"

"Because"—he hesitated—"because *I* want to live forever, too."

"Dan," she said, casually, sitting down on the bed, " 'most everybody wants to live forever."

He looked at her surprised—and glad. "Do they?"

172

She nodded.

After a moment, he took her into his full confidence. "Mom, when you turn out the lights and it gets dark in here, I'm afraid to die." He watched carefully to see what she would say.

She did not act surprised. She waited a minute, trying to get her bearings, searching for the way to say it. "Dan," she began finally, "before Judy was born, she was warm and comfortable and well fed, wasn't she? And I can imagine she might have felt, even though she couldn't talk, 'I don't ever want to leave this. I don't want to die.' "

Dan interrupted. "But it isn't the same. Judy wasn't going to die. She was going to be born."

"Exactly," she said. "Only Judy didn't know what it would be like, so let's say she was afraid and called it dying instead. After she was born, though, she discovered that warmth went on, and food, and being wanted and loved."

Dan was listening intently. She continued. "Someday, when Judy gets a little older, she may feel just like you do now—'I don't ever want to leave this place, earth. I don't want to die.' Only something says to her, 'Why, you're not going to die when you leave here. You're going to be born—born into something even greater, even more wonderful, where love and growth and being wanted still go on.' "

Neither of them said anything for a long minute.

"We don't know, Dan—none of us know exactly—and that's the reason we are afraid. But I have a feeling that we need not be afraid. That dying is something like being born."

173

He stood there, solemn, turning over the brand-new idea in his mind. Then he came over and sat down on the bed beside her. And smiled.

6   TO SEE IS TO LOOK

If you've asked for a big chocolate cake with thick frosting all over it, it isn't quite the same thing to get some flour, eggs, chocolate, a mixing bowl, and a card from Mother and Dad saying, "Love, and make it yourself."

But that was how it was. Larry had been wanting a plane like Ned's for his ninth birthday. Only Ned's was an expensive model, and they could not afford to match it. The next best thing, Ross said, was to get Larry interested in building his own planes.

On the birthday morning, and after all the other gifts, Larry opened the package. There was a tense moment, then his eyes filled with tears. They rushed in with explanations and plans. But it was no use. "If you would use your imagination, Larry," she said finally, half heartbroken herself.

"What's imagination?"

She made up something on the spur of the moment. "Why, it's the thing in you that can help you make something beautiful out of nothing."

It sounded too much like poetry. "I don't want imagination," he said emphatically. "And I can't make anything beautiful. I just want a big silver plane *already made* like Ned's."

174

They decided not to make an issue of it. "O.K., Larry, put the kit away for a while and forget it."

A few weeks later he came into her room one night.

"I thought," he said, "you might want to see it," producing from behind his back a small, crude model of an airplane.

She had not known he'd been at work in the basement; she had not even allowed herself to ask if he'd taken out the kit again. "Why, Larry, you made this, didn't you?"

He was on guard against pity or smothering praise. He knew exactly what he had, that it was not, and never could be, anything like Ned's, and if she gushed or was dishonest . . . "You did a good job, Larry," she said. "You haven't broken the wood once, and you left enough leeway for the propellor to go around smoothly."

What she said was true, and Larry accepted it. He edged a little closer and gave her the plane. "We didn't have any silver," he said, "so I painted it gray instead. It works, and I know the names of all the parts. But it isn't *beautiful* like you said."

She got out of bed and turned off the light. The moon was coming into the room, so she took the plane to the window and held it there for a minute. "Why, it's silver like Ned's!" Larry said.

She thought a minute. The shadow of the plane lay on the polished floor, large and black, the rough edges made smooth. "Look, Larry," she said, and she began to make the shadow glide over the room.

"Here, let me do it, Mom," said Larry. After a minute he brought the shadow to a halt, outlining a perfect black

175

cross of a plane against the pale blue wall. "It's beautiful,
like magic, don't you think?"

"Beautiful?"

Larry stopped because he understood. "Sometimes," he
said, "it's how you look at it, isn't it, whether it's beautiful
or not."

7   JUDGE NOT

They had gone off by themselves for a few days, she and
Ross, leaving the children behind. On the afternoon before
they were to go back, they went canoeing down the river,
stopping to eat their picnic lunch and loaf awhile on the
bank.

She looked at Ross, sprawled out generously on the grass,
relaxed, chewing on a piece of leaf. There was something
about him, she realized, that she deeply envied. Ross had
a fondness for people as natural as the wave in his hair.
And how did he come by it? Most of us, she thought, live
as though it's our job to make other people good, and ourselves happy. While with Ross it was the other way around.
He was apt to accept people as they were and enjoy them.
The disciplines he reserved more for personal use.

She remembered one night when they were first married.
They had been waiting for the late theater train, and a
drunk had come up and accosted them. She had been at
first amused, then annoyed. But not Ross. Ross wasn't
amused by the chap or annoyed. He liked him instead. She
had felt it in Ross the minute the fellow had stepped up to
them. The drunk had felt it too and responded by staying.

The two men had talked, while she had held back. Once, even, they had laughed uproariously, Ross even more than the drunk. She had tried, she remembered; but for the life of her she hadn't been able to see anything so funny. She had realized then, though, as she had so often since, that the main difference between Ross and herself was this very point. His liking for people came without any self-conscious effort, a natural outgoing from within himself, unencumbered by having to judge. She liked people too, but there were so many things she was apt to let get in her way—people's insincerities, their pettiness, their snobberies, their inconsistencies—that often she found herself detained and her appointment with the people themselves postponed indefinitely.

Ross turned over on his side and looked up at her. "What are you thinking about, sweet?"

She threw the pebble in her hand into the water, then felt fondly for his rough-and-ready hair. "Oh, just something about you I like," she said.

8　　　　　　**THE FAMILY BOWL**

She had taken the three children out before breakfast to pick blueberries. The sky was a friendly blue; sparrows chattered at them from the gnarled little scrub oaks; and here and there a cottontail lifted his head to stare at them before scampering.

Larry leaped ahead of them, his long, tanned legs hopping the low bushes, filling his pail in no time. Then he sat down to watch the rest of them. Larry was fleet, like the hare. But if one had been inquisitive enough to look carefully at Larry's harvest, one would have found a few leaves, several twigs, even some green blueberries.

Dan was more deliberate, like the tortoise. With his tongue stuck out the corner of his mouth, he went seriously from one bush to another, as though it were a problem to be solved. Rejecting anything small or medium sized, he picked only the biggest, the bluest, the best. Dan liked a perfect job, and that was good. But it took him a very long time, and meanwhile the rest of them were getting powerfully hungry.

Judy was neither tortoise nor hare. Judy was like a little humming bird, buzzing up to one bush after another in search of sweet. Her pink sunsuit and bonnet brought color and activity to the scene. She worked incessantly. But Judy, oblivious to the future tense, ate as she went along, so that the law of supply and demand kept her pail at low ebb. At long last she came up to her mother, five small berries rattling around in the bottom of her little tin pail. "I want a great big basket, Mommie," she emphasized, "so's to put them in when I get this too full to carry them."

Sometime—not now, but later—she would point out a few things. Larry could stand to throw in a little more carefulness. Dan had to understand a difficult word, "compromise." And Judy? It would be a few years yet, but gradually Judy would have to learn—painful lesson—to fill the little pail first.

They arrived home for breakfast, and she got down an old wooden bowl, a family favorite. "Let's put all the berries in this bowl, shall we? Then we can wash them all together and sprinkle them on our cereal."

They were reluctant. Why not keep them separate instead? "I picked more than anyone else did," said Larry.

"And mine are better than Larry's or Judy's," said Dan.

Judy grinned a juicy, purple grin which said, "And I don't even need the bowl, thank you. I've already eaten."

More important than carefulness, compromise, or completion—perhaps the most important thing to learn—was willingness to put all the berries together in the family bowl.

9   A MATTER OF PRIORITY

They were taking a trip in a crowded bus when he turned to her, "What does that sign mean, Mom?"

"I'll tell you when we get by ourselves, Larry."

That night he returned to it. "What was that sign about, Mom?"

"It said that some people cannot sit in the front of the bus, Larry."

"Why?"

"Because the people in the front don't want to sit next to them."

"Are the people they don't want to sit there Germans?"

"No."

"Are they Japanese?"

"No, they are Americans."

Was she joking? No, she wasn't. "That doesn't make sense to me, Mom."

And how was she to make it make sense?

How were she and Ross to let this child of theirs—this child who, like themselves, was of the majority group,

179

whose skin color would never embarrass him—how would they help him to learn that responsibility went along with his stroke of fortune? How would they keep him, as he grew, sensitive to the inconsistencies all about him, so that instead of becoming numb to injustice and taking it for granted, he would always be saying to himself, "This doesn't make sense to me. This must be changed."

She said slowly, "If we take God seriously, Larry, we can never let things like that make sense."

And this was exactly how she meant it. For he would need, she knew, more than his personal indignation, his common sense, to challenge wrong. The woods were full of tired liberals—people who had been stirred up over this or that when they were young, but who had petered out. A child needed to be rooted in the God who created and sustained moral indignation in man if his indignation was to endure, if his faith in man was to outlast his indignation.

How were they as parents to keep their children permanently sensitive? This was the answer, she believed—a matter of priority—"Thou shalt learn to love the Lord thy God" first. Then "thy neighbor as thyself."

10   WONDER

It was time the children were in bed. The boys were already upstairs undressing, and she was overdue for a committee meeting. As she turned the living-room lights off, Judy stood stock still in her little striped sleepers. Then slowly the child began to bounce, rather than walk, up to the fireplace, where low coals glowed red in the darkness.

She cooed softly to herself, unaware of her parents—Ross halfway up the stairs, Kay in the doorway. Every now and then Judy would stop before the redness, hold her fat little hand up high, and suck in her breath with delight.

As Kay watched the extraordinary performance, framed on either side by ordinary-a-minute-ago and ordinary-a-minute-from-now, she remembered the lines from *Leaves of Grass*:

There was a child went forth every day,
And the first object he look'd upon, that object he became,
And that object became part of him for the day or a certain
   part of the day,
Or for many years or stretching cycles of years.[1]

Tonight it was the fire, and the fire was wonder. Judy herself was wonder. And the living room was full of it.

Just a fire Kay had laid, and lit, and let go down, and would have covered over with the screen, and forgotten—seen with new eyes; become, in that one instant, part of a living thing.

Stop, she thought, lest the moment pass you by. The committee meeting can wait.

11   KEEPING VALUES STRAIGHT

She met a college friend of hers in town, and they spent the afternoon in one of the fancy stores where the "house of the future" was on display—drapes that never fade and refrigerators with revolving innards; white that never

---

[1] Walt Whitman, "There Was a Child Went Forth."

spots, metal that never tarnishes, and "just press this button and watch it do all the work." It was wonderful. They wandered from one room to another, their heads full of bright and glamorous color schemes, stunning flower arrangements, and bedspreads with perky taffeta bows or starched ruffles. It was a native impulse with her, touched off at the drop of a hat, to dream herself in her dream house—antique satin chairs and gleaming silver on polished mahogany, jasmine tea steaming in paper-thin cups, a fire in the fireplace, and white gladioli over in the corner at just the right angle.

But somehow, though the afternoon and its ideas were exhilarating, she was glad to get back home to the house of the present, where moth and rust were still consumer-conscious, and where she didn't press a button so much as she sewed it on every other day. That night, weary and footsore, she soon had her head on the pillow. But before she turned off the light, she let her eye wander around her own room—the big easy chair over there in the corner, sagging and in need of reupholstering, but as it was now, so good for little feet to climb up, and big feet to stretch out, on. There were the curtains and bedspread, simple and plain but therefore easy to wash. She settled back into it all with a sigh of comfort. It was so lived in, so already worn, she had never to worry whether anything could happen to it.

There was something good, she decided, about owning old worn familiar things because that was exactly what she did—she owned *them*. New, glamorous things usually ended up by owning her, and, in turn, the entire family.

The house of the future was fun to think about. But

when it came to helping her keep values straight, she'd settle for the house of the present.

12   NEED

Surrounded as she was in the daytime by food, clothes, and shelter, family, routine, and events, it was easy to slip into a false feeling of self-sufficiency—not a deliberate smugness, just a lack in feeling any sincere need.

It was at night, though, stripped of her daytime props, when she would lie awake in her bed—far off in the distance a train whistling, or the wind rattling away at the side of the house—that the little daily "whats" and "whys" gave way to "What" and "Why." Then she would set her own living over against the bigger Pattern, and lying there in the darkness with no interruptions to help alleviate the shock, she would wince at the total impact of her thirty-five years. Little things would come at her. Little things with big faces—childish habits not put away, doubts, fears, shameful rationalizations. In all honesty she was forced to look at herself—her appalling poverty, her self-centeredness, her great human need.

How did one have the courage to get up in the morning and go on?

Actually, she thought, the human need within is so great, so terrible, so all-the-time, that what we do is to cover it up in order to live with it at all. And then, she went on thinking, we do a strange, extra, terrible thing. We rear up like angry animals as soon as we scent need in the next person. That only terrifies us the more—that here, also, is someone weak like ourselves. Out of our own great

183

need we do not offer others our hand. We strike at them instead. So the German, in his own low period, picks on the Jew; so the Jew, in turn, often refuses to identify himself with another minority group; so the child who is insecure in his family is frequently the playground bully. And, bringing it closer home, did she not tend to criticize in other people the very qualities she most feared within herself?

This seemed to her, the more she thought about it, the greatest of all tragedies: that we human beings allowed need, one of the few things about us which was universal, to be the very thing which isolated us; and that we let consciousness of need, which could bring us all together huddled around a common fire, drive us instead into our several holes, there to shiver like so many animals. Yes, animals. Because as long as we continued to act like this, the spirit of man remained stillborn.

13   REASONS

She went to pick Larry up at school one day only to find him in a fist fight with a "toughie" much larger than himself. As she got out of the car and went over, the older lad noticed her and beat it. Larry stood there shaking with rage, "You old stinkpot, you belly button, you great big piece of cheese."

"Well, now that we've taken care of him," she said, "how about getting in the car and coming on home?"

They started down the street, Larry still sputtering. "That guy's been picking on me. He's three years older

184

than everyone else in the class, and he's the dumbest. He's always hanging around and picking on people."

"Why do you suppose he does it?"

"Why? I don't know. Maybe because he's an old stinkpot."

"And maybe because he feels bad because he's so far behind in school."

"Well, if he feels bad, what's he hit all of us for?"

"Because the rest of you aren't behind in school."

That was crazy logic, but it was the kind of logic that made sense; and Larry had brains enough to recognize it. "Yeah," he said, finally. Then, "But what am I supposed to do? Let that guy beat me up?"

They were home by now, and she got out some graham crackers and milk before going on. Then she said, "No, Larry, we don't want you to let him beat you up. Daddy and I want you to learn to stand your ground and defend yourself. You can punch hard, and that's important to be able to do. No kid will respect you if you can't protect yourself. But, Larry, there's something just as important as being able to defend yourself, and that is to know what it's all about. People never act without some kind of reason. As long as you know why that boy acted that way, even though that doesn't excuse him, you will be more in control of the situation. You could maybe afford to overlook some of his meanness. You might even try to be friends with him."

Enough was enough. She dropped it, and Larry went outdoors to find the gang. But she was glad, in a way, for the incident. For Larry had been asking so many questions about war. Why, why, why? Where did it come from?

185

How did it happen? He might as well begin to learn in this single small episode that it was a rational world he lived in and that men operated on certain laws, just like the stars, and that an understanding and intelligent use of these laws could be, if only man would begin to use it, as potent a weapon as the fist.

14   NO STANDING ROOM

Every so often when she was dusting in the living room, she would stop a minute and open the beautifully tooled leather portfolio that lay on top of the piano. Inside it were all the important family photographs to date.

It was their wedding picture which stopped her today; and as she looked at it, she remembered—the white of the altar, the feel of her hand in Ross's, the rich smell of gardenias and the pounding in her throat as she'd said, "I pledge thee my troth." And she had thought, then, "Nothing can be more perfect than this moment; nothing that life can bring can ever make me happier than I am right now."

So they'd taken a picture of the moment and framed it.

Only now, twelve years later, she knew how much she would have missed if she and Ross had stayed framed to that moment. For there is no such thing, she decided, as keeping intact the affection you pledge each other on your wedding day. In marriage you either grow more and more in love—so that you are always saying, "Do you remember the senior prom or our first year together? We thought we were in love but we really didn't know anything then"; or else you grow less and less in love—so that you go back with nostalgia to the faded gardenia, the old letters, as days that held something no longer true. There is, inexorable law of life, no standing still while you are in love.

Since she was most happily mated, however, the thought she'd just pursued hardly pinched. She went back to her dusting, though, with the vague feeling that if she followed through on the implications, she would eventually feel it. And it did come home when, leaving Ross out of it for the moment, she applied the law to herself. For it meant—since she, like her marriage, was always growing— that she could stop at any given moment and determine which direction she was growing in: up or down, forward or backward.

It meant, bringing it down to where it really hurt, that the end of each day—this day—would find her either a better person, or a poorer one. Only one, or the other.

She finished off the living room in a chastened mood.

15 WHEN YOUR CHILD ASKS FOR BREAD

Watching children accept the world adults have made for them was a poignant experience. It was, she felt, like watching a child open a package, when all the time you knew inside it was a stone, not bread.

Ezra Whitmore was a farmer near where they summered in New England, and a good friend of theirs. Ezra was a forecaster, and whenever they would go to get the milk and give old bread to the lambs, they could count on ten minutes extra.

187

"The frost's coming early this year," he would say, one foot on their running board.

Then Larry would pop up, "How do you know, Ezra, how do you know?"

"Why 'cause! The swallows are all gone and August ain't."

"Is it going to ruin your crop, Ezra? Can you grow things with the frost so near?"

"Yes, Larry, yes." Then Ezra would spit tobacco and rehearse for them the drama of how he was going to outwit Jack Frost, the killer, and save the beanstalk.

Ezra was a farmer, raising crops, and he knew the danger signals when his harvest was threatened.

She was a mother, raising children, and she had her signs and clues too.

"They know there's an atomic bomb. They know the kind of world they live in."

How do you know, Kay, how do you know?

"Why, because. Every so often, when Larry and Dan get to talking about when they grow up, they put something into the middle of their conversation we never put there when we were children. They say, "Dad, Mom, do you think all of us'll get to live that long?"

They know a bomb hangs over them.

And is it going to ruin your crop, Kay? Can you grow things with the frost so near?

Watching children accept the world adults have made for them is a poignant experience. It's like watching a child open a package, when all the time you know inside is a stone, not bread.

188

16   SADNESS IS NEVER SO CLOSE

She tiptoed in to see if they were all tucked in before she left. She'd said good-by to them earlier. She'd told them that she and Daddy were going to take a little trip, that her own father had just died, and that they must go back home for a few days.

"Will you come back soon, Mommie?"

"Yes, Judy."

"I want to go too and say good-by to Grandpa."

"No, Dan."

"Is it going to be very sad for you, Mom?"

"Why—yes, Larry."

She covered them up, and before she knew it she and Ross were on the way. The train drew into the familiar station in the early morning hours, and they got off. But Dad wasn't there to meet them, in his dark heavy overcoat and gray felt, and the stride they were always kidding him about—the stride she had inherited and passed right on to Larry. There was no one to say, "Hello, darling. My! but I'm glad to see you." Only a taxicab driver who took their bags and drove them out to her home.

She wandered around the house all day like a lost child. But by late afternoon she dropped, tired, into her father's favorite chair only to sit there, unbelieving, in the room she'd known so well. It was over. Her own home. Her childhood. Half over when her mother had died. All over now. And big sobs kept rolling up inside of her.

She wiped her eyes and looked outside the window. In the late sunlight a little red maple tree—a thing of exquisite beauty—stood alone, smiling at her. But tears filled her eyes again, and she lost it. After a moment the window framed it again, and it became insistent. "Make room for me. Even in this moment I too am in your line of vision. Take me in."

But she hardly felt she could. It seemed as though it would hardly be fitting if she took her mind off the grief at hand.

"But your father, of all people, would have stopped to take me in.

She wavered. "Would her tribute really be the less if she stopped to drink in beauty?"

"Your father planted me. He cared for me. He loved me."

That was enough. She turned her head full to the window and forgot her crying. "I will enjoy you," she thought, and she sat quietly for a long time, taking in the color, the texture, the lines.

"Is it going to be sad for you, Mom?"

"Yes, Larry. But . . ."

"But what, Mom?"

"It hasn't been *all* sad, Larry. I've found there's been room enough for something more."

"What?"

"There's been room for a thing of beauty to come in and sit down between the sadness and me. And it's made us both glad."

17   **ALTERNATION**

She was grateful that reading the evening newspaper came after saying good night to the children. Reading about Mother Goose, the lugubrious Whing Whang, and Aladdin was good antidote for the blearing headlines, the shocking "realism" of her adult world.

In many ways she had never grown up. She still liked to name the corners of her pie, watch the speedometer when all three numbers turned at once, and open crinkly tissue with big fat bows; she still liked to make the clouds into shapes, and the shapes into stories where fairies had wands, people had magic carpets, and treasures were dug up; and to pretend, when a star was especially bright, that it meant a miracle was about to happen. It was a kind of refreshment—this being able to sit down each evening with her children and enter again the world of fancy and fantasy.

There was the other part about being a parent, too— the part where she couldn't sit down with them to go back into their world, but where she must stand by and watch them stretching taller, inch by inch, to grow into her world of newspaper headlines, a world of pressures and inhibitions, of fear and war, a world where adults hate because they dare not risk to try any other way; a world from which, as they grew up, they too would have to learn how to withdraw if they wanted to keep their precious sanity.

18   **CHILDREN NOT OUR CHILDREN**

When she leaned down to kiss Larry good night, he took her face in his hands. With a self-conscious, nine-year-old grin and a hard swallow he said, "I think, Mom, I'm almost getting too big for a good-night kiss."

She held off—stunned.

"Don't you think so?" He asked it, haltingly, to fill in the silence.

She knew that someday, of course, he would grow up. But so soon? No longer kiss him good night! When just yesterday . . . Then she remembered something, and for her it saved the moment. That night at dinner, and without prompting, he had held out her chair for her to be seated.

Thus did a child leave one stage, but not without entering upon another.

"O.K., darling. We'll just talk together for a while, like we always do, and then we'll say good night without kissing."

He seemed relieved that she had taken it so well. And in his relief he forgot. He threw his arms spontaneously around her and kissed her. That made them both laugh, and it felt good. Rapport had been established again.

After she had left his room, though, she stood out in the hall a minute, alone, with a strange feeling. Ross was gone for the evening. She would tell him about it when he came home, of course. But it would still be primarily her adjustment. It was different for a mother than for a father. She looked back at the closed door. What had Larry said? *I am growing up. And you? You must stand aside and let me.*

Possessiveness, she thought, is a sticky quality, and if you don't wash it off everyday . . . Possessiveness was the one thing a mother had to guard against above all else. Larry was growing up, adding independence to dependence—a good balance—the sign of health.

The dishes were waiting downstairs. And it was a good thing. They would give her a chance to take stock. For this evening meant, if it meant anything at all, that she must be careful to match her child's growth with her own.

19   BIBS AND TUCKERED

She stood at the kitchen sink for the third time that day, for the eighteenth time that week, for the sixtieth . . . In front of her the window sill, and on it, soap, steel wool, scouring powder. Like Miss Millay's "three long mountains and a wood" these were the things that bounded her; over these things she could not see.

For tonight she was tired. Dog tired. And it seemed to her, in times like this, as though most of her life was spent in the eternal battle against dirt. She might begin as dust and end as dust, but why did it have to be her bosom pal in between? This was one of the days when, in spite of herself, housework had gotten her down. She'd begun the day with a washing, and she'd forgotten to check the pockets. A piece of red string had gotten in with the white clothes. That had meant pale pink, but it had made her see red. After that, it was hands down. The rest of the day followed suit until she'd tumbled the children into bed that night —Nobody Knows the Trouble I've Seen—but there was nothing glory, glory hallelujah about it.

She finished the dishes and went in and sat down on the davenport, too tired to wiggle, too tired to read the paper or turn on the radio, too tired, even, to go upstairs to bed. She just wanted to sit. And feel sorry for herself.

Dear God, she thought, when I get to thinking this way, I get in a rut. Help me. Of all the times I need help, now is the time.

One of the reasons she read the Bible each night—dog tired or not—was that it took her out of herself, set her down in her proper place in history, gave her perspective on immediate problems. She was tired tonight, she knew, partly because the work had been hard, mostly because she hadn't liked the kind of work. What was it about housework that really offended her? It was, if she had to say it in one word, her dignity that was at stake.

And what was dignity?

The Gospels in her hand were about a carpenter. And Brother Lawrence, whose book of devotions she was reading, was a kitchen servant in a medieval manor—a humble scourer of the pots and pans. Work with the hands had never been a deterrent to great living. This she knew. She just had to see it again in a new setting.

Housework, she need not fear, nor that such work would get her in a rut, but what went on in the head and the heart while the hands were busy.

20   MORE THAN WANTING

"I've decided," Dan announced one afternoon, bursting into the kitchen for a drink of water, "I've decided that this year I'm going to be good."

"That's fine," she said, looking up from a pie she was fixing to see a blond crew cut, navy corduroy pants, and a

194

black eye grinning at her. "When are you planning to begin, Dan?"

"Tomorrow."

"Why not today?"

"O.K., today." He gulped down a glass of water and took a look at the kitchen clock. "At four o'clock."

"But it's twenty minutes of four."

"I know. That gives me twenty minutes yet."

She waited.

"I want to give Larry just one good kick in the pants first before I begin." Then he was gone like a flash, and she was left to laugh over the ways of small boys.

Only that evening the paper said—and it wasn't talking about small boys—that America wanted to go all out for being good; so did Russia; so did everybody, in fact. But before that happened there were a few licks to get in first, a few deals to square—that boundary line never quite agreed to, that national insult never quite swallowed, that defeat somewhere in history never quite admitted. Shadows, that's all. Mere shadows in the background, while the band plays good will. Because of course we want to do good, and reap good. What sensible man or woman does not?

And shadows aren't very real, are they, when our good will is in earnest. Just the way twenty minutes isn't very long, is it, as long as he wants to be good. Get them over with and out of the way and then . . .

Only sometimes shadows are more real than men.

Sometimes twenty minutes is all the time there is.

195

21   THE FEAR

There was a before and an after The Fear. It was as distinct as all that. Up to this summer she had been afraid. Ever since this summer she had not been.

Always, since she could remember, she had been afraid of the dark. After she had grown up, she'd become objective about it, gone back into her childhood, found out why. She had dissected the Fear, like a scientist, laughed at it, told it to go away. But dissecting it, knowing why it was there, ridiculing it, even, had not been enough to exorcise the demon. Come night again and dark, and if Ross was to be gone and she was to be alone in the house, she was afraid. She'd lock all the doors and toss the night away.

Then that summer when Ross was gone and she was alone with the children, she discovered that Larry too—good-natured, sunny, outgoing, well-adjusted Larry—Larry was getting so he didn't like the dark any more than she did. He'd mentioned it several times before, but one night he met her in the hallway when the others were asleep. "Mom, I think someone's downstairs," he said nervously.

"Why Larry!" she laughed. But it was false. The Fear gripped her too, like a cold hand around the throat. Her heart began to pound. She'd heard the noises too. She'd even toyed with Larry's conclusion.

So what was she to do? She stood there a second looking at Larry. Her brain said, "There's no truth to these noises. You know that. You hear them every night, and you know no one is down there." But her brain was only a very small part of her, and the rest of her paid no attention to it. The rest of her went right on being scared.

She looked at Larry again, and he looked pitiful. He *must not* be plagued by The Fear, ferreting out every little noise, letting his imagination run riot, lying in bed stiff and rigid, trying to get to sleep, not being able to. If only for Larry's sake, if not her own. . . . "Come on," she said deliberately, evenly, and she took his hand. Together they went downstairs. And they sat in the dark. And they told each other stories. At first it was forced, but after a bit it became natural—to sit in the dark and hear creaks and noises all around and still have nothing happen. After a bit, too, the stories got boring.

"Come on, Mom, I'm sleepy," said Larry.

As soon as she was certain that Larry was no longer afraid, that was enough. She went upstairs with him, tucked him in, got into her own bed, and slept like a log the rest of the night.

22　　　　　EXAM, LIFE STYLE

She was cleaning out the attic when she noticed an old carton full of college class notes and old exams. There they all were, tied up in neat little packages: freshman Botany, the History of Economic Thought, the Romantic Poets, Introduction to Art.

On top she found an exam she distinctly remembered taking. Pages and pages she'd written on it till her fingers had cramped. The exam had consisted of one question, "Write the most important things you have learned in this course." She remembered the way everyone raised her hand and objected. What kind of an exam was this? And how could you do a thing like that in three hours?

The professor seemed undisturbed. "Calm down, ladies. What I want to see is how you organize your material. You will be judged as much by what you leave out as by what you put in. And one more thing. Don't start right out writing. Take time out to plan your strategy. It will show up in your paper if you do."

But his words had fallen on deaf ears. Everyone was furious, and she remembered how they'd all gotten together afterwards, over a coke, and raked the professor over the coals.

And yet that was probably the best exam she'd ever taken. At any rate, of all the pages and pages that lay in the carton this one test seemed to her now to make the most sense.

For life never quite came at you in "I, II, III" order with subpoints and sub-subpoints and "take ten minutes to answer this and half an hour to answer that." It came at you all at once with, "Here's a day, with a hundred and one things to get done in it. Now write all you know about living it."

What kind of an exam was this? And how could she possibly get all she needed to in that short a time?

Calm down, ladies. You will be judged by the way you organize your material, by what you leave out as much as by what you put in.

And one more thing. Don't start right out living your day. Take a few minutes out before you begin. It will show up in a very few hours if you do.

23   **COMPARISON**

He was a guest in their home for dinner—a young leader in the Belgian underground movement who had been condemned to die by the Nazis and had been freed the day the Americans had liberated his country. After supper, and the children in bed, he told them the story of his trial. He had had to defend himself, without a lawyer, and in German which he spoke only falteringly.

"The German lawyer, he put me on the stand. Now he know I have left University and been four years in the underground, and that every day I risk my life and the life of my parents, because I live in the daytime in the house with them. Yet the first question he ask me is, 'Do you know what you have done?' I say to him, 'But of course. I know what I have done. It must have value.' And he is very angry to me. He say to me, 'Would you do it again if you had the chance?' And I say to him, 'I do it again.' Then they not let me talk any more, but they take me down from the stand, and I am condemned to death. But I not forget so long as I live, his asking of me, do I know what I have done."

She sat listening to this young man, deeply moved by his calm voice, his noticeable lack of hate, mostly by his strong moral sense: "I have lied and killed and stolen for four years to save the lives of four hundred children. But each time I do it, I know what I have done, and I say to myself, as if for the first time, 'Are you sure you choose right?'"

And what did one say to a young lad like this, besides extending him the courtesy of listening to him, besides thanking him for his share. One offered him, albeit silently, an apology. That all too often among those of us who have suffered least, moral sensitivity has been the dullest, vindictiveness has seemed to linger longest, materialism has been most crude.

24   AN ORCHESTRA

She overheard Larry one day talking to an elderly neighbor who had recently come to live with the family next door.

Larry edged up onto the porch where old Mr. Riker used to sit in the morning. "Mr. Riker," he asked, his curiosity finally overcoming his embarrassment, "what does it feel like to be blind?"

She was about to call Larry back when she realized Mr. Riker was not offended.

"Do you really want to know, child?"

Yes, Larry really did.

"Then go back to your house and ask your mother for a heavy linen towel."

Larry got the towel and returned to Mr. Riker with it.

"Now then, go home and put this on. Come back tonight and tell me you haven't peeked even once."

Larry went away. But he had come back in less than an hour to have the towel off. "Mom, I went over and told Mr. Riker that I thought I knew how it must feel."

"What did he say, Larry?"

"He said, no, I didn't. He said as long as you can take off the blindfold, you can never really know."

The whole thing had evidently touched Larry deeply.

"Mom," said Larry, "I told Mr. Riker I felt sorry for blind people."

"Did you?"

"And do you want to know what he said to that? He said he didn't want me to feel sorry for him. That that way I'd never come around. He said he'd much rather if I just brought my violin over and he'd get out his, and we'd play tunes together, instead."

"Mom," Larry went on after a bit, "I think he's right. He knows 'Reuben and Rachel' and 'The Bluebells of Scotland' and all the songs in my book, and we played for a whole hour, and all that time I never once thought about his being blind at all. I think, rather than me feeling sorry for him, that he and I'll be an orchestra instead."

25   OUR OWN CHOICE

She watched as Ruth made the adjustment—a friend who had married late, who had given up a successful career to do it, and whose husband had then lived only one year. They sat together one evening, and Ruth spoke of the years before her marriage as ones of loneliness, the years since her husband's death as years of aloneness.

It was a good distinction and the clue to Ruth's resources.

Loneliness, Ruth said, was an emotional condition—the period in one's life when one has not succeeded in making contact or finding someone who above all cares.

Aloneness, on the other hand, she meant as a physical condition, not always able to be controlled. You either were with people, or you weren't. But aloneness, according to Ruth, need not be, as was loneliness, a poignant condition. She was alone now but no longer lonely. Memory, intangible but real, was there to sustain her.

But Ruth had, it became apparent as they talked, more than the memory of her husband to hold her. She had discovered God since the tragedy, a God she had admitted but never really known before. And it was that knowledge which was making it possible for her to pick up the thread of her life and go on.

It came to Kay with fresh meaning that the religious man or woman need never be lonely. Christ in Gethsemane was alone. But not lonely. Even with all the disciples asleep, he still had Someone to talk to.

She went back to a verse she had learned as a child, "What can separate me from the love of God?" And she thought again about the amazing answer to that question. "Nothing can separate me—nothing that I can think up, nothing that can happen to me, no mistake that I can make, nothing that anyone else can do to me, or mine."

This was assurance. But man himself had to make it experience. Nothing could separate her from God. Nothing, she realized, except herself.

26   AN OLD MAN'S EYES

Michael and his family had moved into the neighborhood the summer before. They were a cultivated, well-to-do family known to the community as "refugees." She had invited Michael down to play with the boys one day, and the children had all gone out to the back yard.

She found Michael, later, sitting all by himself on the stone wall. "Where are the boys, Michael?"

"They w-w-went away," said Michael. Although his English was good, he stuttered it, agonizing with each syllable.

She went over, Judy at her feet, and sat down on the wall beside him. "Where did they go, do you know?"

"N-n-no, I d-d-don't know."

He looked at her and she saw, for the first time in her life, an old man in a child's eyes.

"What's this you're doing, Michael?" she asked sociably. He had a whole pile of cardboard milk caps in his lap and, one by one, he was turning them inside out and laying them in a neat row along the wall.

"I'm m-m-making plates—for Dan," he added. "W-w-when the boys went away, Dan came back and told me he might l-l-like me if I made him some plates out of these. Then he w-w-went away too."

Poor Dan. Dan would have liked Michael because he couldn't really keep up with the older gang all the time. But Dan would never let himself get shoved off, much less on a pariah.

"You know what would be fun?" she said. "I'll get some tinfoil that I have in the house, and you can make these into real silver plates. Then won't Dan think you're a magic-maker to make silver plates?"

The old-man look began to fade. "Silver plates?" Michael whispered.

She helped him line the caps with tinfoil while Judy played merrily at their feet. Since the boys didn't respond to calling, she let it go at that, and after a while Michael

203

thought he'd better go home. "You come back again sometime, Michael, won't you?" she said as she walked out to the front with him.

For a six-year-old boy he was holding on to her hand rather too tightly. "Mrs. McC-C-Clean," he said suddenly, "I don't know w-w-whether you know it or not, but I'm a G-G-German."

"Why yes, of course I know it, Michael."

He kept strong hold of her hand. Hesitated. Then blurted out, "But Mrs. McC-C-Clean, do you mean you'd still want me to come back and play if I told you I was a J-J-Jew too?"

27   AN UNCHRISTIAN CHRISTMAS

It took a while to do it, but gradually Michael became one of the gang. He was accepted by everybody. Everybody except Chris. Chris's mother still resented the refugees' intrusion into the neighborhood.

One day soon after Christmas Kay looked out of her bedroom window to see Dan, Michael, and Chris building a snow man out in the front yard. Chris said, "Let's not play this any more. I'm sick of it. Let's go indoors and play in my basement."

"I don't want to," said Dan. "I want to play this some more."

"W-we-we haven't f-f-finished this snow man yet," said Michael, a ready second to anything Dan said.

"We've got our old Christmas tree down in the basement," Chris insisted. "And a lot of colored paper still, and a bell. We could play Santa Claus. Come on."

"No," said Dan, "we don't want to play that."

"No," said Michael, and he went on patting the head of the snow man.

Chris looked at Michael sullenly. Then he said, "Michael can't come anyway."

Michael's head came up with a jerk. "W-w-why not?"

"You can't have Christmas," Chris said categorically.

It was Dan's turn now. "Why not?" he asked.

"Because he's a Jew," said Chris, looking straight at Michael and enjoying the flush that came into Michael's face.

"What's a Jew?" asked Dan, dumbfounded.

"Michael's a Jew, and my mother says they don't believe in Christmas."

Dan turned to Michael in astonishment, "Don't you believe in Christmas, Michael?"

She had run downstairs and outdoors, but it was too late by the time she got there. Dan stood beside the snow man, bewilderment written all over his face. Chris stood on the other side, singing in the chant that is as old as childhood itself, "Michael can't have Christmas, Michael can't have Christmas." And Michael? Michael had gone home.

28   SOCIAL ARITHMETIC

"Mom, what's a Jew?" Dan asked as soon as they got in the house.

"Why a Jew is a person," she said. "Just like you are a person. You are a Protestant. Some people are Jews. Some are Catholics."

205

"Then why can't Michael have Christmas?"

"He can," she said.

"No he can't," said Dan. "Chris says Jews don't believe in Christmas."

She said, no time for preparation, "Some Jewish people celebrate the Christmas-tree idea without making Christmas the birth of Jesus. Other Jewish people celebrate what they call Hanukkah. It comes about the same time as our Christmas, and it's a day that has meaning for them just as Christmas has meaning for us. They have a festival of lights, and they give each other gifts. Hannukah is what Michael and his family celebrate."

Dan didn't understand too much of this. All he understood was that Michael wasn't as strange as he had suddenly become that afternoon, and that he needn't be cut off from him because of a word Chris had conjured up out of thin air. He returned to the one thing he wanted a definite answer on.

"But what about me and Michael playing Christmas together? Can we?"

"You can tell Michael about Christmas, if you like, and dress up as Santa and play that one afternoon. I think it would be nice too if we got Michael to tell us about Hanukkah, and you play that together first. He can tell you the story about it and show you some Hanukkah tops and, if his mother says yes, you can have real candles for your festival of lights."

"Gee, that's neat," said Dan. "This way we've got two games to play instead of one!"

THE NEW IDEA

The next few days she decided to keep near the window and see what was going on. It was about a week later that she heard some discussion out in the front yard and went to listen, hidden behind the living room drape.

It was Chris again, at Dan and Michael. "Come on, Dan, we need one more man. Leave Michael and come on and build a fort with us."

"No," said Dan. "Why don't you stay here? Me and Michael've got a tunnel started."

They all stood marking time for a minute. Then Chris came up with, "Dan, what're you always playing with Michael for anyway? You know what Mom says? She says you're a Jew-lover."

She saw Dan wince, as though he'd been struck across the face. Dan didn't know what it meant, but he didn't like to be called a name. She caught herself wanting to cry out, wanting to ward off even this first, this ever so small insult. She stood there behind the living room drape, vulnerable as only a parent can be, wondering once again whether they had the right to ask their children to pay for something that they as parents believed. They had dreaded the first moment when they would have to stand by and let their children face the consequences for what they were teaching them, and where they could no longer save them from the hurt.

She looked at Dan. Dan hadn't liked being called a name by Chris. But he was not going to be cut off from Michael again. "I can too play with whoever I want," he said, right to Chris's face. "Today I want to play with Michael."

Then she looked at Chris. As she watched the bitterness in his face, she realized suddenly that, either way, parents ask their children to pay a price. Chris was already paying a price—a terrible price—and for an old idea. The new idea was still in the making—"a new nation, conceived in liberty, and dedicated to the proposition, . . . now engaged in, . . . whether that nation or any nation so conceived . . . can long endure, . . . the brave men, living and dead, . . . they gave the full measure of devotion." The familiar words came tumbling into her mind. And if grown men had to face such a cost, why then should not children, with that nation still free under their feet, be taught to pay a price for it also?

She wondered if perhaps the greatest gift a parent could give his child was not the knowledge that he must always pay a price if he, in turn, wants to have the nation free to pass onto his children, yet unborn.

30   DEMOCRACY'S ROOTS

At her club that day a beauty expert had given them sound advice. "Take your worst feature," she'd said, "and go to town with it. If you have a pointed face, admit it. Don't try to tone it down. You can't anyway. Instead, do your hair, and wear the kind of earrings and neckline, to help play up the pointed effect."

It was an interesting speech, and a useful one, and the applause was good.

As she went home with some others, they passed a certain public school and some derogatory remarks were made about it. "Going down hill," someone said.

"Foreign element invading it," another said.

She wondered about the applause if the speaker had gone on to carry her point one step further. America, for instance, was a land of different peoples. How about America's taking her differences and going to town with them? Why should she try to cover them up, boil them down in a melting pot? Wouldn't it be better to capitalize on the differences instead?

She remembered an interesting article she'd read once on how the three forms of government dealt with differences between people. Fascism, according to the article, exploited men's differences; communism ignored them; democracy admitted them—live and let live.

But it was more, she could not but feel, than *admitting* differences that was needed. Live and let live could mean a land of individualists, tolerant of each other, to be sure, but unconcerned too. The creative attitude—the kind the speaker had referred to—was needed. And it was here that the relevance of the Christian tradition, which the Pilgrims had brought along with their love of individual freedom, became apparent. For Christianity imposed upon democracy, in addition to the idea of "live and let live," the idea of "live and I'll help you live." It insisted upon a community, not only of individuals, but of individuals who were parts of a whole, "members one of another." And only as a nation was made up of such individuals could it hope to achieve any real unity.

Divorced from the Christian tradition it began in, democracy could not help but become like a cut flower—a set of beautiful ideas, with no roots, no source of nourish-

209

ment. But *with the tradition* democracy could become a creative force in the world, an ideal as well as an idea, a framework in which the brotherhood of man made sense, and against all disillusionment, because it first accepted and believed in the fatherhood of God.

The Better Part

ROSE TERLIN

1   A NEW OUTLOOK

The morning sunrise after the dark night has always been a symbol of a universal desire—the longing for a new beginning, a fresh start. How often we long to recapture the moments in our lives when a freshness of spirit, a newness of outlook, welled up in us and we felt we could "mount up with wings as eagles." Embarking on marriage, starting one's first job or tackling a new one, bringing children into the world—in all these the sense of great adventure came shining through the nervous apprehension and lifted us beyond ourselves.

It is not necessarily that we are defeated by our failures or that the memory of past frustrations dims the vision of the dawn. It is the humdrum monotony, the seemingly deadly routines of our daily lives, that defeats us. It is true of every important relationship in life—husband and wife, children and parents, all personal and professional relations. So we are restless and bored, seeking to escape from the dull, stale monotony that dims our lives.

What we need is not excitement for escape, but a new outlook, an awakening of the spirit of eternal sunrise within us by which we lay hold of—no, are *held by*—the indwelling God of eternal life, the God of new beginnings, the God of beginning again.

"Thou madest us for Thyself, and our heart is restless until it find its rest in Thee." [1]

2   THE WAY TO GAIN

"Whosoever shall seek to gain his life shall lose it; but whosoever shall lose his life shall preserve it."

It has been said that if we lost all of Jesus' words save these, we would still have the center of the Christian gospel—the "good news" of how man comes into possession of his life, of his own true self. A. E. Housman in his moving essay, "The Name and Nature of Poetry," says that these words of Jesus constitute the profoundest utterance ever to cross human lips.

Here is the law of life, stated in the form of a paradox. How many psychologists will attest to the truth of the statement that he who seeks to gain his life loses it. We have heard so often that he who seeks to gain wealth and makes that the driving force of life may end up embittered, lonely, and unhappy, if not impoverished. But its meaning is more universal than that. Those who seek always to protect themselves, their prestige, their egos from hurt end up with no prestige, no self-development, no growth of the living psyche. They are doomed to the death of

[1] Augustine.

mere existence, to the neuroses and the hell of the divided being.

This anxious concern for the self is rejected by Jesus because it doesn't work; it simply does not produce the desired results. There is no hint of moralism here, no suggestion of "sin," but a simple, challenging statement which accepts as valid man's desire for "life," eternal and abundant, here and now.

3   HALF IS NOT ENOUGH

"Whosoever shall seek to gain his life shall lose it; but whosoever shall lose his life shall preserve it."

How shall I lose my life to gain it? Surely not by acting in accordance with this particular virtue or avoiding that particular vice. The religion of Jesus is not a catalogue of specifics, but a law that goes to the roots of human personality. How then do I accomplish this transforming act? By yielding the will—last outpost of the self—to God. Meister Eckhart illuminates the way for us when he says, "There are plenty to follow our Lord halfway, but not the other half. They will give up possessions, friends, and honors, but it touches them too closely to disown themselves."

"It is just this astonishing life which is willing to follow Him the other half, sincerely to disown itself, this life which intends complete obedience, without any reservations that I would propose to you in all humility. . . . When such a commitment comes in a human life, God breaks through, miracles are wrought, world-renewing divine forces are released . . ." [2]

This statement that we find life by yielding our self-centeredness, by recognizing honestly and renouncing completely our egocentricity, makes clear how ultimate the demand is. Anyone who has ever glimpsed the rewards in creativity, freedom from fear, integration, life bubbling within like an ever-refreshing stream does not count the cost too great.

4   A THOUSAND WAYS TO ONE

"Whosoever shall seek to gain his life shall lose it; but whosoever shall lose his life shall preserve it."

The words of a modern novelist and a modern philosopher bring challengingly before Christians the meaning of these profound words of Jesus:

"I do not believe there is any other way of saving one's soul today. He is saved who overcomes his individual egoism, family egoism, caste egoism, who does not shut himself up in a cloister, or build himself an ivory tower, or make a cleavage between his way of thinking and his way of acting. He is saved who frees his own spirit from the idea of resignation to the existing disorder. Spiritual life has always meant a capacity for dedication and self-sacrifice. In a society like ours spiritual life can only be a revolutionary life. One must not be afraid, one must not be obsessed with the idea of security, even of the se-

[2] Thomas R. Kelly, A Testament of Devotion (Harper & Brothers), p. 52.

curity of one's own virtue; spiritual life and secure life
do not go together. To save one's self one must struggle
and take risks—one must lose one's self." [3]

"There is no escape. You must say yes or no (according
to the light you have seen). There are a thousand ways of
saying no; one way of saying yes; and no way of saying
anything else. . . . But commitment is never merely a series
of prunings. . . . It is a tremendous decision." [4]

5   WHAT IS DECISIVE?

"Not everyone who sayeth unto me Lord, Lord shall
enter into the kingdom of heaven; but he that doeth the
will of my Father who is in heaven."

These words of Jesus are among the most challenging
in the New Testament. Every individual who professes
to be Christian, and every Christian institution, stands
under the judgment of these seemingly simple phrases. To
take them seriously, even for a day, is a revolutionary experience. For Jesus is saying that it does not matter what
a person professes; it is what he *does* that determines his
destiny. Here in one sentence Christ blasted the whole Platonic world of *idea* and substituted the affirmation that
action or behavior is determinative. In Plato's world people stand on their heads; Jesus set them on their feet.

Here one moves out of the realm of speculation and
mystery into the real world. Jesus did not say that
one had to have a correct concept of God, that it was a
person's idea of God, or his creedal affirmation or church

[3] Ignazio Silone, *Bread and Wine* (Harper & Brothers).
[4] Gregory Vlastos, *The Religious Way* (The Woman's Press).

affiliation that was decisive. Rather, it is whether he meets
the demands of God which he apprehends through his
conscience. Perhaps if with all his heart a person accepts
this motivation for his behavior, his knowledge and understanding of God will grow amazingly.

6   THE KINGDOM

"Not everyone who sayeth unto me Lord, Lord shall
enter into the kingdom of heaven, but he that doeth the
will of my Father who is in heaven."

In this statement, Jeus defined the goal of religious living—entering into the kingdom of heaven. The words
sound stale, even empty, to us after two thousand years
of Christian history. How can freshness and challenge be
infused into them? Playing a certain game may help.

Pretend you are a Chinese student who has never had
contact with any Christians, but in the college library you
have found a New Testament and started to read Matthew's gospel. Being an intelligent, rational person you
ask two questions. What does this religion of Jesus Christ
offer? How is the goal achieved? It seems to offer the kingdom of heaven—the regnancy of God among men, the con-
quest of the evil and injustice that have bedeviled men, the
enabling of the individual to realize his fullest potential-
ities to become a good tree bring forth good fruit.

As you read the parables, this kingdom of God does not
seem another-worldly mystery. It is a natural process—a
seed in the ground being transformed, a grain of mustard
seed growing into a great tree, yeast in a measure of dough,
pervading and transforming its whole nature. The goal

that is offered is supremely challenging—that the person accepts the regnancy of God may be insignificant, but, relative to his capacity, he can achieve great things of enduring value. Such is the power of God among men to whom he has access.

7   THE IMPORTANCE OF THE WILL

"Not everyone who sayeth unto me Lord, Lord, shall enter into the kingdom of heaven, but he that doeth the will of my Father who is in heaven."

Christianity has traditionally placed more emphasis on the fruits of religious living than on the process by which these results are achieved. But since this is a universe of law, in which no effect is attained without its appropriate cause, it is well for us to focus more on the method of achieving abundant life than on the description of its glories. In this statement Jesus says that the method is doing the will of God.

Repeatedly, this phrase is decisive for him, "For whosoever shall do the will of God, the same is my brother, and sister, and mother."

"My Father, if it be possible, let this cup pass away from me: nevertheless, not as I will, but as thou wilt."

This emphasis on the *will* is significant. There is not much discussion of it in the sermons we hear. There is more emphasis on "right thinking," on concepts of God—intellect—or on love, sympathy, and so forth—emotions—than on the will. Modern psychology has stressed the importance and the deviousness of the will of man. It is not "as a man thinketh" that he is, but as he *wills*, using his

217

thought processes to justify what he wills to do. Jesus said we must relate our will to God's—will what God wills, and we will find abundant life.

8   UNDERBIDDING GOD

"Thou shalt love the Lord thy God with all thy heart, and with all thy soul, and with all thy strength, and with all thy mind."

The most striking feature of this passage is the totality of devotion called for. Jesus did not reply to the lawyer's answer by asking, "And what do you mean by God?" He approves an answer which calls for infallible devotion apart from any notion of concept. Perhaps he believed that if a person actually gave such devotion to whatever he called God, however thin and meager the content of his conception, and proceeded to act on this devotion, his experience and knowledge of God would be enriched immeasurably. Perhaps it is only after such an act of commitment that one can sincerely sing of the glory and grace and mercy of God.

We are always trying to underbid God—to buy freedom in terms cheaper than the most absolute bondage. We try to be children of God without giving the loyalty, the love, the devotion of will and mind and heart which such a relationship demands.

Oh Lord, our God, the king of all that is, to thee we present ourselves anew with all that we have and are. Hallow us through thy spirit that we may rightly use our powers and gifts, our time and all that is ours in thy service. Amen.

9   **A BASIC ATTITUDE**

"Thou shalt love thy neighbor as thyself."

How convenient it would be if being a Christian required us only to "love God," practice the virtues approved in the most respectable society, and avoid such obvious malfeasance as stealing, alcoholism, murder, and so forth. But the Christian life is more difficult and more adventurous than that! We must love our neighbor!

"And who is my neighbor?" asked the lawyer. The story of the good samaritan must have been startling to the little group who heard it. The characters are carefully selected to make a point which was certainly revolutionary to the hearers. An unknown man is beaten, robbed, left injured by the wayside—not an uncommon sight in those days. A priest passes by, and this man of God crosses the road to the other side. A Levite does likewise. Both of these are religious men, with racial and religious status in the community. But a Samaritan, a racial and religious outcast, comes by and treats this man as if he were his own brother.

What would happen in America if we began to practice an ethic which treated all men, irrespective of creed, color, or station in life as if they were equal with ourselves? To love your neighbor as yourself would seem in the exposition which Jesus offers the inquiring lawyer to have very little to do with emotions or with sentiments or with being kind to those less blessed than you. It is not that out of one's blessings, in wealth, position, majority status, one is decent to those less favored. Rather the capacity to behave spontaneously toward all men as God requires springs from a basic attitude in which one stands equal with all men—stands on the same ground as all the rest of the human race—before a just and merciful God.

10   THE LAST OUTPOSTS

"Thou shalt love thy neighbor as thyself."

It has been said by Forbes-Robertson that one should not try to "look at the moral law apart from national life" because "God is a social being, a being of relations." The cultivation of private piety, which so often encompasses the approved description of a Christian in our individualistic society, is futile because it fails to produce the fruits of Christian living in the individual as well as in society. We are conditioned for good or ill by our relations with people. Loneliness and isolation have been called "the most frustrating ills to befall men."

True love for others enlarges the imagination. It develops the capacity to identify one's self with others, to see things as they do. What does loving our fellow man mean but identification with the fate of all men, daring to look at our fellow human beings, their needs and desires and aspirations, as God sees them?

If we are to worship God with our hearts and not just with our lips, then we must do it by turning again to God, meeting his demand for us, for our neighbors, and for our nation. It is only as we yield the last outposts of ourselves that God may enter in, that we can go out into the world to transform it. If we do not go out into the world and take on its burdens, if our only answer to suffering human-

ity is to be sorry for our share in creating suffering, then
our very rebirth is stillborn.

11   **LET US PRAY**

Prayer is the decisive element in the Christian faith
and the chief source of insight, clarity, and spiritual refreshment. But not the prayer of "vain repetitions," of
theological formalities, of perfunctory mumblings. Nor is
it the prayer of half-mechanical mutterings to which we
give only part of our attention, much less our powers of
concentration, on a Sunday morning in church.

The prayer that is the decisive element of the Christian
faith is that prayer entered into alone where both an attitude and an act are involved. The attitude is one of profound self-examination, of opening the heart and will and
mind to the searching finger of God. It is an attitude of
passionate desire to know the truth about one's self, to
discover the area of reservation from the total self-dedica-
tion that is the decisive requirement for finding life. It
is an attitude of complete devotion and deep listening to
God, with complete willingness to do anything which may
be required of one. Prayer is an attitude of heightened
consciousness and intense concentration in which the
total personality is confronted by God.

Prayer is an act—an act by which the individual re-
dedicates himself to his one supreme devotion. It is an
act in which an individual sets his feet upon the path to
"life."

"When thou prayest, enter into thine inner chamber,
and having shut thy door, pray to thy Father who is in

221

secret, and thy Father who seeth in secret shall recompense thee."

12   LET US PRAY TOGETHER

Group worship is an important resource for Christian living and for the extension of the kingdom of God. The Christian religion is paradoxical in many ways. One significant way in which two opposites are held together, and each given its place, is in this tension in Christianity between the role of the individual and the role of the group. One can stand before God, assume complete responsibility as a child of God, only as an individual. Yet the concept of the *kingdom* of God is a social concept. It bespeaks a group of people in whom God is regnant, and who as a group have power to do great things. God's way of justice and peace in the world can be significantly achieved only through group action.

Thus group worship, which is different from prayer, renews and inspires us by the wonderful sense it conveys of the power of a group through which God is working out his purpose. In these days, we cannot do that which is necessary to achieve a community unless we face the broken character of human life in our day—unless we stand before God intensely aware of what is happening in the world—the suffering, terror, degradation of the very gifts God has given the human race. As we stand as a group before God—who perhaps in this day needs sensitive human beings to share his grief—let us always ask ourselves what we are *doing* as a group "to proclaim release to the captives, . . . to set at liberty those who are oppressed." (Luke 4:18, R.S.V.)

13   "DELIVER US FROM EVIL"

It is repugnant to the modern mind to beseech the Deity to work miracles on behalf of the petitioner—to grant immunity from the suffering, tragedies, misfortune, and even daily problems of individuals. Indeed, the deeply religious person prays to be spared no suffering, no mistakes, no difficulties essential to their insight and understanding of the nature of God and man.

What, then, is the evil from which we seek deliverance? The ends of religious living are wholeness, integration, freedom from all that mutilates the psyche, and maximum capacity for growth of the personality. When the Christian prays for deliverance from evil, therefore, he prays that he shall not waste any of himself. He prays for light to see his "blind spots" so that he can see himself as God sees him. He prays for the insight to recognize his hidden motives, his evasions, his areas of darkness—the evil from which he must be delivered to serve God with his whole heart.

"O holy Lord God, who searchest the hearts and triest the reins of the children of men, cleanse me from all hypocrisy and give me truth in the inward parts, that being pure in heart, I may see thee in thy kingdom." [5]

[5] Stobart, *A Book of Private Prayer.*

14   **ON FAITH**

"Faith is not something we believe in spite of the evidence; it is something we dare in spite of the consequences." [6]

Faith is belief manifesting itself *in action*. It is a willingness to venture beyond the established certainty. If one's righteousness is in mores and laws and regulations written down, how much open-mindedness can there be? The attitude of mind which asks for these certainties exhibits a lack of faith; it is a demand born of fear. Then men and women of vital religious faith are those who move through life with spontaneity, flexibility, the capacity for growth and adventure. They possess that quality which has been called "the glorious liberty of the children of God." People who are afraid of "breaking out" are not God's freed men or freed women.

"Our Father, help us to act on the bit of truth we know. If we say we believe in brotherhood, give us the determination to make full and creative life possible for all people. If we say we believe in love, give us the courage to take the risks involved in loving intelligently. If we say we believe in prayer, give us the willingness to face ourselves fearlessly, to think courageously about the problems confronting us, to work for the achievement of a radiant life. If we say we believe we have responsibility to share life, give us a sense of our need to reconsecrate ourselves. May we fail none—not those witnesses who have gone before, nor ourselves, nor the youth who follow. Forgive us our failures, send us forth with resoluteness, that

[6] Sherwood Eddy.

the power which is as available to us as it was to Jesus—
and which he used—may be ours." [7]

15   THE LAW OR GOD?

"In Christ Jesus, neither circumcision availeth anything,
nor uncircumcision; but faith working through love."

"Circumcision is nothing, and uncircumcision is nothing; but the keeping of the commandments of God [is
everything]."

The Christian religion emphasizes the necessity for faith.
All of us long for the fruits of faith—wholeness, courage
to face adversity, power to "move mountains." But what
precisely is meant by faith? Is it an intellectual assent to a
creed? Is it a kind of resignation which says, "I cannot
understand the ways of God, but I accept what happens
as his will"? Is it pulling oneself up by the bootstraps,
forcing oneself to believe something which cannot be
demonstrated in experience?

It is significant that Jesus in his teachings recorded in
Mark, Matthew, and Luke used the word "faith" very
little, whereas Paul used it continuously. It is illuminating
to read the magnificent letters of Paul with the question in
mind, "What is this 'faith' that produces salvation?" How
Paul struggled to make it clear! He used one kind of language for the Corinthians, another for the Galatians, and
so on, that they might understand and, by acting on that
understanding, be transformed and filled with the power
of the Holy Spirit.

[7] Jane Saddler.

In his letters to the Galatians, Paul sets forth the anti-thesis of faith—namely, righteousness understood as living by rules, codes, regulations. Circumcision was a religious rite; a testimonial to acceptance of the law as the norm of righteousness. Paul boldly affirmed that adherence to law is the way of death. But obedience to God "maketh alive."

16   OUR ROLE

"Ye are the light of the world." "Even so let your light shine before men that they . . . may glorify your Father which is in heaven."

These words of Jesus are startling when we stop to think about them. They suggest that the role of the true Christian is to reveal God to men, a rather presump-tuous and terrifying position. Yet apparently Jesus believed that human nature could be so transformed, that men could so become instruments of God, that their lives would be a revelation of him. This role is not terrifying when one considers the God whom Jesus revealed to men—the understanding Father, the Creator, and the source of the life "that maketh all things new."

When we meet a person who is characterized by free-dom, spontaneity, who is fearless, unself-conscious, cre-ative, deeply possessed of honesty and integrity without seeming to try to be any of these things, we feel that this is the way God meant personality to grow. We feel we have caught a glimpse of his will for men.

"Grant to us, O Lord, to live in such continual com-munion with Thee, that Thou mayest become more real than everything earthly, and that Thy Truth, Thy Goodness, and Thy Beauty may more and more manifest themselves in our lives." [8]

17   LEAVING OURSELVES OUT

One of the surest signs that we are losing our perspective and sense of proportion is that we are very anxious to be proved right about something. If we are really committed to truth, it is unimportant whether we are right or wrong. The only important thing is to be *real*. To be anxious to be right is a certain sign of fear. If we are really out for truth, our activity will provide its own corrective. Insignificant truth is useless for the purposes of our growth. Doing the right thing for the wrong motivation is as bad as doing the wrong thing.

In the moral realm, we learn more from our errors, for God uses our mistakes as well as our insights to reveal himself to us, provided we are possessed of "the single eye." If we are genuinely seeking for truth, we'll discover right and wrong.

It is wonderful to be free of the burden of regrets, of anxiety and fear! We simply do the best we know to do and observe the results as dispassionately as a scientist conducting an experiment. If we are honestly trying to do what is right rather than doing what we want to be right, then we can evaluate the results objectively. Since our prestige is not involved in the outcome, we can have a clearer eye to see the truth. One rejoices in the people one knows who have achieved this freedom. They are delightful to work with, and they even develop a sense of humor!

[8] Dr. J. H. Oldham, A *Devotional Diary* (1930 ed.).

18   WHEN WE ARE MOST HUMILIATED

"O come, let us worship and bow down: let us kneel before the Lord our maker, for he is our God." "Holy, holy,
holy is the Lord of hosts, the whole earth is full of his
glory."

It is precisely at the point of our greatest need that
God's greatest opportunity exists. Who will blame us if
we try to turn our faces from the great issues of our own
lives and of our world and make our little peace with
little things? Yet, salvation for us as individuals and for
our nation is to be found only in facing the full horror of
what our hands have wrought and in turning back to
God—stripped and humiliated, utterly emptied of pride
and confidence in ourselves, and desperately seeking to
follow the ways of God. God will not deal with less than
the whole of a person—the mind and heart and soul and
strength, the will, the social attitudes and behavior, the
things we face and the things we refuse to face.

Oh, God, whom we dare to call Father, we cannot
come before thy face in this day with paltry little prayers.
We ask only the grace to give all that we are and have,
that thy will may be done on earth. We do not ask that
thou wilt spare us suffering; rather we beseech thee that
we may be spared no suffering essential to our salvation.
Forgive us the triviality and pettiness of our efforts for
good before the magnitude of evil. Bind us inextricably
with all thy children. Lift our hearts, clarify our vision, and
strengthen our hands to do thy work, that we may be
worthy to be called thy children. Amen.

19   RHYTHMS

The Christian life is full of rhythms. Professor Hocking calls it "the principle of alternation." There is the rhythm of suffering and joy. The Christian suffers because he identifies himself with the fate of all men, because he is sensitively aware of the tragedy of human existence and the heartbreak of man's rejection of God's way to his own doom. But the Christian also rejoices, for he is daily aware of the goodness of God and his power to transform life. The joy of the Christian is the joy of a man whose burden is lifted and whose life stretches as a zestful adventure before him.

There is the rhythm of activity and rest. The Christian is active because as a child of God he is eager to accomplish God's ends. The Christian is quiet, "waiting upon the Lord," secure in the inner knowledge that God works through him in activity and in rest. The Chinese have a proverb that "there is a time for fishing and a time for mending nets." The person who has worked hard in a cause he believes to be right must have his time of withdrawal from activity that a new, creative refreshment may take place and the heart and mind be prepared for the next period of activity. These rhythms of suffering and joy, activity and waiting, symbolize a profound truth about the religious life—the Christian sees himself as an instrument, not as god. His concern is to be a good, responsive instrument in the hands of life.

20   FRIENDSHIP

"Our chief want in life is someone to make us do what we can." This statement of Ralph Waldo Emerson, the great essayist, may be an overstatement but it does contain a kernel of profound truth. We have all had the experience of accomplishing some difficult task or overcoming some great obstacle because someone who had confidence in us expected that we could do it. The often unspoken faith of our friends is a source of inspiration and power, even when we are not consciously aware of it.

Like all good things, this too may be evil. For it can mean that our security rests too much in the high opinion of our friends. We may feel our status is threatened when our friends are disappointed in us. When this is true, our norm for action is more likely to be protecting our own self-esteem than serving God—love of self rather than love of God.

If our attitude in meeting the expectations of those who know us best is not fear of disappointing them and damaging our self-esteem in their eyes, but rather the knowledge that they can see us better than we can see ourselves, then our friends and loved ones are indeed a source of insight, power, and inspiration.

21   THE DIVIDED SELF

In developing the life of the spirit, much insight may be gained from considering the contrasts set forth in the New Testament. They increase our understanding of both the goal and the process of religious living. There is the house built on rock that endured all manner of storms

and the house built on sand that collapsed in the first
tempest. There is the futility of saying "Lord, Lord" set
against the glorious achievement which springs from doing
the will of God. There is the good tree from which alone
can come good fruit and the evil tree which cannot produce a single good fruit. There is the broad way set against
the narrow, and no other road. There is life contrasted with
death, and no other possible fate is suggested for man.

So it is with the religion of Jesus. There does not seem
to be any room for compromise or for doing some good
here, practicing a high virtue there, and then considering
oneself virtuous. It is radical in the sense that it goes to the
roots of human nature and concerns itself with the whole
direction in which the personality is set. The life of drift,
procrastination, opportunism, and expediency, of good in-
tentions, shallow enthusiasms that wane in action, and in-
decision stands in vivid contrast to the picture of Christian
personality presented by Jesus in his ministry. It was the
sublime purpose of his life to redeem men from the divided self.

22   WHOM DID JESUS APPROVE?

Have you ever thought about the people whom Jesus
spoke of with approval? They have two outstanding characteristics—the capacity for decisive, radical action and
the capacity to live out beyond themselves.

Consider the characters in the parables of the pearl of
great price and of the treasure hid in the field—men who,
with joy, sold all they had in one decisive act to possess
the ultimate. It is not the halfhearted or the fainthearted

who win the kingdom, but those who "rise day and night" until their end is achieved, those who hammer, hammer, hammer stubbornly at the door until it is opened. It is the men and women who by one decisive act have come to possess the "single eye" and the whole heart.

Then there were the people who could live out beyond themselves, beyond the narrow confines of social approval and conservative respectability—those who would eat with publicans and sinners, those who had a boundless enthusiasm for life in all the ways it manifests itself.

Almighty God, search deeply our hearts and make clear to us the reservations we hide even from ourselves. By the might of thy spirit enable us to yield all, that we may possess all. Enable us to possess that courage to dedicate our whole hearts to thee that we may have the freedom and boundless enthusiasm of the children of God. Amen.

23   LIGHT TO LIGHT

When one contemplates the long stretches of history since man made his first impress on his environment and the vast reaches of the cosmos in which his individual life is set, one is moved to say with the Psalmist, "What is man that thou art mindful of him?" What one person does or fails to do seems insignificant in the long stretches of time and the glorious dimensions of the universe. Yet, if ever there was a faith that attested to the power of the individual, that redeemed man from a cosmic pessimism and sense of futility, it is Christianity. It is a faith based not on philosophical speculation but on a life that was lived and which was so potent it transformed men and history.

"Brief, O God, may be the flame of our individual lives, but let us not forget that to the kindling of each an ongoing universe has bent itself.

"As we move in the vast stream of time, let us shelter each flame from the winds of the night, let us cherish each bright flowering of the aeons. Let no bruised reed be broken, no smoking flax be quenched.

"Thou who didst create light out of darkness, teach us to join light to light that we may together make a clear white path for the race of man as it goes forward into the uncharted dark." [9]

24   THE WAY OF LIFE

Religious literature in all ages and in the midst of many different theological emphases has stressed continuously the profoundest insight of the Hebrew-Christian faith—that human life without God is stunted, broken, frustrated, tragic, and self-defeating.

> Thou madest us for thyself, and our heart is rest-
>   less until it find rest in Thee. . . .
> When I shall with my whole self cleave to Thee,
>   I shall nowhere have sorrow or labor, and my
>   life shall wholly live as wholly full of Thee. [10]

[9] Abbie Graham, *On Being Immortal* (The Woman's Press, 1942), p. 42.
[10] Augustine.

Lord, what is my confidence which I have in
this life? or what is my greatest comfort
out of all things that are seen under heaven?

Is it not Thou, O Lord my God, of whose mercies
there is no number?

Where hath it ever been well with me without
Thee? or when could it be ill with me,
when Thou wert present? . . .

I rather choose to be a pilgrim on earth with
Thee, than without thee to possess heaven.
Where Thou art, there is heaven; and where
Thou art not, there is death and hell.[11]

Let a man be satisfied that his God demands thus and so,
and he is forever free of the torment of divided counsels.[12]

25   WHOLENESS

One of the deepest unspoken prayers of our age is to
be delivered from the bondage to fragments. We earnestly search for wholeness, for unity, for a sense of universal-
ity. Our intense individualism, in contrast with the sense
of "one world" which gave even brutish existence in the
Middle Ages a quality of security we lack, has left us with
a profound sense of alienation and frustration. It is essential for us, at times, to recall and contemplate the
unity of mankind throughout the ages, under one God.

[11] Thomas à Kempis, *Imitation of Christ*, Chap. 59.
[12] John Brown.

In the words of John Donne, "All mankind is of one Author, and is one volume; when one man dies, one chapter is not torn out of the book, but translated into a better language; and every chapter must be so translated; God employs several translators; some pieces are translated by age, some by sickness, some by war, some by justice, but God's hand is in every translation, and His hand shall bind up all our scattered leaves again for that library where every book shall lie open to one another."

26   STRETCHING TO MAKE ROOM

The sense of sharing life with others, the communion of spirit which comes from trying to see all human beings as God sees them, is one of the precious gifts of the religious life. There is a feeling of identification with all people everywhere, of stretching one's spirit to encompass all of God's creatures, which gives a sacramental quality to even humdrum days. Abbie Graham expressed it in these words:

"God lives not, I think, in bread and wine but in the breaking of bread, in the sharing of wine. Bread unbroken does not fortify the heart but bread divided among all who know hunger will sustain the spirit. There is nothing wrong with communion tables except their length. They accommodate too few. God is not geared to feed the few. He is at his best with multitudes." [13]

"Eternal Spirit, breathe into the hearts of living men the expectation of the host, the hope of comradeship for

[13] *Ibid.*, p. 26.

all earth's children, the quickened impulse for a world at peace. Make our feet messengers of succor and relief. Bring to our eager souls all the glory born in Bethlehem, the confidence of man in man, the love of God cradled in a human heart. Amen." [14]

27   REAL CHRISTIANITY

Every age has its own peculiar virtues which are necessary to its culture. The nineteenth century Protestant church preached prudence, industry, and sobriety as the hallmarks of a Christian. That these virtues were essential to the progress and enhancement of our growing industrial enterprises did not prevent their being universalized as the greatest of all Christian virtues and, indeed, the highway to heaven.

In the middle of the twentieth century more sophisticated Christians do not so readily make these attributes their criteria for sound Christian character. Our middle class Protestant virtues are now good taste, respectability, refraining from giving offense, moderation—"nothing too much." One must not get too enthusiastic, passionate, concerned about anything. It's such bad taste, and besides, it "doesn't get you anywhere." It only makes other people uncomfortable, which obviously isn't Christian.

The difficulty with this concept of being a Christian— this practicing of specific virtues—is that it doesn't work. The fruits of real Christianity for the individual are life, insight, capacity to develop one's individual character and

[14] Stephen Hole Fritchman, *Prayers of the Free Spirit* (The Woman's Press, 1945), p. 44.

personality to its greatest potential. In community life it
is the ending of exploitation, discrimination, depredation
of man to man and the developing of a free, wholesome
community. Have men and women who have revealed
God through the ages since the first prophets came out
of Ur of Chaldees been characterized supremely by prudence, industry, sobriety, moderation, respectability, and
"good taste?" One suspects it is true that the "children
of darkness are wiser in their own generation than the
children of light"!

28   THE ROSE OF THE FOUR SEASONS

In one of the most excellent books [15] for personal devotion Olive Wyon tells the charming story of a visit in
Brittany where against the wall of a cottage, in December,
she found a climbing rose bush in full bloom. On asking
its name she was told, "It is the Rose of the Four Seasons."
Later, still haunted by the phrase, she came on this prayer
of Thomas Aquinas: "Grant, most Merciful Father, that
in Thy Presence my spirit may receive wisdom, and my
powers of action the glory of triumph: in Thy Presence,
where there is no danger, but many mansions, and the
perfect concord of wills; where there is the charm of
Springtime, the light of Summer, the fruitfulness of Autumn, and the repose of Winter. Amen." [16]

"No danger, but many mansions!" Here is adventure
and exploration, at all times and seasons, in fair weather

[15] *The School of Prayer* (The Westminster Press, 1944).
[16] *Ibid.*, p. 121.

and in storm, in new life and in death, in fruitfulness and
in aridity, in the warmth of loving and of being loved, in
the coldness of rejection, in peace and placidity, in storm
and confusion—one climate of "perfect concord of wills,"
but many seasons of searching and apprehending.

29   INSIDE OURSELVES

A story is told that Abraham Lincoln one troubled
twilight left the White House for an evening walk alone.
A boy crashed through the hedge and was knocked down
as he collided with the President's long legs. "Is it getting
to be that a Southern gentleman can no longer walk the
streets of Washington without being knocked down?" he
demanded truculently. Lincoln is reported to have put
his hand on the boy's shoulder and said quietly, "Son,
the fellow who is in your way is inside you."

How many of the hurts and bumps of life come because
the pressure and tension is inside ourselves! One sometimes wonders whether modern urban life is really as complex, as full of tension and obstacles to be overcome, as
conducive to hecticness and frustration, as it seems—or
whether these things are due to the loss of that central
core of spiritual serenity, which loss is the curse of a secu-
lar age.

"O God, by whom the meek are guided in judgment
and light riseth up in darkness for the godly; grant us in
all our doubts and uncertainties the grace to ask what
Thou wouldst have us to do, that the spirit of wisdom
may save us from all false choices, and that in Thy light

we may see light, and in Thy straight path may not
stumble; through Jesus Christ our Lord, Amen." [17]

30   INTEGRITY

"Watch integrity and look upon right."

The spiritual pilgrimage that is the Christian way of
life imposes one discipline more difficult than any other—
the discipline of *integrity*. Integrity means emotional as
well as intellectual honesty, and our very virtues render
it most difficult of achievement. It is easy to know when
one is being intellectually insincere; telling an outright
lie. But our conditioning is such that we do not even *know*
when we are being emotionally insincere.

We learn from the cradle to exhibit feelings we do not
really feel. We strive to dragoon our emotions into conformity with what we conceive to be our duties. We begin
to live to please others, to wear a mask we think they will
approve, and thus we destroy our own inner integrity.

Jesus placed much stress on "the single eye," the "pure
in heart." Modern psychology is continuously revealing
to us the atrophy of the soul, the inhibiting of creative
personality which comes from emotional dishonesty. The
Christian discipline of prayer—opening the heart to the
searching finger of God—is the essential condition for
emotional sincerity.

Search me, O God, and know my heart: try me, and
know my thoughts:
And see if there be any wicked way in me, and lead me
in the way everlasting.

[17] William Bright.

31   MAN AN INSTRUMENT

"Thou madest us for Thyself, and our heart is restless until it find its rest in Thee." [18]

We live in a profoundly restless age in which human beings find themselves without either arms or armor for defense against the corroding acids of insecurity and fear. People have never so longed for security, certainty, stability, to know "who" they are, to be "found," to be whole, free, functioning, effective human beings. Yet never have we witnessed more evidence of the lost spirit—neuroses, alcoholism, divorce, adultery, on the personal level; and hypocrisy, imperialism, discrimination, group hostility, and even hatred, on the social level. Churches, educational institutions, welfare agencies, psychoanalysts have all multiplied without stemming this tide of personal and cultural disintegration.

These gloomy meditations on our times may be irritating to contemplate, but they are not new to Christian history. A just and righteous God is revealing himself in these very woes that beset us. For basic to all Christian teaching is that insight that man is not an end in himself. He is an instrument. The pretensions of modern civilization have sought to make man an end in himself. But man only finds himself when he gives himself away to something greater than he is—and he dares not give himself to anything less than the God revealed in Jesus Christ.

[18] Augustine.

A Time for Everything

JOSEPHINE JOHNSON

1   **ECCLESIASTES 3:1–8**

To everything there is a season, and a time to every purpose under the heaven:

A time to be born, and a time to die; a time to plant, and a time to pluck up that which is planted;

A time to kill, and a time to heal; a time to break down, and a time to build up;

A time to weep, and a time to laugh; a time to mourn and and a time to dance;

A time to cast away stones, and a time to gather stones together; a time to embrace, and a time to refrain from embracing;

A time to get, and a time to lose; a time to keep, and a time to cast away;

A time to rend, and a time to sew; a time to keep silence, and a time to speak;

A time to love, and a time to hate; a time of war, and a time of peace.

2   **TO EVERYTHING A TIME**

And blessed are they who have learned the rhythms of the invisible clock whose hours and minutes are immense and soundless. The great clock of the seasons and the years, and the small clock of the intuition, whose timing is guided by the heart. Some of us are born with an inner ear attuned to these immense and soundless rollings and to the infinitesimal ticking. Others of us acquire this sense by slow and painful experience—the way of knowledge is a long road—and by the gradual discarding of immense loads of trivia, childhood fantasies, and corrupt, unnecessary burdens of self and pain.

3   A TIME TO PLANT

This sense of timing is probably the essence of wisdom, and therefore not easy to acquire. But is is as vital in raising children as in raising food—or armies. We must know the time to plant, and the time to expect the harvest, or pull up the weeds—and be able to tell the difference. The seed of wisdom is not a pill to be taken at hours on prescription, and sometimes—to shamefully twist a metaphor—it is as well sown if it goes in one ear and out the other. We harass our young children with knowledge. We cultivate their minds with bulldozers and expect a harvest like a seed catalogue overnight.

There are four words that sum up books of knowledge for the parents: foresee, forewarn, forestall and forebear, but the greatest of these is forebear.

I recall—not long ago—"helping" my child of seven work outdoors on an airplane he was making. I was fascinated by my own ideas of how it might be done—by the wonderful gadgets out of old fuses and bits of wooden construction toys, the things to pull out and the things to push in. He worked with me patiently for awhile, and then he said suddenly, with great restraint and quiet, "Mother, isn't there something you would like to be doing in the house now?"

4   A TIME TO EVERY PURPOSE

In every sphere of life there is this need for timing and the pull of contradictions, the play of opposites, but never so hourly, and so persistently, as in the home with children. The breaking down and the building up, the weeping and the laughing, the getting and the losing. To have children is a double living, the earthly fountain of youth, a continual fresh delight, a volcano as well as a fountain, and also a source of weariness beyond description, when the body goes on functioning by will power alone, or by prayer, or by pride, or by the hidden reservoir of power which triumphs over—or at least deals with—tantrums and germs, landlords and dust, dirt and blown fuses, sorrow and pain, rage, and the dull rebellion of the flesh. Nothing, however, has contributed more to my joy of living, to my sanity, to my sense of direction, and to my belief in the goodness of life, than my husband. And like most good and wonderful things in life I have never been able to find the words to do justice to him—to his kindness, his patience, his strength, his humor, his complete understanding; to his both endearing and enduring qualities, his sense of honor and his sense of irony, his versality and his love. And since I cannot express it as adequately as I wish, I must let that which is most fundamental of all go with these few words.

5 TO EVERYTHING A SEASON

An awareness of the richness of seasonal change is a gift. To know the whole world of nature which goes on unmindful of man and his scientific horrors, his subliminal darkness his antiseptic life—is a healing experience and a source of happiness that has no relation to age or circumstance.

I have somewhat outgrown what a friend so concisely spoke of as my "passionate love affair with the vegetable kingdom," but if the intensity of the love has been tempered by time and redirected, nevertheless it is still there as an unfailing source of peace and pleasure—and reality. The legend of Antaeus is far more than a myth.

We live above the meeting place of two rivers and are separated from the heart of the city by a half mile of the Ohio. Where the Licking joins the Ohio, the waters are thick and muddy. But on clear days the surface changes from brown to silver and reflects sheets of sun and blue sky and, toward evening, slow small waves of red glassy light. The flat muddy shore is strewn with small red shells, the dry red bodies of little crawfish, and driftwood smoothed and twisted into strange living shapes. We have found gannet-like birds carved by wind and water, alligators, and a great, long, satiny limb like a brown boa constrictor. The children climb up on a huge drifted stump at the water's edge and watch the coal barges moving by with a curious swiftness, and the silver foam pouring over the paddle wheels.

Once three little boys in a leaky boat which they were

bailing out with tin cans asked Terry to cross the river with them.

"Terry can't swim," I said.

The answer came swift and reassuring, "Oh, that's all right, ma'am! None of us can either."

6   TO EVERYTHING A SEASON

After a snow when the black trees along the shore are rimmed with white and a stillness is all through the dry vines and the cold underbrush of the bank, the movement of the coffee-colored river, heavy with syrup-like mud, is like that of a live reptile thing; and small trunks and branches of trees, still covered with frosty snow, are carried down swiftly in its current.

In spring and summer the river is alive with lights at night; and in the warm, sad air of spring evenings the monotonously gay music from the *Island Queen's* calliope comes through the flowering apple trees; and the lights from all her decks are multiplied in the water. In the day the warm, watery spring light of the clouds flows up and down the river, and the sky and water seem to merge in the pale blue and pearl-like air.

In the hot summers I like to remember snow, too, a long way from this river—a great snowstorm falling in southern Utah, and the sheep herders driving their flocks down to winter pastures, the heavy sheep covered with a frost of snow, and the melancholy baaing of the sheep coming faintly down wind through the whiteness.

Once even in May we were surprised by a sudden flurry of snow coming down from the mountains without

warning and disappearing as suddenly in the sun and heat;
and the next morning there was a rime of snow over the
pale sage brush, and two beautiful and ghostlike deer
leaped and vanished into the desert.

7   TO EVERYTHING A SEASON

One day in the city I saw two great gray and dappled
brewer's horses being pulled into the curb, and they
seemed powerful and alive and alien—somewhat more real
than anything else in the city. They made the windows
of gadgets and gilt jewelry and candy boxes and women's
hats seem more tawdry and artificial than usual, and the
faces of the people tighter, more hurrying, more empty and
more fearful.

It gave me more nostalgia for the country again than
I had felt in many months, and I remembered the great
gray Percherons on my uncles' farm, the sound of their feet
thundering across the field, and the excitement we felt as
children watching these enormous creatures when dis-
turbed suddenly by a gadfly or some less explicable urge.
They started tearing across the pastures in the summer
evenings, the earth shaking and echoing under their giant
hooves. It brought back to me the good strong smell of
sweaty hides, mingled with harness leather and hay and
night, and I remembered coming back in the darkness
from long horseback rides through the country and seeing
the black shapes of the Percherons against the night sky
and hearing their welcome whinnies.

Those were wonderful rides in the days of comparative
innocence when the "vegetable love affair" was at its

height, and I can remember nothing that evoked a greater, more solid joy than that which I found in the fields and woods. If this sounds like the official password to the most sentimental of all classifications—the professional friend of bird and flower and beast—it stands anyway, and I don't care. People can do far worse than go on bird walks and paste up maple leaves in a book.

Because of the summer heat the riding was late in the evening and ended in darkness, and so the scents and odors of the oncoming night are remembered more vividly—the sweet, malty smell of oat fields, the rich, warm smell of flowering corn that was like an actual warmth in the cool evening air, the dry smell of dust and manure from the pastures, and the intoxicating sweetness that came up from roadsides and cold ravines, of wild grapes in bloom, sudden ephemeral gusts of odor that were passed too soon, and sometimes even the racy and musky smell of skunk, not too unpleasant and even companionable from a distance.

8   TO EVERYTHING A SEASON

In the city yard here in Kentucky are mock orange trees, thorny, blackened with the inevitable omnipresent soot that penetrates everything including the human lungs. The orange trees drop great green balls of wrinkled fruit, fine for explosive baseballs, but nothing else. In spring the black soil is covered with purple violets, and in the summer the cucumber vines that cover every inch of the slope above the river are filled with thousands of murmuring bees, and there is a blackbird that gives a cry exactly like a boy whistling at a pretty girl—quite startling, and it whistles even in the winter.

But it is not country, and it is not even a substitute, and the earth fulfills itself only through the black "soup" and mud pies that the children make. We are luckier, a thousand times luckier, than most; but for the time being we too live an artificial life.

9   A TIME TO DANCE

In the highly stylized, artificial, and mechanical world in which most of us live—in which we have gotten about as far from the real sources of happiness as possible, and take our pleasures by prescription, our relaxation in the role of spectator, and our energy outlet in commercial competition—there is still, thank God, one way of being, participating, and having fun without paying somebody else to have it for you. There is still the minor miracle, the communal joy generated by communal dancing—square dancing, folk dancing, and the play-party games.

To melt ice, break down inhibitions, build up confidence, and burn up fear and pettiness is a marvellous thing, and it deserves all the loving and lavish advertising usually reserved for vitamins and soap flakes. In dancing the unpleasant people become quite bearable, the dull revive, the sophisticated lose their polish, the cynics lose their barb, and the people you like anyway become more scintillating than ever. As for yourself, it is worth all the creaking next morning to have had the illusion of being wholly alive and without sin, and unconscious of gravity for a few hours.

248

10   TO BREAK DOWN AND TO BUILD UP

The contradictions of modern life and the continual play of opposition, which up to a certain point are growth and necessary to growth, and beyond are destruction and a tearing apart—combined with the normal ambivalence of the human heart—have led many women into what seems an impossible juggling act of balance. And to those to whom this state of contradiction has become intolerable —and with the demands of career, society, and motherhood, an impossible challenge and heartbreak—I recommend, with a grain or two of salt, a book called *Women— the Lost Sex* by Lundberg and Farnham, which is an exhaustive study of this problem with definite and concrete suggestions for its solution. It recognizes that the almost impossible has been exacted of women, that they have volunteered in droves for these kamikaze missions of modern living, and that society has loaded them and their graves with honors. The authors suggest that the wreaths be reserved for the foot soldiers and the living, and some sanity and order be restored to life.

11   A TIME TO EMBRACE

There is something sad and stupid about the woman whose sole interest is in the care and feeding of a family, but there is something infinitely neurotic about the woman who joins committee after committee, harried and haggard, rushing from conference table to platform, and whose mind is so preoccupied with the timetable of the meeting that she has no space or patience for the timeless, the aimless and yet remorseless agenda of her childrens' lives.

"A time to embrace and a time to refrain from embracing"—and the woman who tries to embrace every cause, every committee, every movement, will find herself spread so thin she is brittle and useless, no more substantial than a thin shell glass—and as easily shattered.

12   A TIME TO BE BORN

There likewise may come a time in any life when no appeal to pride, no sympathy from anyone, no demand on the bootstrap philosophy of life, no shame by comparison with the greater trouble of others, no prayer can be of any help in lifting us out of the continual presence of despair. When we think repeatedly as in the poem by Countee Cullen "I see death drawing night to me out of the corner of my eye," and when this burden of guilt, the faceless and nameless old man of the sea, becomes too great, when the anxiety is a sickness, it is time to look for help, to stop hunting the nonexistent bootstrap and get the aid of psychiatry—the "physicianing" of the soul if you will—and to do surgery on the spiritual cancer, which is real and as deadly as the malignant cells of the flesh.

There is "a time to be born"—and born again, free of accumulated, encrusted sores of fears and prejudices, old hates, of cancerous wounds, old prides. And there is a time to die—a time for the blue, unburied child of our young years to be decently interred—and to get on with the living.

13   A TIME TO KEEP

Among the convictions liable to come between friends and to "set a man at variance against his father, a daughter against her mother," to disrupt gatherings, and to place the individual in the category of the dangerous eccentric, none is quite so effective as that of pacifism. And conviction it is that survives every form of discouragement the majority of men can give it. For those of us fortunate enough not to have to face the choice between the army and prison, the loss of jobs, the social ostracism, there is still the duty to speak and not be silent. And there is a duty not to rely alone on a belief that peace is wonderful, but to learn the relation between peace and social change, between social injustice and total war, and to take the deadly, passive implication out of the word pacifism—as have the young men who spoke out, who made their choice and went to prison for conscience sake.

14   A TIME TO HEAL

In prison perhaps they knew "the peace above all earthly dignities. A still and quiet conscience." The peace which religion has brought many who have learned to rest as they run, who have found quiet even in the center of a storm, who are sustained and impelled onward by the knowledge of a goal worthy of all the living and dying, the incredible suffering and despair of mankind's history.

In the middle of the war my little boy drew a picture of a clock with its hands pointing to an hour marked seventeen. "That's the hour to stop the war," he said. Long past the eleventh hour. And long past the seventeenth hour

only some hope, some inner sense of universal meaning
and of strength greater than force of arms or the ingenuity
of science or the collective might of the state, can sustain
us and give us the necessary courage and imagination to
create peace as the hands of the clock move faster and
faster toward a later hour.

15   A TIME TO BUILD

In a world of destruction whose time is that of rending
and tearing down, the Quakers have chosen the time of
building and healing. They have through work camps and
young peoples' groups, through countless activities,
brought a dynamic force to work, based on belief in the
power of love and service, the achievement of peaceful
ends by peaceful means. They have gone beyond the doing of things for those who need help. They are doing
with them. And the doing *with* is a patient factor in changing old patterns of fear and ignorance. They attempt to
rebuild confidence and tust, to heal misunderstandings and
old wounds. Their work among Negroes, miners, Mexicans,
mountaineers, Japanese-Americans, and share-croppers goes
on unceasingly in the United States, and abroad they are
trusted likewise on the strength of their singleness of purpose to act and act effectively with a purity of motive and
means to distribute food and clothing and do what healing is possible in a corrupt and ravaged world.

16   A TIME TO LOVE AND TO HATE

We talked recently in a fellowship of our underlying
personal attitudes toward our condemners—the spirit in

which we tried to revoke evil and meet our adversaries. The close re-examination of motives is of great value and sometimes fundamental to the achievement desired. Do we wear this righteous humility like a red flag? Do we rejoice unduly over the downfall of an adversary? Is our pacifism a form of personal grandeur, and are we—as a friend of mine admitted—so belligerent in our peace that we antagonize people?

To come without personal hate to a problem involving human relations, no matter how unsavory or wrong or wicked the problem may be, gives a greater power to solve it. To distinguish the act from the actor is the difficult divorce. Social workers know they cannot become involved in hatred, no matter how deserving of it the cruel and ignorant parent may seem, if they wish to be of lasting service to the children in the case.

17 BREAKING DOWN AND BUILDING UP

In my private confessional of errors, in the long list of hours I would live over differently, among those that loom the largest are certain speeches I have made in bitterness and sarcasm against social injustice. It is not the attack on these injustices I regret, for I would make them again and with greater vigor, but the tone of contempt, the bitterness that was substituted for factual knowledge and experience. And the sarcasm in personal conversations also, the heat that accomplished nothing and was in a sense a by-product of the despairing knowledge that I was accomplishing nothing but must appear to be.

"A time to break down and a time to build up"—but

the breaking down was too easy and the building up too difficult, and much time has been wasted in hot and clever —and usually only hot—words, many enemies made, and the injustice itself fattened and warmed and strengthened in a great wind of irrelevant words.

18   **A TIME TO LAUGH**

All of these worthy words, and classical illusions, these *big* serious subjects aside, the things that gives the days their color and taste are not the sermons and mottoes and the image of the "good parent." The seasoning and edibility lie more in small pleasures, deviations—even eccentricities.

The privilege—about once in six months—of sitting down in a clean room in an empty house.

The fascinating corruption of the ladies magazines with their beautiful pictures of food.

The squashy, delicious taste of gumdrops.

Reading *Thus Far and No Further* by Rumer Godden, a beautiful book about a year on a tea plantation in the mountains of India.

Eating rice and fish all mixed up with herbs after the children are in bed, and talking to my husband alone without the buzz of little voices.

The writing of lists of "things to be done."

The eventual marking off of everything on the list.

A clean desk.

Reading the dictionary without purpose.

Reading books about Africa and hippopotamuses.

Seeing *Porky Pig and His Gang* next to *The Poetics of Aristotle* on the book shelf.

19   A TIME TO KEEP

And among the unforgettable things that come to mind is the beautiful smile of a young Quaker nurse who was leaving the comfort and ease of a visit at Christmas time with friends to go back down to the share-cropping country and continue her self-chosen work of visiting and nursing in the cold poverty of the farms. When she spoke of going back on that gray December evening, she said, "I'm so happy I feel almost selfish."

And I recall reading the wonderful simplicity of Marian Anderson's words, "Religion, the treasure of religion, helps one, I think, to face the difficulties one sometimes meets. I do a good deal of praying."

And I remember a letter I had during the war from a friend, one of the loveliest people I have ever known and one whose life is a greater precept than any sermon. I don't remember the exact way she put it, but her belief in the spiritual resources beyond words but not beyond grasp was profound and very moving. "I know that help is always there," she wrote, "even in the moments of great doubt when I have to pray, 'Lord, help thou mine unbelief.'"

20   AND A TIME TO CAST AWAY

And religion can also be an ugly thing. More depraved in some of its middle-class respectable aspects than in the unprintable rantings of fundamentalists in London parks, or the hysterical leapings at revivals.

I sat in the office of a prominent minister in the city while he spoke over the phone about buying a Negro church building. The matter concerned crossing that in-

visible line between white and Negro districts. And the
minister became apoplectic with rage. "My parishioners
have thousands of dollars invested in this community,"
he shouted. "I have a thousand invested in my own church
alone. You can't do this thing! We can't afford to have
these values go down!"

And so the real-estate values of the church were firmly
mortared. "How firm a foundation ye saints of the Lord!"

In spite of the magnificent and backbreaking efforts of
some, it has been said with terrible truth, "The church
is the largest Jim-Crow organization in the United States."

21   A TIME TO SPEAK

No Negro can be understood solely as an end and a
beginning in himself. He is a sentence out of the context
of the history of his race. A sentence more easily misunderstood, misjudged, than that of the white man who is likewise isolated as an individual from the long chapters of
his childhood and forebears.

We have lived on that uncertain terrain—that uneasy
merging place of North and the South, where the swamp-
land of prejudice still seeps under the harder upland soil
and the intellectual and economic emancipation still wars
with ancient superstition and economic bondage. The very
house we live in on the Ohio River seems to have a history
both as a station for the passage of slaves northward into
freedom and southward into bondage. And it is not always possible in this meeting ground to know when it is
wisest to speak and when to keep silent—but there are
times when one must say, like Jeremiah, "His word was in

mine heart as a burning fire shut up in my bones, and I was weary with forbearing, and I could not stay." The "nigger" and "coon" stories cannot be heard with smiles and polite applause, and it is better to dismay the nice, pleasant people in the nice, pleasant home and ruin the peaceful evening. It is worthless and hollow pleasantness when built on mutual support of one another's prejudices.

22   A TIME TO WEEP

I recall an incident at Christmas time one year when plans were being made for the school children to go from house to house caroling. At the music institute where the program was arranged, the question came up of a group of Negro children's joining the carollers. Partly out of conservatism, partly out of consideration, one of the directors objected on the grounds that the Negro children might be insulted at some home. There was a silence, and then the Negro teacher said quietly, "Our children are used to being insulted."

23   A TIME TO HEAL

There are ways in which each person has in his power to hasten the day when such insults will never be heard again. One of the most fundamental and simple things, and yet one that can implement the laws and the statutes and the philosophies, is the cultivation of Negro friends— friends on a home instead of a committee basis. To sit down and eat and drink with friends and talk about something besides the race problem.

It is sad but true—this story of an educated, liberal white woman who prided herself on her civic responsibilities and her broad outlook and who, seated beside a Negro woman of major accomplishments and leadership in her own right, could think of nothing whatsoever to say except, "You must be very proud of Marian Anderson."

24   A TIME TO CAST AWAY STONES

The things that children say have more than seldom a universal application, a meaning beyond the moment; and the words that come now to my mind are those of Annie on the streetcar when she and Terry sat up together in a seat without me, and in the heady feeling of riding alone like adults, she turned to Terry and whispered loudly, "Let's pretend we're *people!*"

God help us—let's pretend we are people, that we are grown up and no longer afflicted with bed-time bogey terrors and racial myths. That we can use the knowledge and experience that time has provided us, and grow up to meet our years!

25   A TIME TO LAUGH

It is with relief that I can write of a little scene *without* tragedy; and no parent can resist the temptation, given an audience, to repeat some matter concerning his children. It is one of the things we live by!

Mr. Terry Cannon, six, comes to dinner at a restaurant with his wife, Mrs. Annie Cannon, three. "We left the children at home," he explains.

"That must be quite a relief, to get away from home sometimes. How many children have you?"

"Seven. And they all have diptheria."

"Oh, my!"

"And you know diptheria isn't just a cold. It's a big disease! They have to have eight bottles of medicine. And they cost ten dollars!"

"And are you glad to be out at a restaurant, Mrs. Annie?"

"Y-E-S."

"She means 'yes.' She just likes to spell it. Say 'yes,' Annie. Restaurant owners don't like you to spell."

Mrs. Annie giggles and says nothing.

"How old are your children?"

"All six."

"Were they born all at once?"

"All but one, and she was born eighteen months later. That was Clara."

"What a lot of babies for Mrs. Annie to take care of all at one time! She must have been a very busy mother helping them all to grow up strong and healthy."

Mrs. Annie obligingly looks important.

"What do you feed your children for breakfast, Mrs. Annie?"

"Hamburger and chewing gum and mashed potatoes, and that's all."

"Oh, I see. Well, what do the children play?"

"They play post office and hide-and-go-seek. They play post office first. To get it over with."

Mrs. Annie gets up and wanders around pooching out

259

her cheeks with bananas. Mr. Cannon adds up each item
of food and arrives at the total in his head.

"C'mon," says the lady of the house. "Le's go!"

"Annie!" says Mr. Cannon. "Mind your restaurant manners."

Mrs. Annie laughs loudly behind the bananas, and they
both depart, after Mr. Cannon meticulously, but somewhat reluctantly, pays the bill.

26   A TIME FOR CREATIVE EXPRESSION

Since Ecclesiastes fails to mention a time for writing, I
will just have to intrude it here, because it's a fairly fundamental part of the business of living. The writer's advantage, in some respects, over those whose expression lies
in other fields, is in the privilege of a double—sometimes
a triple—living. Pleasure multiplied in the mirrors of
words, and pain siphoned off in words. The precise description, the re-creation of almost anything from a vase of
hyacinths to human emotions, *is* a privilege—no matter
what any writer may tell you about the honest, and plaus-
ible, agonies of creation. The ability of expression entails
also considerable responsibility, but a discussion of this is
a complete volume in itself, and volumes have already
been written.

Seldom was there a parent who, surveying the plump,
dimpled perfection of her child at one, two, three, or four,
did not wish to pop him into a bottle or tie a brick on his
head, and keep the little fellow in that state of warm,
translucent innocence for all the years to come. Happily
this impulse is defeated, but the writer can have his cake

and eat it too—preserve the child forever in those years
and at the same time leave him free to grow.

27   MAKING TIME

But how does one find the time to write? These translucent, innocent little ones are not interested in the preservation of their moment, nor do they give a rap whether you
write a word for posterity or not. The answer is, I don't
know. I just do—or I just don't. Under pressure from outside, or from writing for obligation—for pleasure—for
mitigation of pain. One writes for all reasons, under all
conditions, for better or for worse, and one doesn't write
at all. It becomes primary to be put above all household
work—or secondary to be put aside. Of course, it is obvious
I am not talking as one of those who write for a living.

The largest portion of my writing was done before I
had children, but the last novel, *Wildwood*, was written a
page a night after the children were in bed. I believed that
a small possible goal was better than a big impossible one;
and since a year has 365 days, I thought I should come out
in the end with a book 365 pages long. Naturally this didn't
come out with mathematical precision—but a book was
completed.

28   WORK WITH ONE'S HANDS

I have since thought of many additions to this book—
and others—so many ways of changing the thought from
despair to a reasonable hope; but when a thing is printed,
it seems past and done and about as workable as a statue

261

finally cast in bronze. And the old clay model has dis-
appeared. If in his heart the author regards each finished
book as only a printed epitaph for the glorious volume it
was *going* to be, he hopes that nobody else regards it as
such. And he is content if the epitaph does some justice
to the dream. Writing is not—to me—like painting or
modeling or any creative work which is real pleasure in the
process. Painting is one of the purest pleasures I know
since I do not take it too seriously, and I believe that the
therapeutic effect of work with one's hands, creating rather
than passively watching, is almost a mystical source of
happiness and health.

You may not be a great creative artist, but there is something dynamically splendid about even a great, big, terrible paper rose—if you make it yourself.

29   MORE ABOUT WRITING

The sources of fiction and models for characters are infinite and not easily analyzed. "Did you write that book,
Hollywood, Mother, or didja' just copy it?" Terry asked
me. And many a reader assumes that the latter is all too
true—that all the people are out of life and pinned on
paper still squirming. It is true that the author is there
still wriggling around in various guises, and that scraps of
father, mother, husband, sister, lover, son and daughter,
friend and enemy, live again in wholes which—we hope—
have integrity of their own. It would be cynical to say the
author seems only to be trying to make the prosaic mysterious, and to give credulity to the impossible; and even
were it true, to object would be to set up an impossible

standard, conformity to which would strangle fiction. However, I would rather write than write about writing, and will leave the job of analytical criticism in more competent hands. Let me add only one thing more—the honest craftsman may be also a man of vision, and his job is to foresee, forewarn, and not forbear.

30   A TIME OF PEACE AND OF WAR

The time of war is officially past; the time of peace is with us—or at our throats, as the lady said of Christmas—and over every nation is the memory of crimes that seem beyond the imagination of men, that were beyond the conception of beasts—Dachau, Bucherwald, Bataan, Hiroshima, Nagasaki. And no declaration of peace can wipe out the memory and restore the dead, the crippled, and the insane. Only the realization of the enormousness of the tragedy, only years of expiation by action and sacrifice—action and vision in proportion to the incredible depths to which all nations have sunk.

For more than ten years one nation after another has thrown overboard all claims to law and decency and godliness and humanity. They have sacrificed their sons and their sons' children, and have clung only to the pitiable, vicious little images of national pride and honor, of outworn phrases and outworn modes of living, to graven images of selfishness, to tin gods of white supremacy and tariffs, race, empires, cartels, to myths of yellow peril, to fear of the new and fear of each other, to weapons useless as bows and arrows, to weapons as deadly as poisoned boomerangs, to black magic rituals of spheres of influence and untouchable borders.

31   HELP THOU OUR UNBELIEF

If there is to be peace, it must be a whole peace, a world peace, international disarmament, international government, international understanding. And there must be evidence of good faith given, not each nation demanding of the other what the nation itself—or those who represent the people, and not to be confused with the people—is afraid or unwilling to do, each saying, "This charter does not apply to things of my possession," each unwilling to preside at the dissolution of their already crumbling empires.

There is, however, hope left that the same material forces which have brought us close to the completion of world suicide can at least provide those material things over which wars are fought and in such abundance that the incentive for war will be lost. But that transitional period of overcoming our blindness to this simple fact— the time and effort necessary to the recovery of sight— will require all the intellectual and spiritual resources left in man. Lord, help thou our unbelief!

Prayer

MAUDE ROYDEN SHAW

1 TO PRAY AND NOT TO FAINT

How hard it is to pray! Should our Lord not have warned us of this? He tells us to pray as though it were the easiest thing in the world. Or does he? No, after all I think he warned us, for he "spake a parable unto them to this end, that men ought always to pray, and not to faint"—"never to lose heart" as Moffatt's translation puts it.

He knew, then, that we were likely to lose heart. He wanted to help us. He "spake a parable" to us to make us realize that it is important that we should pray and go on praying. He even takes as an analogy for God an unjust judge—he evidently wanted us above everything to remember that we must not lose heart, we must not give up praying. We must not say, "I'm no good at praying; I had better get up and do something."

We must not stop praying. That is the great thing.

We are to leave the rest to God.

2 GOD WILL LIFT OUR PRAYERS

My thoughts turn again to our Lord's saying that we are to pray. Often I feel too unspiritual to do so. It seems to me that I am not good enough. I keep finding myself guilty of wrong motives when I try. If I pray for the world, is it not because I am afraid of war and its dreadful consequences? If I pray for a friend, is my love worthy—is it unselfish enough—for my prayer to be heard? If I pray for myself, is my desire for an answer based on selfish considerations? Can God hear a selfish prayer?

But our Lord did not say *good* men should pray. He did not say our prayers must be perfect in sincerity and purity of heart. He said we were to pray.

Will he then sift out what is honest in my praying and use it, leaving the rest aside?

Yes—so it seems. So I now realize.

Lord, receive my prayer. It is the best I can do.

3   FEELING AND PRAYING

Sometimes I want to pray and prayer is a willing and easy service. Sometimes I have no wish at all to pray. Then it is difficult. And is it not insincere to pray when I feel nothing, and the things I ask for move no emotion in me?

Our Lord told us to pray. He did not tell us to feel. Even the emotion of love is interpreted by him in terms of service. He told us that to love one's neighbor as oneself means to serve him. One cannot command one's emotions; and the good Samaritan was commended not because he felt what we call "love" for his enemy but because he did him a kindness—he "took care of him."

"Then said Jesus unto him, Go, and do thou likewise."

Here is a saying of Thomas à Kempis that helps me continually. It is this, "Do what lieth in thy power and God will help the good will." And yet another from the same source, "Lord make that possible to me by Thy grace which by nature seems impossible."

Help me, O Lord, to pray when my heart is cold and unmoved. I cannot feel as I would, but thou hast compassion, and I have only to obey. Hear my prayer.

4   PRAY WITH FAITH

I think again of this truth, that Christ did not command us to feel. Sometimes we feel too much. It happens that we are in some great strait—we are helpless in the presence of suffering or danger to ourselves or to someone we dearly love. We pray in an agony. We besiege the throne of grace with prayer.

Our Lord however told us to pray *with faith*.

"Go in peace: thy *faith* hath healed thee." To pray with faith is not pray in an agony. It is surely to pray with calm and conviction.

I think the storm and stress of agonized petition is a barrier which prevents the answer from reaching us. God wants to answer. He wants the good of those we love, and our good, a thousand times more than we want it. He is more ready to hear than we to pray.

"Be still, and know that I am God."

5   LOVING BY SERVING

My mind dwells on the parable of the good Samaritan, remembering how it follows on the saying that we must love our neighbors as ourselves, even if the one needing our love is our enemy, for our Lord illustrates his saying by telling of the "love" shown by a Samaritan to a Jew. The Jews "had no dealings with the Samaritans."

How is it possible for me to love an enemy? By serving him; "Go, and do thou likewise."

We are not asked an impossibility. We can do something even for an enemy. This is what Christ asks of us.

It seems to me as I ponder this hard saying and two others—"Love thine enemies" and, "Pray for them which despitefully use you"—that they throw light on each other.

A friend said to me, "How soon one becomes attached to the people for whom one prays!"

She had been telling me that to pray for one she hated would be hypocrisy. I knew—and she knew—that our Lord would not command anything that was not utterly sincere. So I suggested that she think of herself as going into his presence with the man she hated—her employer in an understaffed office—and standing there before him until she knew what he was asking her to do. She did so and saw herself vindictive and her employer cruel and both in great need of the mercy of the Lord who had no rancor even for Judas Iscariot. A great pity for them both flooded over her, and she prayed for both as in a common need of forgiveness and grace.

The story of Simon the Pharisee, found in the seventh chapter of Luke, helps me here.

6   FAITH, NOT AGONY

Let me think again of the frantic prayer of the woman of Canaan. It seems to me that she was frantic. She "cried unto" Jesus, and his disciples were angry with her and said to him, "Send her away; for she crieth after us." Their embarrassment suggests that she was making a scene in the street and one which, unless he put a stop to it, would do their master no credit. "Send her away."

How strange that our Lord was silent and, worse still, rebuffed her with insult when at last he spoke.

But the end of the story is that the child was healed.

I think he could not answer her prayer while it was one of agony and not of faith. When he rebuffed her, she saw his face and knew his power. Instead of crying out, she spoke with assurance. She spoke with faith. That was all that was needed.

"Her daughter was made whole from that very hour." The whole story must be meditated upon in the light of that fact.

7   OUR NEED OF THE INCARNATION

In meditation on the story of the woman of Canaan and her outcry, my memory recalls the words of the Old Testament prophecy about the Messiah.

"Behold my servant whom I uphold; mine elect, in whom my soul delighteth. . . . He shall not cry, nor lift up, nor cause his voice to be heard in the street. . . . He shall not fail nor be discouraged."

How greatly we needed the Incarnation! How necessary it is for us, when we are perplexed or in agony of mind, to turn our eyes to our Saviour and see how he met the human difficulties we human beings meet from day to day! His whole mind, I now see, was bent on relieving the petitioner, on saving her child. To this end he acted, and even by a rough rebuff sought to awaken in her a sense at once of his power to heal and of her right to the healing she asked in the name of a mother's love. "Love conquers all"—she suddenly saw that and claimed the victory.

It seems to me that we cannot measure the force of our own faith or how far our will is wholly identified with the will of God. I think of a mother praying for her child in war. But here we have a world which deliberately accepts war, and we know there can be no war without death. Have we a right to ask that the deaths should be of others' sons—not ours? Does not this sap the strength of our prayer, or make its fulfillment impossible?

Here I cannot see clearly. I only know that pray I must, and leave the rest to God.

8   CHRIST IN OUR STRAITS

Our Lord, we are told, prayed in an agony in the Garden of Gethsemane, so that "his sweat was as it were great drops of blood falling down to the ground."

There are aspects of the Incarnation which we cannot understand. This is one. But as I meditate on it, I believe that I do understand with my heart, and I remember the great saying of Pascal, "The heart has its reasons that the reason does not know." Pascal was no sentimentalist; he was one of the more brilliant and incisive of all Christian intellectuals.

I do not know how Christ could ask of his Father something that his Father could not grant. I do know that if he had not, at least once, known the agony of apparently unanswered prayer, he would not have been with us in our most dreadful straits. When I realize this, I adore him, Son of God and Son of Man.

9   SAVED BY LOVE

When our Lord prayed in an agony, his prayer was not answered. When he reached perfect submission to the will of God, he said, "Thy will be done," and it was done.

It could not be God's will that Jesus should be crucified. No. It was his will that the world should be saved by love alone; and, if the world's Saviour used any other weapon, the world would not be saved. If this meant that the Saviour must be crucified before men could believe in the perfection and power of the love of God, then he must be crucified.

How horrible! The mind recoils; the flesh shudders. Surely there must be some other way? Surely so hideous a crime need not be the price of our salvation? Surely men will believe without that? No—they will not. We will not. *I* will not.

"Greater love hath no man than this, that a man lay down his life for his friends." If this is the price, it must be paid. The Saviour is willing. Calm assurance comes now.

"Thy will be done."

"Rise; let us be going: behold he is at hand that doth betray me."

271

10   BE STILL

One night I too was praying in an agony. Someone I
loved was very ill—so ill that everyone thought he was
dying. I woke in the night, and instantly my thoughts went
to him. I was wide awake. I uttered a cry to God that he
might be sleeping peacefully—resting and so, in repose,
gathering strength. In a kind of vision I thought I saw his
spirit like a little flame wavering in the draught. I saw
myself watching it and trying to hold my breath lest I
should help the wind to blow it out; but I could not hold
my breath or control it because I was gasping and weeping
with the passion of my desire.

God took hold of me saying, "Be quiet. Be calm. I can
use your prayer and the love that makes you pray, if you
are quiet. If you are in such agitation, you may blow out
the little flame that already wavers and flickers. Hold your
hands round it. Protect it with them. It will live."

11   IS WAITING WASTE?

A very wise spiritual guide advised me to begin my
prayers by being still. This is the way to avoid being in a
state of agitation which puts the answer I plead for out
of my reach. He said I should give a quarter of my time
to this stillness, giving a loving attention to God. If I had
an hour, fifteen minutes; if four minutes, one.

I find this difficult because I am in a hurry to ask God
for the things I want so badly. How often I am in a hurry!
Today I am specially anxious and in haste. I have a day's
work before me. I cannot, I really cannot, waste any time
in waiting.

Waste? The word falls on my own ears with a sudden and new significance—*waste?*

Is it waste then to listen to the God to whom I have offered myself and my life?

12   DOING IS NOT ENDURING

When our Lord said, "Thy will be done," he meant that he would do it. Rising from prayer he went immediately to meet his enemies and carry through to the end the action that was needed. His prayer ended, and he said, "Rise, let us be going: behold he is at hand that doth betray me."

He taught us to use the very words he used, "Thy will be done." How often have we used them with no idea of *doing* the will of God! All we have thought of was enduring it. When sorrow has overwhelmed us, we have thought we reached a high level of faith and devotion if we could accept our grief as coming to us from the hand of God and therefore to be borne without resentment.

This cannot be what Jesus meant. He never told us that suffering came from God or that it was his will.

His will is to be *done*—not endured.

13   GOD'S WILL IS HEALTH

"As he was praying in a certain place, when he ceased, one of his disciples said unto him, Lord, teach us to pray. . . . And he said unto them, When ye pray, say, Our Father . . . thy will be done."

How joyful is the will of God for us! I find God in

Jesus Christ, and there I see that God's will for us is life
and health. There is not one record of Jesus' inflicting an
illness on anyone—not one. Nothing about its being a
proper punishment for our sins, or a spiritual discipline or
the like. On the contrary, he dealt with illness and de-
formity as an enemy. He spoke of it as the work of the
devil and made haste to "cast it out."

"Shall not this woman . . . whom Satan hath bound, lo,
these eighteen years, be loosed from this bondage on the
Sabbath day?" And without waiting for the Sabbath day
to pass, he set aside criticism and healed her.

14   STRENGTH AND UNDERSTANDING

Since Jesus always healed the sick and never in a single
instance refused or rebuked the plea for healing, how is it
that so many good people are ill?

The weight of the world's sickness lies on my soul and
shuts out God. There are so many, many sick today. Some
are healed by scientific methods, some by spiritual power.
Why not all? At least all who pray and put their trust in
God? Jesus "healed them all," we are told, unless their
own doubts made healing impossible.

"He could there do no mighty work. . . . And he marvelled because of their unbelief." Yet even there, "he laid
his hands upon a few sick folk and healed them."

I have tried to understand this, and I have failed. It is
here that there comes again to my mind the strength that
lifts me up even when I do not understand, "Men ought
always to pray and not to faint."

274

15   THE SINGLE EYE

How can one "pray always"? If it means that one must always be addressing oneself to God, I find it impossible. Indeed I find it would, for me at least, be wrong even if I could do it. I cannot think of two things at once—all I could do would be to keep my mind jittering between two thoughts, my God and my work. And this would prevent me from concentrating on my work.

Some tell me that they can do some kinds of work automatically, with their minds fixed on something else. Women especially say this—women far better and more religious than myself.

And yet I wonder if they are not mistaken. People who are really musical don't take their knitting to a concert. Unmusical people might, but wouldn't it be to conceal, even from themselves, the fact that the music bores them?

"If thine eye be *single* thy whole body shall be full of light." Not if one eye is fixed on the sky, and the other on one's work.

I distinguish, then, between what are called "acts of prayer," that is to say, conscious lifting up one's thoughts and offering one's work to God; and "states of prayer," that is to say, a dependence on him every hour and every moment, which is like the dependence we feel on someone we love and trust and whose presence we desire at some ordeal because we know it will bring us strength. I have known such ordeals and remember well how my last look has been toward that person and my first a turning toward him again to seek, if it may be, his approval. In between I have been utterly concentrated on doing my best.

Such an attitude towards the Friend who is God is indeed to "pray always."

16   STOP SHOUTING

Lord, I am busy and have a busy day before me. I feel equal to it, but it is as difficult as it is interesting, and I find it hard, even now at this moment, to put it aside and listen to thee. Perhaps the thoughts that come into my mind are really from thee. Perhaps they are actually the answer to my prayer for thy guidance. How shall I know?

A Quaker once told me that she was praying in great agitation, so great that she really felt breathless and stopped for a moment. God said to her, "I have something to say to you when you stop shouting at me."

Lord, I wait. I stop shouting. Soon I shall learn from thee, and by experience, which are the thoughts that come from thee and which are my own fancies. Forgive me if I am slow. I have followed my own fancies so long that I am confused by them. But thy voice will make itself plain to me if I will listen.

17   TRAINING THE EAR

I am often baffled by my own uncertainty in making decisions. Even as I listen for the voice of God and think I hear it, I am in doubt. Is it God's voice I hear or my own wish? Modern psychology in helping has also done something to perplex us further. In its light we find depth beyond depth of self-deceiving. I have asked God to sort

out all that is sincere in my prayer and forgive the rest;
but how am I to sort out all that is true in what I think I
hear from him?

To this I have no easy answer. There is no easy answer.
But I know that one who listens to an orchestra can, with
his trained, attentive ear, know one instrument from another. His trained—not only now attentive—but trained
ear. So shall I at last know the voice of God from my own.

18   PRACTICE MAKES PERFECT

One learns to pray by praying. When I first began
seriously to pray, I took much interest in the experience of
others who had gone far along the road I wished to tread.
I have been perplexed by the amazing number of books
written by those who know the way. I found most of them
interesting, some enthralling. I was absorbed in them and
read first one and then another. Soon I found my appointed hour of prayer all too short and felt, as I read
these spiritual books, that I was getting on.

But I was not praying. Just as one who reads books about
swimming still cannot swim when he ventures at last into
the water, so I read but did not pray.

Reading is good. I should read every day. But how much
more I learn by praying! How much more I learn from one
experience of my own!

And how ready is my God and Father to give me this
experience when I trust myself at last to him.

19 IN THE LIGHT OF HIS COUNTENANCE

Having waited silently on God, what can I ask for? Not all the things I meant to ask are fit to be asked.

Madame Chiang Kai-shek tells us that she, having a great confidence in her mother's prayers, once asked why she did not ask God to destroy the Japanese nation. Her mother was silent for a moment and then said, "How can you ask me to pray God to do something which in a human being would be utterly shameful?"

Merciful God, forgive us our shameful prayers! How dare we approach thee with such words on our lips, such wickedness in our hearts?

"Whatsoever ye shall ask in my name, that will I do, that the Father may be glorified in the Son."

In my name . . . that the Father may be glorified.

In the light of his countenance I look at the prayers I meant to offer. Some of them are too silly, some too wicked for me to pray them now. They cannot glorify the Father.

20   PRAYER MEANS ASKING, TOO

It is often said that prayer does not mean asking. But it does. "I pray you"—that means "please."

Even when one is silent before God, one is asking.

A modern writer, comparing the attitude of the scientist to truth with that of the saint to God, says of the former, "He asks; he seeks; he knocks. . . . His desire to know Truth grows until the heat of desire may be fitly described as an unceasing knocking at the door. . . . This need may grow to be a great necessity, a crying aloud of his whole nature."

So should be the "crying aloud," the "great necessity" of the Christian who prays to his God, whose name also is truth.

Is this not petition? Is it not the most urgent, the most clamorous of all petitions? And in our piety are we to know better than our Lord who said to us, "Ask and it shall be given unto you"?

21   SPECIFIC PETITIONS

If we pray, we must pray in Christ's name.

Does this mean that we must ask only for spiritual gifts?

I do not find this in Christ's teaching. He gave us two prayers—one we call the Lord's Prayer because he gave it to us, but it is for us and not for him. He could not pray "Forgive us our trespasses" who had no trespass to be forgiven. There is another prayer which is in a still deeper sense *his*—the Lord's—prayer, for he prayed it himself.

"Jesus . . . lifted up his eyes to heaven and said . . ." The rest is in the seventeenth chapter of John. It is a prayer. It cannot be that the prayer our Lord prayed to the Father which we are allowed to hear holds no light and truth for us.

Let us listen.

"I pray for them [his disciples]. . . . Keep them in thy name that they may be one. . . . Sanctify them through thy truth. . . . I pray also for them which believe on me through their word . . . that the world may believe that thou didst send me."

Here are petitions, very definite petitions, for certain people in definite need.

22   INDIVIDUAL PRAYER

When we hear Christ pray, there is much in it for others, little for himself; but intercession is often difficult unless we are willing to be definite in our petitions.

I meditate upon this seventeenth chapter of John. I see our Lord with his disciples on the last evening of his life on earth. They are very few, for many now "walk with him no more." They understand very little of all he has taught them, and he "has yet many things to say unto them" but they "cannot bear them now."

And upon these few depends the salvation of the world!

"I pray for you: I pray not for the world." That sounds strange on the lips of the Saviour of mankind: but he is thinking of them now because on them his saving work now hangs.

How definite, how individual is his prayer! He knows exactly what these friends of his need. He prays for that need.

I also think of each one for whom I pray, and as my mind dwells on them prayer is easy.

"How do you pray for people?" I asked a friend.

"I think about them with God," he answered.

23   DAILY BREAD

I have learned much about prayer from the seventeenth chapter of John. Let me now meditate on the prayer our Lord gave us for our own use. It is very short. It must contain, I think, only the absolutely fundamental things. There is not a word we can ignore. Clearly it is intended to be not only the prayer we are to use—but the pattern of all our prayers.

How startling to find that it contains not only worship but petition, and petition not only for spiritual but also for material things.

"Give us this day our daily bread." I do not think that Jesus, the carpenter, meant anything here but bread—the bread that he and poor people all over the world earn by the sweat of their brow. "Man does not live by bread alone." No; therefore the petitions that follow are for forgiveness, guidance, deliverance from evil. But without bread he cannot live at all; therefore he is to ask first for bread.

It is a very great mistake to try to be more spiritual than Jesus was.

24   A PSYCHOLOGICAL NECESSITY

"Ask and ye shall receive." But "your heavenly Father knoweth what things ye need before ye ask him."

Why then ask at all? Surely it is not for us to tell a God all-loving and all-wise what to give us?

There is no right giving where there is no wish to receive. God himself, if he respects the freedom he gave us, cannot compel us to accept his gifts. Sometimes I feel that, in prayer, I hold my hands clasped so tightly that it is impossible to put anything into them.

If I hold them out and open them, this is "asking." It is not a matter of words, but of a state of mind. We ask because we truly want—we ask because we cannot help asking if we truly want. I believe it is a psychological necessity;

and it brings us an answer because it finds in us an asking.

How often am I struck with the need for absolute obedience to the example and teaching of our Lord! How often, in obedience—even in blind obedience—I understand what I saw no sense in before I obeyed.

I learn to pray by praying.

25   MARYS AND MARTHAS

"Martha, Martha, thou art careful and troubled about many things. . . . Mary has chosen that good part which shall not be taken away from her."

People, especially overworked housewives and comfortably cared-for husbands, often say to me, "I should like to say a good word for the Marthas."

They need not trouble. Everyone has a good word for Martha. We all like to be waited on. We must not encourage Martha to wait much on God, or we may get less waited on ourselves!

Well, our Lord, too, waited on us. He came not to be ministered to, but to minister. He was a much "busier" person even than Martha. Could he have meant her to do less? It seems to me that he meant her to seek the source of power that she might do all she had to do with greater ease; sometimes "to sit at his feet and hear his word."

I have never yet heard anyone say a good word for Mary. Except our Lord.

26   THAT GOOD PART

Our Lord certainly commended Mary. He cannot have meant she was to do nothing but pray. He spent long hours, whole nights, in prayer; but when he had prayed, he said "Rise up, let us be going."

In prayer he found the strength he needed in order to preach, to teach, to heal, to travel up and down Palestine; to respond to the clamor of the people in their need even when he had hoped to go apart and rest awhile; to go forward to Golgotha even when he had suffered the agony of Gethsemane. He prayed in Gethsemane, and *therefore* he could face Golgotha.

I know, though so often I forget, that I too can be—I am—less Martha-like when I have been with Mary "who also sat at Jesus' feet and heard his word." I do not do less work for that; I do more, and more quickly, and better.

Prayer is not "quietism" when it issues in work.

27   GOD IS NOT IN OUR IMAGE

Thou art coming to a King,
Large petitions with thee bring.

It is a lovely thought—too lovely for us to realize easily. Sometimes I find myself making a bargain with God—"If you will grant me this prayer, I will give up something else." Again and again I must remind myself that I am praying to one whose care for me and those for whom I pray is immeasurably greater than my own and that there is in him no huckstering spirit of a bargainer. He is more ready to hear than I to pray, more able to give than I to ask, more powerful to help than I have any knowledge of. I forget all this so easily. Why? Because my own spirit is so mean, my thoughts so poor, my giving so ungenerous. And I make God in my own pitiful image.

"Jesus," wrote H. G. Wells—himself a skeptic—"was too great for his disciples. . . . Is it any wonder that to this day this Galilean is too much for our small hearts?"

28   REAL HUMILITY

Our Lord said, "He that humbleth himself shall be exalted." Yet what a bad name this Christian virtue has! Humility. It suggests Uriah Heep.

It suggests to me now that we are very pagan still. We easily think ill of a virtue Christ praised.

"Two men went up into the temple to pray." The Pharisee said, "Lord, I thank thee that I am not as . . . this publican."

The publican *did not compare himself with* anyone, but "beat his breast and said, Lord, be merciful unto me, a sinner."

I see that this is humility. It does not lie in comparing oneself with other people, even to make oneself ashamed. One might have thought that, in contrast to the Pharisee who compared himself with the publican, the publican might have compared himself with the Pharisee and felt abased. He did not. He stood before God and in that Presence implored mercy.

29   MERCY

Let me too ask for mercy. I cannot judge others. They have temptations and difficulties of which I know nothing. Whether they are better or worse than I, also I do not know. I know only that I am so unlike my Master that I must ask forgiveness.

I look at him—only at him. In the light of that white flame of love, purity, and goodness, I see myself unloving, impure, and evil.

I cannot endure the sight. I look up to Christ again and, being helpless, beg him to help me, to forgive me, to teach me to forget myself, to forgive myself. And he answers:

"Behold I stand at the door and knock. If any man hear my voice and open the door, I will come in to him and will sup with him and he with me."

30   LIGHT

Today I lay down my burden of sins and perplexities. The burden of them is intolerable. Only God can carry them. I lay them at his feet. "He knows what He does among His great stars." I do not know. I pray for light, and light is given. I ask forgiveness, and I have that too. I ask for guidance, and behold the next step is shown to me.

More than this I must not expect. That God would give it if I could bear it I firmly believe; but instead he gives me so much of the light as my dazzled eyes can endure, so much of knowledge as I can perceive. I shall know more. I can be patient for I know, now that I see, how little I could understand if it were told to me and how poor a use I make even of what I know and understand. I leave all to the God and Father of mankind. "He knows what He does among His great stars."

Mists and Mellow Fruitfulness

BONARO W. OVERSTREET

1   INTO THIS NEW MONTH

The sun and stars do not break up eternity into thirty-day cycles. Their schedule provides for no momentary slowing down to celebrate accomplishment, nor for any speeding up to dramatize a new beginning.

But we who live under the sun and stars have a recurrent need to say, "There—that much is done," and to say, "This is a fresh start." Out of our human need we design a calendar pattern that can be imposed upon the endlessness of time.

And though all our logic may tell us that the first day of a new month is just like any other day, yet our feelings tell a different story. With some flick of thought, some quickening of the spirit, we acknowledge the difference—ahead of us there is a month in which anything can happen; in which no mistakes have yet been made; in which we can begin again.

286

2   DEEP RHYTHM

For convenience man devises his ticking clocks and squared-off calendars, and by them he measures many endings and many beginnings.

But more deeply moving than their precise rhythms are those of the natural world. The calendar may say "October second." But blue grapes on a frost-touched vine say "autumn." Corn shucks; the call of crows; the crisp, small sound of dry leaves and the odor of leaf-burning—these say "autumn"; these say "harvest."

These say the time has come for reckoning the well-dones and the ill-dones of the year.

These say the time has come for counting our resources —in barn and bin and cellar, and in our own hearts.

When frost whitens the woodpile beside the house, it is good to know that logs can be translated into winter warmth. It is even better to know that we have prepared yet another defense against the cold—to know that all who share our roof have so planted and tended the seeds of understanding that their faces around the winter hearth will glow, not with firelight alone, but with confidence and love.

3   OF GATHERING, AND OF LETTING GO

Autumn, season of earth's maturing, asks that we also be mature. For upon our human nature it makes a double demand.

It asks that we prepare for the future—that we be wise in the ways of garnering and keeping.

But it asks also that we learn to let go—to acknowledge the beauty of sparseness.

The homely satisfaction of smelling apples in the bin or of counting our jars of applesauce on a pantry shelf is only half the experience of being human in October. The companion half is that of walking out through the thinning orchard, where dry leaves run ahead of us along old furrows.

The child in us may ask perpetual summer, may ask to hold on forever to one kind of beauty.

But the mature human being in us knows how to walk with the wind through lean orchards—how to watch while the birds fly south—how to acknowledge that the life of man is both a gathering and a letting go.

4   NO HASTY PREPARATION

Poplar trees yield their yellow leaves to sudden morning wind. And a woman, glancing out of the window as she washes dishes, feels a tug at the heart—here it is again.

Hands idle a moment, she marshals what she needs for the understanding of autumn—a philosophy of life and death, the two strangely one.

And she remembers a schoolbook story about an old man, homely of feature and shining of spirit, who lived and died in Athens a long time ago—a man named Socrates.

Queer to remember him so. . . .

But there was that thing he said when he was told that he should prepare himself for death, "Know you not that I have been preparing for it all my life?"

The woman alone in her kitchen nods to herself, "That's

how it is. You can't get ready for loss at the very moment when it happens—not for the loss of poplar leaves, nor for the loss of a person you love. You get ready for all the lettings go by being as wise as you know how in all the moments of living."

She looks out at bare trees—and smiles—and goes on with her dishes.

5   THESE FAMILIAR PLAYERS

Like actors who return each year at a stated season, fields and orchards present once more their great morality play.

The plot is ancient, familiar to many generations.

It is the plot of good seed that produces good harvest, of well-tilled acres that reward the labor of hand and plow.

Also it is the melancholy plot of unpruned branches bearing small, bitter fruit.

It is, in brief, earth's great morality play of cause and effect.

We cannot fix the date when man gave up the ways of a nomad to become a farmer, to become a planter instead of a follower of wild game in its seasonal migrations.

But on that day he signed up as an actor in this annual drama. He began to discipline himself by its strict logic. He wrought from its plot both law and poetry—"Whatsoever a man soweth, that shall he also reap."

6   UNFINISHED LESSON

If the workings of cause and effect were everywhere as visible as in the world of seed and harvest, much human folly might reach a happy ending in wisdom.

But many of us who applaud the logic of earth's morality play when we see it acted out on the stage of field and orchard, are baffled by that same logic on the stage of the human spirit.

Knowing better than to plant weeds to reap grain, we yet go on hoping that we can somehow plant seeds of self-interest to reap peace and love.

Ever since man first became farmer and craftsman, he has been gradually maturing his sense of realism—of cause and effect—on the physical plane.

On the spiritual plane he too often remains an unreasonable child. Planting seeds of willfulness, he watches as only a child would watch for a harvest of strength and well-being.

7   **CONCERNING THE WISE**

There have been men and women whom we have called wise and good. We have met them in the pages of history and have been blessed in meeting some of them in the flesh.

Wherever we have met them, they have changed our feeling about life—have revealed to us that the business of being human is more than a routine, more than a calculating exercise in self-interest. They have surprised us into a new sense of spiritual drama.

When we try to puzzle out what distinguishes these rare people—why they seem to walk in light instead of in our common darkness—we find an answer essentially simple. They accept the logic of earth's great morality play as universal logic—as the cause-and-effect logic of man's spirit no less than of the seeded field.

They know that what that morality play forever declares is that harvest does not come without planting— whether it be a harvest of grain or a harvest of love.

8   THE REPEATED INSIGHT

Those who have been wise in the logic of life—not expecting justice to spring from injustice, nor mutual understanding from special privilege—form a fellowship independent of time and space.

Christ instructed, "As ye would that men should do to you, do ye also to them likewise."

Confucius advised, "Do not do to another what you would not have another do to you."

Rabbi Himmel summed up thus the spiritual law, "That which is hateful to thee, do thou not that to another."

Lincoln said, "As I would not be a slave, so I would not be a master."

And an ordinary living woman explains to her small son, "You wouldn't like it if Johnny did that to you. So you see you can't do it to him."

Wherever the words are spoken, wholeness and glory enter into life. For these words declare man to be craftsman and husbandman of the spirit no less than of the soil.

9   REASON FOR GRATITUDE

Sometimes when we pay special tribute to our heroes, we make it sound almost as though we were grateful to them for having done so much that we can afford to do less.

Because they struggled for freedom, we can simply enjoy freedom—take it for granted.

Because they worked for the common welfare, we can concentrate on our own private affairs.

Because they ran risks, we can play safe.

Unintentionally we make it sound as though their great gift to us was a gift of exemption from effort.

But surely their true gift is very different.

They have given us, not exemption from effort, but design for effort. From them we learn what is really worth spending ourselves for—justice for all; freedom for all; understanding among all.

Their gift, moreover, is a gift of evidence—by having lived and worked they have given testimony that greatness of spirit is possible to human nature—that human nature we all share with them.

10   THE UTILITY OF GREATNESS

Too often we turn into empty sounds the full truths spoken by saint and prophet. Upon our natural voices we impose tones of stereotyped reverence. Then, with minds wandering or fixed upon our own concerns, we give lip service, and only lip service, to insights that make all the difference in human affairs between greatness and mediocrity, between peace and strife.

It is not thus that greatness is rightly honored. Greatness is honored only when we try to make our own daily behaviors fit the standard that greatness has set up.

We do not build our physical houses by guess work.

We rely upon measuring rod and plumb line. For we do not want those houses to be skewed products of impulse and error. We want them to stand weatherproof—solid and true.

We can scarcely afford, it would seem, to be less exacting when we build the houses of our spirit. To those whom we call great we are indebted for spiritual measuring rod and plumb line. But it is we ourselves who must decide to place our confidence in these.

11   FOR MEASURING

For measuring lumber we have our physical yardstick.

For measuring behavior we have our spiritual yardstick— do unto others as you would have others do unto you.

That is the precise and universal rule—the Golden Rule. To house it with honor we build our churches and cathedrals—while we stow away our physical yardstick in any workshop corner.

Yet it often seems that wo place more trust in the latter. For when our eye says one thing and our yardstick another, we accept its judgment. But when implse and self-interest say one thing and the Golden Rule another, we argue the case. We say that it is, of course, a good rule in principle and in general; but to apply it with literal precision would go counter to practicality and common sense.

Then we are appalled—and inclined to blame the whole make-up of things—when the house of our spirit turns out to be a jerry-built affair that slants precariously before the storms of circumstance.

12   CENTER OF THE CIRCLE

The maps were wrong—the ancient maps that showed not only the earth, but the ends of the earth.

And common sense was wrong.

Columbus was right; the world was round. After all the proofs that it could not be so, the world was round.

Here was a new fact for mankind to wrestle with—to wrestle with as once Jacob wrestled with the angel, until it blessed him.

For a round world has its own peculiar blessing to give— not to navigators alone, but to all who care for the dignity of man. On a flat world some humans might claim to be at the very center of things—the true center—while others were crowded to the unwanted, precarious edges. But on a round world every individual is a center point. The circles that can be drawn around the spot where he stands will, in the end, include all men and all portions of the planet.

13   UNIT OF DIGNITY

It might be a good spiritual exercise to practice every morning—this exercise of feeling at home on a round world, where every living individual is equally a center point.

To think of ourselves at the center comes easy. We feel our own feelings, think our own thoughts, hope our own hopes. We know the intensity of these.

We may not be powerful, or wealthy, or eloquent. But we feel too much not to have some significance. We can readily believe that the modest human unit that is ourselves has some inherent dignity, some inborn right, some personal relationship to the whole make-up of things.

Spiritual maturity, however, requires us to feel with equal intensity the fact that every other human being is a unit of significance, to feel that each stands strongly center of a meaningful scheme.

The woman who lives on the wrong side of the tracks—she too is center. The woman who lives on the other side of the world—she too is center.

That is the lesson of a round planet assigned for our learning.

14   WITHIN OUR KEEPING

One kind of very practical circle can be drawn around each of us—the circle of our influence. This circle, however constricted it may seem, we dare not neglect. It is in our keeping.

Perhaps we cannot preach brotherhood to crowding multitudes. But our circle of influence is wide enough to include the family dinner table. There we can, by word and attitude, make human brotherhood seem well worth working for.

We cannot feed all who cry for food in this hungry world. But within our own community there are people who hunger for both bread and love. Surely our circle of influence is wide enough to embrace some of these.

We cannot be heard for truth in every place where falsehood is loud-spoken. But where we live and move—within our own circle of influence—we can try to speak truth, and we can refrain from all damaging rumor that might spread from our tongues to the tongues of others to breed misunderstanding and cruelty.

Each of us, in brief, has one peculiar geography lesson to learn—we must study to feel the outlines of our own circle of influence.

15   DRAWING TOGETHER

Houses scattered at the edge of town—where streets end and country roads begin—enjoy all through the summer months a privacy of green. Around each of them, hiding them from one another, stand beech trees and oaks and maples.

Within their tree-walled privacies families work and play, virtually unseen by other families that work and play a hundred yards distant on either side. They work and play in a leafy remoteness from the lined-up houses of the town and the square business blocks—even though these are within easy walking distance.

Then, in October, the leaves come down.

Houses draw suddenly close to one another—houses that show white and friendly among silver beeches, among oaks and maples. In the chill twilight friendly smoke climbs wraith-like from neighbor chimneys. Friendly lights shine from neighbor windows.

It has happened again. Human beings have put off their summer mantle of separateness; they have drawn together for the time of cold.

16   SEASONS OF THE HEART

It is not accident that we human beings, generation after generation, draw upon the natural world for symbols to express our heart's caring.

For our spirits have their own seasons.

There are times when we stand seemingly on our own, independent—like houses hidden from one another among summer trees.

And there are times when we need the reassuring knowledge of one another's presence—like houses that reveal their mutual nearness when leaves fall and nights are cold.

It is right enough that there should be such spiritual seasons of privacy and of drawing close; for each of us is an individual self, not quite like any other; and each of us is part of something very much greater than himself.

It is right that there should be spiritual seasons.

But a great loneliness surrounds any person who—even in the green summer of well-being, and of apparent self-sufficiency—forgets his need of those neighbors who are briefly out of sight behind clustering trees.

17   A TASK AND A HOPE

How shall we define the sorrow of our age—its sprawling tragedy? How explain the fact that twentieth-century man, triumphant in many things, is yet man afraid?

May it not be that our trouble is simply this? With short-sighted, fair-weather confidence in our little selves and our little groups, we have tried to go it too much alone—each individual, each family, each little clique and class and nation.

297

Now in the soul's bleak weather we learn at last that we must learn the art of mutual trust, of mutual aid. We must learn the high art of community-wide and world-wide neighboring.

We talk of "one world." But one world will never be built *in the large* by people who cannot build it *in the small*.

Here, once more, we encounter the wisdom of an old story—the story of the widow's mite. Any person, however modest, builds one world if, by word and attitude, she helps one person to look at another with new understanding, if she helps one person to look at another as neighbor.

18   MUCH IN LITTLE

It is easy to believe that only big things are important— big efforts, big accomplishments.

But we must, for our common salvation on this earth, practice to see that all good things are important; all beautiful things are important; all generous acts are important; all work lovingly and expertly done is important.

This is the meaning of the story of the widow's mite. We, like the widow, may feel apologetic about the smallness of our gift. We may wish that we had wealth and power to bring to the cause in which we believe.

But the meaning of the story remains unshaken—if the *quality* of what we do is such that our action, written large enough, would make a world of generosity and confidence, then what we do is important.

A woman on a crowded streetcar smiled a warm human

smile at a woman of another race who was thrown against her when the car jerked to a sudden stop.

She smiled—and her smile was important. It had in it the rightness of man's relationship to his fellow man; therefore, it was important.

19   THREE KINDS OF WISDOM

Christ talked with folk—not unlike ourselves—who needed more than an abstract definition of rightness. They needed to visualize right action—action that they could emulate in their own lives. Therefore, the story of the widow's mite.

Centuries later the philosopher Kant talked with folk—not unlike ourselves—who needed more than scattered examples of rightness, who needed a principle. He said, "So act that the maxim of thy act is law universal." Do, in brief, what would be good for all men if practiced by all men. Again, the stress was upon the *quality* of behavior, not the size.

Now psychologists speak up. They declare that mental and emotional health comes, not from the bigness of what we do, but from its wholeness. If all our actions—even the smallest—confirm and support one another, and confirm and support the ideals we profess to believe, then we are in good health.

Kant would say Yes to the story of the widow's mite.

Psychologists would say Yes to it.

20   **THE OPEN DOOR**

One of the loveliest words in our language is the word "hospitality." It holds in keeping our will to move toward other human beings, not away from them.

The symbol of hospitality is an open door.

At any time of day or night, in any season or in any weather, an open door symbolizes our nearest approach to true civility. But there is something peculiarly right and beautiful about the opening of a door in the autumn dusk. In the shaft of warm light that stretches out into the grayness, both those who welcome and those who are welcomed stand strangely glorified.

And an onlooker who happens to view from a distance this little drama of the open door is himself glorified. For he sees in the shaft of light not particular individuals who chance to be friends; he sees in dark silhouette figures who symbolize the age-old, world-wide human impulse toward hospitality.

21   **THROUGH THIS DOOR**

Fortunate among the world's children are those who grow up in homes rich in hospitality, where the door is psychologically open even when physically closed, where friends and neighbors take pot luck.

Greatly to be pitied are those children—however many "advantages" they may enjoy—who grow up in homes where guests are regarded as problems, where even the entertaining of a neighbor is prefaced by so much hectic cleaning and cooking that the family comes exhausted to an event from which all easy joy has been drained.

Before we wear ourselves down to the point of jitters by our determination to have no speck of dust visible to guests' eyes, we need to stop and ask what impression of those guests we are, by our nervousness, giving to our children. Do we want our children to think of them as people who come to see us because they like us—or as people who come intent to criticize?

Our boys and girls can scarcely learn to make friends easily—and to feel at home with the human race—if they grow up seeing us worried about the opinion of every human being who crosses our doorstep.

22   THE WELCOMING MIND

A hospitable door that opens wide to welcome guests is one of the beautiful objects of this earth.

But even more beautiful is a hospitable mind that opens wide to welcome ideas and experiences that come visiting from other minds.

We stand in danger, today, of becoming as suspicious of unfamiliar viewpoints as were our primitive ancestors. We stand in danger of becoming again citizens of the tribe—just when we most need to become citizens of the world. But our tribes are not now natural groupings of blood kin. They are those of class, race, political party, or religion. With a primitive distrust for those whose opinions challenge our own, we huddle in our little groups—hoping to make security out of a bright pretense that all right-minded people are much like ourselves; and that all who are not like ourselves are less than right-minded and can be kept outside.

But here and there among us are individuals who practice a new civility for a new world. They open their minds—and hearts—to learn what life looks like from unfamiliar angles. Across the tribal lines of class, race, party, culture, and religion they practice the high, beautiful art of mental hospitality.

23   THROUGH ANOTHER'S EYES

Basic to mental hospitality is the art of listening. Many of us never do listen. We keep still—most of us—while another person talks. But keeping still is not the same thing as listening.

Often when we have said our own say, we turn our minds loose to wander at will—and call them back only when we have a chance to do some more talking.

Often we spend our intervals of enforced silence preparing what we will say next.

But a state of pleasant coma is not a state of listening. Nor are we listening when we rehearse future words with which we hope to make a good impression.

These shabby imitations of listening leave us exactly where they found us—absorbed in ourselves.

To listen is to move out of our own concerns into those of another, out of our own experiences into those of another. It is to look at life with borrowed insight. It is to lend our own mind and heart—to lend them with such active will that they bring back to us from the-person-not-ourselves a kind of understanding not previously our own.

24   ALL ALIKE

"Human beings are all alike." "Human beings are all different." We make these conflicting remarks many times over.

Similarly we say, "Pretty much the same things happen to all of us," and, "Life treats us so differently—gives us such contrasted experiences to think from—that we speak a different language even when we use the same words."

Curiously enough, life itself encourages us to voice such contradictions.

We are all alike; and the same things happen to us—we know joy and sorrow, hope and fulfillment and loss and loneliness.

We are all different; and different things happen to us— if we have known always an atmosphere of love, we do not know how it would feel never to be wanted; if we are members of a majority group, we do not know how it would feel to belong to an outcast minority; if we can give our children the care they need, we do not know how it would feel to bear the constant fear of their starving.

We are all alike.

But we can feel our alikeness, feel our common destiny, only if we so practice the art of listening to one another— with ears, minds, and hearts—that we can understand our differences and our different slants on life.

25   STANDARDS

One person, we describe as "interesting" and "important"; another, as "uninteresting" and "unimportant." But what do we mean? Interesting and important to whom?

Dull and unimportant to whom? To us, or to himself? To us, or to those who have built their love and hope around this person we so easily label?

Most of the judgments we pass upon others probably tell more about ourselves than about them. Our judgments tell chiefly whether or not these others fit into our own scheme of things—whether they make us feel interesting and important.

Sometimes, if we are honest, we can catch ourselves in this not-quite-honest act of imposing our own interests upon mankind in general. We can notice, for example, how we listen to people.

Do we listen to what they say merely in the context of our own interests, our own experiences, our own moods, even? Or do we try to hear their words in the context of *their* interests, *their* experiences, *their* moods? Do we try to feel why the things they say are important *to them*? Do we try to imagine ourselves in their life roles?

When we talk, we want other people to make some reasonable effort to understand what we are talking about and why we think it worth saying. Here it would seem, then—in this whole area of talking and listening—is one more instance of our need to practice doing as we would be done by.

26   **SYMPHONY**

October is a symphony of permanence and change, of one rich mood played off against another, of silence played off against earth's flutes and trumpets and violins.

There are days when the sky achieves such blue perfection that we are lulled into doubting that any cloud could trespass. Here is not just "sky," but "Sky"—a kind of Platonic ideal, faultless and changeless. Under the sky, landscapes lie faultless. There are signs of past change— thinning branches, weeds, seed-heavy, slanted by the winds of yesterday. But for this one day, or brief succession of days, our planet tells of *being*, not of *becoming*. It *is*; and we *are*; and time itself refrains from breaking the spell.

Then—a dry leaf stirs—and turns upon its rustling neighbors. An abrupt gust grabs a handful of yellow leaves from a tree beside the road. There is a running of wind in the grass of a stone-walled pasture. Crows call. Gray clouds lump above the horizon.

We turn up our coat collars—thrust our hands into our pockets.

October is a symphony of permanence and change.

27   SHAPES OF WORDS

Each autumn there is a first morning when our invisible breath becomes visible, and the chill that scrolls our words frostily upon thin air is no respecter of wisdom or folly.

A boy calls to his dog.

A young wife says good-by to her husband at the door of a house not different from other houses along the street where it stands, "Good-by—I'll be watching for you."

A bitter-faced woman looks across a hedge at her neighbor's place and says to her daughter-replica: "The amount of time Mrs. Smith spends just walking around that garden of hers—even now when there's not a flower left—it makes a body wonder when she does her housework."

A grocer, unlocking his store, exchanges a word with a passer-by, "Feels like winter's coming—and it's going to be a tough one for a lot of folks—all over the world."

On a station platform one commuter says to another, "You mark my word. This country's going communist. All these refugees—if you ask me, most of them come straight from Moscow."

We talk—each of us after the manner of his own mind, his own heart; and the noncensoring cold writes wisdom and folly alike, kindness and cruelty alike, in frosty whiteness upon thin air.

28   RECURRENT IMAGE

Most of us, watching our breath white upon autumn air, have had, now and then, the feeling that we could almost read the frosty scroll of our own words. We have felt those words stand clear before us, visible for judgment— and have wondered whether we would like the look of them if they could be read—by ourselves; by friends and neighbors.

We have wondered—and the thought has linked us with earlier folk who, back through the ages, have many times wondered—what difference it would make in human behavior if the spoken words of all of us were visible for all to read; and if ugly words and beautiful, stupid and wise, bitter and generous, all took shapes appropriate to their kind.

It is an ancient thought—given permanence, for example, in the fairy tale of the princess who, endowed with wealth and beauty, was yet so ugly in spirit that toad-words hopped from her mouth when she spoke.

It is an ancient thought—and yet newborn where, on the first cold morning of autumn, a woman vents her irritation in words of unaccustomed sharpness. She sees before her the white breath of her speaking—and suddenly knows that she would not want to face her own words if the shape of them matched their spirit.

29   THE VOICE OF ACTION

"In the beginning was the Word. . . . And the Word became flesh and dwelt among us, . . . and we behold his glory."

That quick summary of one great event is, in fact, a summary of all that is more significant in human history —the history of the race, and of every member of it.

A woman says to her husband, "We ought to be doing more than we are in our local church to bring about fellowship with other churches. It does seem, with the world the way it is, that all who care about the spiritual future of man should be coming together—forgetting old differences—proving that, regardless of creed or class or race, the church of God can move like a mighty army. Surely there are enough of us, if we'd just get together, to provide the great affirmation for which the world is starving; enough of us to prove that evil and cruelty and self-interest are not going to have things their own way. We should begin right now, here in our own church."

This is what a woman says to her husband as they sit together, late at night, in front of their living-room fire.

Her words promise a better world. But only if her words become flesh—if they become action, if they become program—can anyone else ever behold their glory.

30   FROM GHOULIES AND GHAESTIES

It was an old folk prayer against primitive dark and the frightening sounds of that dark:

> From ghoulies, and ghaesties,
> And long-legged beasties,
> And things that go boomp in the night—
> Good Lord, deliver us.

Today we meet ghosts chiefly as a Halloween fiction—children laughing under borrowed bedsheets. And only with the eyes of our imagination do we see witches fly dark across the moon.

Where once human flesh grew rigid with the fear of unknown sounds in the forest night, we identify familiar sounds even in darkness—the stair that always creaks when the wind blows; the Virginia creeper that scrapes against the walls and taps a window pane.

Yet we are still afraid. Perhaps, in fact, the fears that haunt us now are more corroding fears of "ghoulies and ghaesties." For we are, now, most of all afraid of our own human kind, and of the faulty social arrangements we have made for living together.

Our fear is a commentary, not upon the mysterious universe, but upon our prevailing reluctance to live up to the law that God has given for life without fear—the law of human brotherhood.

A FUTURE TO MAKE

So long as we humans feared chiefly unhuman forces—ghoulies and ghaesties, and long-legged beasties—it was natural for us to ask unhuman aid, to pray for miraculous deliverance.

But when we fear chiefly our own human kind—people distorted by our combined social blunderings—it seems, somehow, less than gracious to ask that God perform repeated miracles to save us from the consequences of our having tenaciously refused to trust the law he gave us when "the Word became flesh."

We were told—we were shown—that love casts out fear; that where men live as brothers, in a system of mutual self-respect and mutual confidence, fear is obsolete.

We have, in brief, been given once for all a rule for escaping fear—and Christ demonstrated that what we were told made sense; that it accorded with our nature; that it could be applied in practice; that it could be utterly trusted.

The world's confusion shows that we have gone as far as we dare go in violation of God's law—to go further is to commit racial suicide. We have a new future to make—and a law according to which to make it. If we build well, trusting our human fellows and trusting the Creator who told us to trust our human fellows, man's fear of man may, in time, seem as quaint as the primitive fear of "ghoulies and ghaesties."

Roads and Vistas

BLANCHE H. DOW

1   **ROADS**

November has a way of her own. Crisp air, swaying Spanish needles, echo of honking geese held in memory from the night, motors passing on the road.

The secured peace of warm houses, fire and book, radio, food and light and comfort—these may satisfy in December, but now every venturing impulse is stirred. To take to the road, that would be the thing.

Well to be bound by contracts, held by responsibilities. Good that in this moment of temptation we cannot throw our obligations lightly away. Travel must be by remembered roads, but there is happiness in that.

Streets that curve hold a promise and so do roads that wind. They raise enticing questions. Curves are inseparable from charm. Lights and shadows play on them in new geometric patterns. Delicate angles, pot-bellied curves, amusing, bemusing. Strange and familiar constantly blended. Satisfaction of the known, stimulation of the new. Comforting, provocative combination.

The road we have traveled gives assurance, stability. It is familiar, comfortable. The known road straightens. Its hazards have been met and passed. Success, remembered, sustains us.

The winding road is exciting. Its prospect is tonic. The problems of its untried passage, still unseen, fail to frighten. In time they will exact solution, and that will test the integrity of our journey's purpose, the validity of our chosen roads.

2   WORK IMMORTAL

No roads are more beautiful than those of our western prairies in a good wheat summer as they cut through the shining grain.

Bronze-gold in Kansas, the wheat, like a rich Byzantine mosaic, with the dark blades of the corn and the sweet alfalfa's purple.

Long alternate rectangles of Montana, plowed fallow fields and strips of grain. Invisible becoming visible from moment to moment, then fused by the vigorous road, like a day's mistakes, into the soft blur of the past.

Oats and barley and rye in Alberta, and wheat. Powerful, moving, cumulative force of repetition. Acres that merge with acres. Warm ripened grain without a boundary. Elevators cutting the sky. Houses and barns, gray against the ground, dwarfed by the immensity of the harvest. In that great panorama only the sky holds its own.

Are men and women here forgotten, lost in the greatness of the thing they have produced?

Men and women are never forgotten. In time and space their gifts endure.

The houses and barns along that road say this to us as we pass, "Men plowed and planted and prayed over these fields. Women worked and watched and waited. They felt fear, loneliness, always fatigue. They knew the menace of drought and flood. When the hot winds blew, when the shallow river beds filled and overflowed, washed out the seed, sickened the young plants, with patience not short of heroic they planted again these endless acres."

Wheat means everything to them—safety, freedom, their part in a better world. To it they give themselves daily. Bread for themselves and bread for their brothers.

Work that exercises all their powers, work that demands complete dedication, work that relates itself to the whole of life is a present part of their immortality.

3   THE STRAIGHT ROAD

Straight roads offer fulfillment.

Monotonous? Perhaps. So is the day's routine, but it is the basis of our effectiveness.

Genius alone may transcend the ordered modes and routes of travel and, to our slow wonder, arrive in heady flight at that destination toward which we laboriously push.

Geese, last night flying south, circled in dizzying nearness to the ground, so close that one saw the soft texture of their breasts. For a moment the village lights had seemed to offer warmth and safety. But their mistake was clear—they were off their course; they had turned away

November ROADS AND VISTAS

from the straight road, lost their direction; failure threatened the whole migration. The great gray leader gave a rallying call, and with a surge of power they were up and on.

Bleak, the straight road? Yes, in contrast with the winding side road's charm. It would be pleasant, perhaps, to turn away. It might even offer advantage. But the plain road insists. It is clear, direct, unswerving. Its demands pound like a hammer on conscience, that inner determining mind.

Straight roads move without compromise to destination. "Loitering in winding ways" may lead to "brambly wildernesses," but wilderness offers only recreation, escape.

Recreation and escape are like lace. They must grace and trim. Real journeying is of firmer fabric.

The stretching miles may frighten. Their beauty is stern, but it is unmistakable. They promise and they fulfill.

4   TO ENRICH THE JOURNEY

Roads and minds have much in common.

Ulysses, bound for Ithaca, Aeneas, "tossed about much on land and on sea," Dante, toiling the steeps, Pilgrim, caught in the morass, are truer than fiction. They are a symbol of life. They are an interpretation of its mobility, of the drive which the spirit imposes on the outward act, of man's compelling urge toward something greater than himself, his yearning to discover through experience the greatness of God and by discovery to draw near him.

Swift, straight travel and the side road's recurring appeal

313

must be weighed and reconciled, adjusted, fitted together
to justify and to enrich the journey.

Likewise established truth and the mind's unquenchable
thirst for more.

Truth is not static any more than life. Like the road it
continuously reveals itself. It cannot be fenced in. It is a
living force. It draws us as the road draws us to an expanding world. It grows as we grow, moves forward as we
move. It clarifies the journey, reveals each new succeeding
stretch, illumines and ennobles what had seemed the little
progress of our day.

Routine need never be gray or dull, responsibility never
fail to reward if we relate them to the whole, fit them into
the reaches of the long and thrilling road.

5   BEAUTY

"As the mountains are round about Jerusalem," sang the
poet, and he saw in the familiar scene the illustration his
heart burned to find.

The beauty of the world, present or remembered, is a
source of refreshment, stimulus, even when it awakens
questions we cannot answer:

> No universal hymn is quite so deep
> As waves off shore;
> Their cadence in his heart who hears would keep
> Forevermore.
>
> In sunlight when the wind is strong,
> The while they fling

314

Their foaming crests the yellow sands along,
They shout and sing.

When tides steal out, consuming form and mass,
Too small to leap,
Essaying still the graying sands to pass,
Pearl-edged they creep.

But when the tides mount and their volume grows,
They crash like thunder,
Impelled by that no finite being knows,
Consumed with wonder.

The deep plays on eternally in strains profound
For those who hear;
O, may its music evermore be found
Within my ear!

6   TELL ME THE ANSWERS

Gray gull,
Gray gull,
Where are you going,
Taut wing cutting the thick mist through,
Into black night, or into bright morning,
Only one need, that direction be true?

White gull,
White gull,
What are you seeing,
Skimming blue surface, drenched by salt spray,
Diving in vain for fish that elude you,
Circling and diving, then up with your prey?

Quiet gull,
Quiet gull,
What are you dreaming,
Poised on the rock, eyes fixed on the sea,
Unstirred by the deep sounds of wind and of water,
Silent and calm in your long reverie?

Gray gull, winging your path through the cloud,
White gull, tireless and strong to your task,
Quiet gull, growing in calm for the morrow,
Tell me the answers the spirit would ask.

7   ALL ANNS

Ann, who is two, fell out of the swing and cried. Her
cut head bled, and the blood added fright to hurt. Her
world was broken to bits. What had been pleasure had become pain.

It was a lovely morning. The sky was deep. Fat sheep
that were clouds moved lazily across blue pastures.

She pushed herself off the bright sand up into the dark
of the apple tree. Out and up and down and back. Chest
expanding, spine tensing. Moving in long curves through
space was like having a magic carpet. Or wings. Like a
bird. Out and up and down and back.

And then a rope gave way. The bright circles stopped.
The long rhythm broke. The security of her familiar world
was shattered, and Ann cried for her mother.

It was more than the hurt. She wanted her world restored. She wanted to feel again the comfort of her
mother's arms, the healing of her mother's likewise-griev-
ing voice. She had to have her identity reaffirmed, her

sameness with a steadier force than she, her inseparability from the loved source of her being.

We are all Anns. Our bright mornings suffer sudden clouds. Disasters fell us. Fears torment. We must have re-affirmation of our source. We must establish anew our identity with, feel again our inseparability from, God.

Then our world, too, will be restored.

8   ONE WORLD

The modes of what we call culture often bring us to grips with attitudes that are fundamentally right. Our need of oneness, our quest for identification, is true, and we should satisfy it, whether that comforting establish-ment is limited, as in Ann's case, to the one essential human source of security, or whether, with an extended awareness of all people, we yearn to be one with them, one to assuage their pain, one to share in their hope.

Only the realization of the equalness of human person-ality can bring us together.

The identification we seek must be divorced from con-descension. Conscious superiority kills it, even when it stems from traits to admire.

Mind is mind, trained or untrained; spirit is spirit with its undiscovered power. This is to be remembered. Life is life, and immeasurably precious; personality is personality. Cultivation, accomplishment, expression are all questions of comparison. They are considerations apart from the ac-ceptance of equality which is the necessary basis of union.

Enthusiasm for our particular convictions, our culture, may lead us to regard those that are different as negligible.

Eagerness to impart, to convince, may move us to ignore, to minimize, and thereby to breed difference.

Enthusiasm and eagerness are vital attributes, but perception and the desire to learn are prerequisite to their effective expression.

Moslem and Christian seek the same God. Illiterate and linguist speak the same language. If we could but learn it, we would have more to unite than to separate us.

It is one world we want.

9   A NEW WORLD

For those who recall November, 1918, the implications of this week are deeply serious. In the quarter-century enactment of the tragic drama of forgetting we have been both spectators and actors. Our roles may have been those of supernumeraries, but, drifting across the stage in the wake of players whose parts were more vitally involved in the action's progress, we have lost sight of the inevitable last act, have forgotten the first.

To forget is to fail. We could easily forget again.

To insist day after day upon the ruthless following of effect upon cause, to keep always within the mind the things one would like to forget, not with morbid motive, but that one may never cease to see the difference in the weights of those values which once made themselves desperately clear—these are no easy infinitives. They require will and perseverance and constant effort.

They are practical, realistic methods of approach to the attainment of goals which are set by nobler aspiration.

The Latin Americans call a certain day, with its impli-

cations of a new world's discovery, the "Day of the Race."
We might well rechristen day after tomorrow, well resolve
to mark that day by a renewed allegiance to the cause of
peace, humanity, the world which has to be.

The one world must be a new world or it will be no
world. No day is too short, no life too humble to hold a
prayer for it, to make an effort toward it, to bring its realization nearer.

10   **LEST WE FORGET**

Lest we forget—the world is a prompter's book, and
the cues are endlessly repeated:

> I went to eat this noon
> Into a little street off Montparnasse
> And Notre Dame des Champs;
> Where one could read or rest or dream,
> Lost in the pleasure of thus sitting silently,
> A stone's throw from an avenue that conjures up
> Such spirits of the past
> As Plato, Pindar, Aeschylus;
> And Notre Dame des Champs,
> Symbol of heart and faith of rural France,
> A virgin who delights in flowers and grasses,
> The winds across the fields, the hallowed mood
> That follows on the silence of the wood.
>
> Into that quiet came the raucous scraping
> Of crutches 'gainst a stone;
> Harsh and discomforting it broke
> Into the rhythm of that reverie,
> A sudden, searing summons of return

To one who thus could lose himself in dreaming;
A man pushed wearily the chair
And dragged his broken body into place.
To see him turn
Was like a cutting lash across the face.
"Don't think I fail to read what you are thinking,"
To me in silence flashed his vivid glance:
"Citations, medals, monuments
We've had in plenty;
Treaties, too, that broke in spirit
Before the minds that framed them
Left the table.

"Where are the promises you made us,
You people who are safe and whole and sound?
Have you forgotten what it is to lose your sons?
Or see them coming back to you like this?
Allies or enemies, there's no distinction
In measuring the massacre of war.
Which are the minor questions, politics
Or human understanding and regard?
Are they the boundaries of land, of sea,
Or human hearts that pulse with love of living?"

11   ARMISTICE DAY REMEMBERED

The prompting goes on:

He pushed himself away;
It was a hurt to watch him,
Twisting the trunk
To give his shrunken limbs
The semblance of a motion.

320

His going charged the quiet of that place
With heaviness that knew no lessening.
The living city throbbed around me still,
Touched to warm color by the autumn sun;
The grass was barred and crossed with tender shade,
While falling leaves made amethyst the path;
Stored wisdom whispered still in Montparnasse,
In Notre Dame des Champs, the grace of faith;
But ever through it now I heard the plea,
Silent but no less fervent, of the maimed,
Who drag their heavy feet across its beauty:
"We stumble painfully along this weary road,
That you may hold the horrors of past difference
Forever blazoned on your memory.
You, who have within your careless hand
The power to save or slay men,
Look on us,
The tragic fragment of a harrowed past,
And keep them whole!
O, lay aside the shallowness of self,
Give all, take nothing
But a need to share.
Then, and not before, shall quarrels cease
And you will know the blessedness of peace."

12   THE SAME COIN

Happiness and sorrow are opposite faces of the same
golden coin. Experience is its inexorable mint. One is
only as deeply incised as the other, and the depth of the
incisure is measured by the values we cherish.

We should like to keep the coin always bright side up.
We shrink before the implications of its downward face.

We distrust our strength, reluctant to put it to the test, preferring to postpone the inevitable schooling.

Both faces must enter into the fullness and service of life.

We go trembling out of a warm room into the cold night, spinal column rigid, limbs and torso tense, teeth chattering. The body in resistance to the rigorous air denies its normal capable responses. Only the will to breathe deeply, rhythmically, naturally, will afford relaxation, release the diaphragm, bring freedom from the wretched shivering.

Cold and warmth are complementary manifestations of the body's climate; happiness and sorrow, of the spirit. Happiness and sorrow determine our ability to see with the heart.

Jesus felt happiness, suffered sorrow, and so identified himself with us. He enjoyed the warm hospitality of Lazarus' home. He wept when Lazarus died. He joined in the bright festivities of Cana. He felt the harsh blow of betrayal.

To follow that example in his experience, to welcome happiness and sorrow, to know through them identification with the race, is to know something of the sublimity of God.

13   BOTH TREE AND FRUIT

Happiness and sorrow are not moods. Moods pass. What we casually call happiness today may be compounded entirely of sunlight and warm food and laughter. Not to be passed over lightly. A neighbor's thought, a

gesture of kindness, a commending word, any one may
kindle the brightness of the day, enhance its glowing quality.

Make no mistake. Such days are to be prized. If we can
help to make them, that is our obligation.

But nightfall and solitude may dispell the mood. Friends
may seem to fail, commendation yield to sterner criticism,
a troubled mind deny the body's ease.

Likewise our seeming sorrow, mood-induced. Slights
which are magnified, suspected slurs, the "slings and arrows of outrageous fortune" may bruise us, blind us, tear
the frail protective covering of our ego until we seek outlet in self-pity, equally deadly whether silent or spoken.

But happiness and sorrow are manifestations of character. They are both means and end in its formation.
They nourish the tree of living and they are its fruits.

The Benedictine monks have always known how to
graft. Through their skilled ministration those twisted trees
at Boscherville have for generations borne apples on some
limbs, pears on others. The tree of living likewise yields
two fruits, but naturally, simultaneously, and equally rich
in flavor and substance.

We must partake of both.

14   **REAL UNION**

Happiness and sorrow are cumulative. Not in the im-
position of an oppressing load. Rather in the clarity, the
depth, the beauty of their revelation.

They push barriers away. They make clear the heights.
They bring the vast horizon nearer.

They are an open gateway to a world outside oneself.

Even as they surcharge the heart, the mind in fine co-operation points the way to the self's extension, to the expressive action which provides relief and thereby release and growth for the moved spirit.

Pent within, happiness, as sorrow, consumes, exhausts, corrodes. Freed, the sudden stream finds its compelling direction toward companionship, identification, union.

Of all its needs, the world needs union most.

Another's happiness I, too, have known. I know, for memory makes deep experience everlasting.

His sorrow, too, is mine and mine is his, for we are one.

15   EVER-CHANGING PATTERN

There is, it seems to us,
At best, only a limited value
In the knowledge derived from experience.

.   .   .   .

For the pattern is new in every moment.[1]

"The pattern is new." Unless the knowledge gained from experience is reconditioned in each new situation, it is a rigid and a dangerous guide.

Here is an affirmation, a new call to the mind and heart. As time permits no hiatus, as the physical universe has no point of fixity, so the mind and the spirit must be forever taut to the vital process of creating.

[1] T. S. Eliot, "East Coker," *Four Quartets*, Harcourt, Brace and Company, 1946.

Yesterday's formulas, as formulas, are outworn. Today's new pattern must have new interpretation. Experience, knowledge, hope, faith must be merged in a new synthesis which takes mind and imagination and prayer. The three are inseparable.

"The pattern is new." Sometimes the change is sudden and devastating. Sometimes it is serene and slow, so natural, seemingly so like the old that we fail to see it. Abundance and need reverse. Sickness and depletion seem to defeat. Ability finds its too small measure. Only the flowing stream of life is constant. Only its changes are unfailing.

To deny it, the ever changing pattern, is to hide our heads in the sand. To defy it is to battle life and time, invincible antagonists. To retreat from it is to know frustration where there might have been fulfillment.

It is no literary or dogmatic accident that Mary, bereaved of her great Son, becomes to all who ponder on her gentle spirit the symbol of the generous heart. Age knows the diminution of its powers, but it knows, too, the compensating balm of wisdom and nobleness and the realization of wholeness. Life amputates more than limbs. Readjustment, rehabilitation, reconstruction are our constant imperatives; courageous will, creative mind, aspiring spirit our means.

16   TIME

Time may be a bugbear, or it may be blessing.
It may take wings, or it may weigh like lead.
We misuse it, abuse it. Exhausting ourselves with much

busyness, we disclaim that we have it. But time is the first natural resource. It is an essential raw material. Among the gifts of the physical world its unvarying solar measures alone are equally bestowed.

Time is a river and our little boats its traffic. The still deep waters push hard against the oars and give us poise, power. Rocks and rapids try endurance, skill. Soft, light-flecked shallows provide pleasure. The stream and the scene have infinite variation.

Time has three tenses: yesterday, today, tomorrow, separate but inseparable. Each has its identity, its purpose, its value, but each is unmeaning out of sequence.

We are afraid of time for the reason that we are caught by its external processes, absorbed by its minor calculations. We miss the inner meaning which would calm the fear. We divide and subdivide, arrange, subtract. A year, a month, a week, and then the minute fractions of the day. Going, going, with seeming acceleration. The flight is final. We cannot hold it back. Our store diminishes. Our fingers cannot stay the advance.

But the flow is more important than the fraction. It is endless. It is of us. We are of it. The continuity of life, its greatest balm, moves through us and around us in time's stream.

To feel the power of time's continuing flow is to be comforted, to know calm instead of fear.

17   **THE RIVER**

Wrapped in torn shreds of mist, the winter day,
A shivering hag, so nearly spent, so old,

Would on my heart her clutching fingers lay
Bloodless as yellowed parchment, wrinkled, cold.

The plane trees stand in rigor, stripped of leaf,
Their stark boughs fixed like bones against the sky;
Bare buildings round me rise, dim halls of grief;
The chilling gust mourns dully, "All must die."

The towers of Notre Dame no longer gleam
Transformed by light into a rising prayer,
Grim sepulchers of ages rather seem,
Stone harbingers of those who once walked there.

Dim, faintly drawn against the sky of lead,
The penciled ribbing of the Pantheon's dome
Today speaks of naught else except the dead
Who spend their rigid night within its tomb.

Only the river moves, the ancient Seine,
Older and younger than the world it sweeps;
Bearing eternally a deep refrain,
Fighting this gray paralysis, it creeps
Into my heart; I sudden cast away
The clutching fingers of the death-like day,
To hear the moving truth I groped for long
Profoundly uttered in the river's song:

I am the living river. Tired? Yes.
But what in river's life is weariness?
Worn with the seething traffic that I bear,
These tethered wooden barges that I wear
Bruise my soft stream, cut cruelly my breast,
But at day's end in ocean there is rest;
Engulfed by it, I'll be content to know

I merge my shallows deep within its flow;
Lost? No. I am found forever
For as I pass I have been, I am
The river.

18   CHOICE IN MEMORY

The past is the tense of memory and art and wisdom. It is rich, rewarding. It furnishes us for today. In it we have built reserves of appreciation, of power. On it we draw for knowledge and nourishment and restoration.

Leaves are burning outside today, and the sweet, bitter smell brings back a child's thrill in the changing year.

Light sifting through the golden hickory trees. Nuts on the ground, pointed quarters of the hull curling to show the delicate ridges of the shell.

Branches bare against the sky until they catch for the moment the rare, soft mantle of snow.

Pale blue petals of the first Johnny-jump-ups in the new spring grass.

Warm summer scent of white clover, with the soft "zrrr" of the greedy bees, sucking the sweet.

Memory has its function of enrichment and of teaching. It is a book of many chapters, and we choose from them for rereading. Warped or embittered or egocentric, we might revert so insistently to negative experiences of the past that memory would offer imprisonment instead of freedom, impoverishment instead of wealth.

"You amaze me," said my mother to her four grown children as, gathered after long separation, half laughingly, half ruefully, we recalled the deprivations and the hardships of earlier days in a New England parsonage. "I don't remember those things at all. I remember only the fine and the happy ones."

There is the voice of wisdom, the will that chooses and rejects, the mind and the imagination that make life positive and rich.

19   THE BREADTH OF ART

Out of the memory-laden past comes art.

Art is the poignant record, fixed in fine form, of how man has tried and failed, climbed and fallen, stretched for the stars with fumbling hands, earth-fastened feet, caught, in spite of the limits of his finite quality, glimpses of his infinite source.

Rivera has done a simple portrait of a little Mexican girl, looking with enormous, solemn eyes at the world into which she has been thrust. Here is something more than representation. The head is far too big for the body, the eyes too big for the face, but the pathos is the pathos of all underprivileged, all misunderstood children. Into one child Rivera has put children.

Dvorak has caught in his *New World Symphony* the nostalgia of new Americans for the Old-World homes to which they would not return, but to which they are still tied by the heart, the nostalgia of the race in its sense of removal from its source. His homesickness is all homesickness.

St. Gauden's *Grief* speaks of the nobility, the dignity of all sorrow, the beauty of death.

In art the past particular transmutes itself into the

present universal. One grief becomes all grief, one joy, all joy. Art reaches out to every heart in warm embrace and healing comprehension.

20   WISDOM

Wisdom is a learned lesson of values, a disciplined ability of judgment, yet so broad and so tolerant that to associate with it such words as "lesson," "discipline," seems somehow to contradict its import. It is not so.

Consider grandmothers. Are they truly less exacting than mothers? Are their hopes less ambitious, their standards less high? Or, in the process of living, have they forged for themselves a truer scale of values? Have they not perhaps a finer confidence in the long result so that the minor setbacks, shocks, failures of today seem less significant, can be more tolerantly supported? May not the subtracted time between two generations give breathing space, provide a moment's chance to see from afar, to enjoy a perspective denied the closer view?

Wisdom sets great store by intention, less by convention. The one is related to character, to personality. It is deep-seated, educable. In it lies the promise of the future. The other belongs to the temporarily accepted mores of a group. It is fluid, impermanent.

Grandmothers have lived through the revolt of one generation against the imposed conventions of its predecessors and seen its impermanent quality. They accept mistakes with calm. Mistakes are human, inevitable. To help right them, to show how to right them, to encourage and to sustain, that is the wise function of living. Grand-mothers know it.

Patience, understanding, loving are wise antitheses to intolerance, misunderstanding, scorn.

21   BETWEEN AGES

Children have no consciousness of time. It is a bound-less provision like air and light and play. They accept and enjoy.

Natural, legitimate, right, the enjoyment of a gift.

Old people treat time with gentleness. The present is gracious. Quality transcends quantity. Today is a gem to polish and hold.

Wise to cherish a jewel, to enable each facet to catch the light.

Between the ages lies the danger zone, the desert of lost values. There it is that we reach with greediness for every satisfaction. To choose may mean to lose, and we shrink from the responsibility of choice, sacrificing serenity to strain, depth to drive, peace to push.

We are like travelers planning to go everywhere, scholars striving to know everything, politicians trying to please everyone, and all for the loss of a word. We cannot say No to ourselves.

There is no brighter symbol of the mind's true freedom than No. To lose it is to lose our sign of choice.

Opportunities, obligations, experience crowd the years between childhood's careless freedom and the earned quietness of age. What are the values we prize? What are the principles to which we give service?

To free ourselves from the pressure of unimportant things would relax strain, relieve worry, set free our power.

22   NEED OF CREATIVENESS

Today is only a point in time, the intersection of yesterday and tomorrow.

We move so gently out of the past into the present that the change is hardly discernible. Yet the change is constant, and only the creative mind can meet it.

In this moment which is now, the synthesis for the future must be achieved.

The future is for the young in heart. Numerical age has less bearing on that qualification than one thinks. There are young octogenarians and there are old people of twenty.

Tomorrow is made by those who dream, who have vision, which is constructive hope, and visions, foregleams of the finished plan.

"It is quite impossible," wrote Polybius two thousand years ago, "to make a good start in anything without in anticipation mentally embracing the completion of the project or realizing in what sphere and to what purpose and for what reason the action is perfected."

Tomorrow will be both new and old, but, however familiar its elements, they will exist in a new combination, in new quantitative proportions, with new qualitative significance. A new situation will pose new problems, exact new solutions.

23   BRIGHT WORDS

There rises before us one of those New England winters into which the Pilgrim Fathers put the heroism of their effort and the courage of their hearts.

A new world theirs and a new life. Freedom, justice, opportunity were the shining words which pointed to the future.

Must our times deny that hopeful prophecy?

The world is gray-faced with fear. Doubt hangs over it, a heavy mist. The anxious mind, hardly convalescent, reverts like a poor invalid to the nightmares of its sickness.

Where is reason, that tonic to depleted courage? Where is the sustaining sermon of the past?

The world is tired. Inevitable aftermath of the mad, careening journey into which we allowed ourselves to drift and to be drawn.

But, given patience, tiredness is cured. Given resolution, confusion yields to direction. Given faith, courage comes.

Pondering the lonely ocean they had braved, driven by forces they could not measure, beset by doubt and deprivation, the Pilgrims established our tradition of steadfastness.

In three hundred years the physical continent has been conquered. The next three hundred call for something far more difficult. We have ourselves to conquer.

Freedom and justice and opportunity are still the bright words of our future.

24   OUR FOREFATHERS

This was a promised land
To those grave Pilgrims who sailed out from home,

Preferring dangers of a world not known
To 'prisonment of spirit and of mind.
How many aching hours they must have strained
To catch the first glimpse of a rising sun
Upon a stalwart shore!
Sick with discouragement and out of heart,
Alone upon that turbulent expanse,
How tortured must their minds have been with doubt!
Was freedom worth the sacrifice of ties,
The loss of comfort and the tranquil ways
That seasoned modes of living ever breed?
What of their own capacities?
Achievement is so limited by time,
Would they live long enough to raise their homes,
To plant their seed,
To tame a wilderness,
By fixing in it faith,
And law,
Fair-minded and concerned
For all who constitute the governed,
And, against the future, learning,
Knowledge, the will to keep
Through time undying
The noble sum of what the race has done?
Doubt passed with night;
Came one bright day
They cleared the ocean mist
And saw the land:
Rock reefs stretched sturdy passage for their feet,
Green spires of forest laced the shining sky,
A hemisphere gave welcome;
Their courage answered it with deep conviction.

25   THANKSGIVING MEDITATION

We are those Pilgrims' sons;

.   .   .   .   .   .

Deep in our veins there flows
The course of that they willed us,
Unsparing and immortal.
Three hundred years have failed to dim
The brightness of their vision for the land;

.   .   .   .

There's nothing new in danger:
It is a constant,
As much a part of each man's journeying
As tides are of the ocean;
But only ignorance or mad caprice
Would disregard the tides—
Each crashing wave reverberates with battle,
Fogs thicken,
Unknown currents swell,
The sea bears threat of doom.
These rugged rocks that once were stands of strength
Today we vilify as hard and sharp,
Tearing the feet,
Their climb not worth the passing pain of effort;
Will yields to opulence,
And mind to ease,
Breeding dull idleness
And ultimate decay.

.   .   .   .

Like summer playboys on a pleasant sea
We loose our sails regardless of direction,
No mind to winds, no eye fixed on the sky,
To sight the fleecy omen of the squall,
Refuse to think beyond the moment's magic

335

Until the mad blow strikes.
Then while the green waves rise,
And the deep heaving swell
Sucks down our craft
Like a poor prawn
Caught in the claws
Of some great oscillating crab,
We scan our crew to find a sailor,
One who does not treat our sailing carelessly,
Who knows the rule of compass and of chart,
Studies the cloud,
Hears the full voice of ocean,
Who knows to reef and tack,
To fix the jib and to release the boom,
Who meets the coming storm,
Provisioned for its onslaught.

26   WE WORKERS

We must have leaders
Clear in thought
And sane in judgment,
Who never have forgot
The purpose of the Pilgrims
And the long charge they left us;
We must have leaders who stand erect before the door
Of time which stretches like a continent,
Self-pledged unto that vision of the future,
A future made for man,
Not nations, states, nor vast majorities,
But man, the race:
He must be free to educate his power,
Strong to his work, despising weariness,
Intent that every goal achieved

Shall serve the purpose of the total man;
Faith is one bulwark of the growing dream,
Belief in God,
However one conceive him,
And law
And learning are two others.
The future holds and draws,
The structure grows.
We workers hold the promise in our hands;
Working, we build the greatness that may be
When will is tempered by humanity.

27   PARADOX

"To give is to have."

Epigram or paradox, the ingenious phrase incloses a truth.

To give thanks is to have thanks. The Anglo-Saxon "thanc" meant "thought, favor, liking." To have thought of the things we like and by silent or spoken prayer to dwell upon them on this day will renew its moment, will restore its meaning.

It is the golden time of harvest. It measures the reward of plowing and planting and tending. It defines life in the beautiful symbol of earth and its yield. It is a moment to feast but in awareness of the meaning of the feast.

The simplest feast may be holy and rich by the spiritual quality which ennobles it. The richest may be barren and base in its heavy descent into gourmandism.

To give thanks is to think of blessings, and blessings are gifts from God. They are our mercies, our benefits, the sources of our happiness.

Blessings are the pattern of our lives; they should be the pattern of all—quiet beauties of the outside world; magnificent phenomena of nature, sunrise and sunset and starry nights, hills and valleys and plains as vast as oceans; the constant miracle of procreation, birth and growth and fruition; human relationships that do not fail, friendship and family, love and loyalty; work to be done that challenges every power; opportunity, need.

Tragedy, frustration, sickness are rare with us. We pledge ourselves to make them rare with others.

To give thanks is to have thanks. A thankful heart is a happy heart.

28 PROPER EQUIVALENCE

He is only four, but judged by the taut resolution of his will, he might be twenty. "Are you going to be cross on my birthday?" asked his mother this morning, as he objected to dressing.

"Is this your birthday, mother? Well, I'll tell you what to do. Put my clothes on the bed and tell me to put them on and, if I fuss, don't pay any attention."

In that instant the child was aware of his whole situation—compunction that his irritability should mar a day's perfection; acceptance of authority as a source of order in this world; relegation of ill-humor to the list of unimportant things.

Four years have made him aware of the conflict we wage—antagonism against co-operation, truculence against conciliation, mood against reason. Conventional reserve

has not yet stayed his outward turbulence. The will to be
well-considered does not modify his expression.

But he has a rare gift of understanding. His penetration
shatters any illusion of authority based solely on added
years.

Order, that balance between authority and freedom;
security that requires each member of a family to help
make its happiness; understanding that prevents the scud-
ding clouds of irritation from obscuring the sky's deep
blue—these are essentials of family living, and the child
recognized them.

Regard for personality is a two-way passage. Children
respect, parents consider, but respect and consideration
must move in both directions.

Then only will today and tomorrow, adulthood and
childhood, achieve their precious proper equivalence.

29   **KINDNESS**

An air age is an age for poetry, for the poet, like the
plane, may take the short highroad of the heavens for
his proposed journey.

Even an everyday rhyme may have a code of conduct,
a set of values, an unforgettable sermon, packed within its
brief extent. My mother used to say,

> Boys flying kites haul in their white-winged birds;
> You can't do that way when you're flying words.[1]

Not great poetry, but obvious truth.

[1] Will Carleton, *The First Settlers' Story.*

We were hard at it on the front seat of the car, with all the freedom of an intimate small group demonstrating its cleverness in the verbal vivisection of an absentee.

"She is so silly," said one.

"So slow," came the rejoinder.

"So lacking in chic."

"So satisfied with herself."

Suddenly from the back seat came the voice of a seven-year-old boy, "She is always agreeable."

It was the truth. We had forgotten it. She was always agreeable.

David never falsifies. He had heard our careless damaging remarks and had not been amused. He had weighed their import, considered their cruelty, and had studied in silence to find the courteous retort which would be the truth.

Such a gentle reproof from the lips of a little boy! Such a beautiful example of natural kindness, of innate consideration!

"She is always agreeable," implies much more than even the sturdy words seem to say.

30   AMERICAN WOMEN

Women of the United States have a greater obligation than any women in the world.

Why more than British women? Because we are less tired. Because we do not have the long list of things to forget which must rise with soul-shaking frequency to undo them. Why more than Chinese? Because we have never been hungry. Because we are Christian. Why more than Russian women? Because we have had for a hundred years the means to expression which they have had for only twenty.

Historians have assigned to women the role of conservers. We are creators as well. Women share in every creative process which centers in the group. We work creatively with foods, textiles, physical resources, but above all with human materials.

Who would say that women have not shared equally with men in reconciling differences, discovering aptitude, strengthening weakness, curbing arrogance, sustaining courage, stimulating achievement, healing hurt? If the theater of our operation has been limited, it has not been trivial or mean. If restrictions have fostered undue preoccupation with detail, their removal should enable us to see the whole and to relate the part to it.

The age-old sickness of mankind, dangerous to the death today, will find its cure only through the mind that can create, that can meet the new situation with a new solution, that can move and adjust and reconcile.

The responsibilities of her new, extended citizenship must challenge every thoughtful woman. The world's desperate need demands her full creative potential.

A New Government

LOUISE DUDLEY

1 A FORM OR A FORCE?

"Now when they beheld the boldness of Peter and John, and had perceived that they were unlearned and ignorant men, they marvelled; and they took knowledge of them that they had been with Jesus."

For all the Christian world the month of December is dominated by the birth of Christ. Sometimes we are so occupied with the good customs that have grown up with the celebration of Christmas, the sending of cards and the giving and receiving of presents, that we pay little attention to the real meaning of the day. So for this month we propose to use the coming of Christ as our central theme and in particular to ask ourselves what we expect of the Messiah.

Is the coming of Jesus to be to us a form or a force? Do we want to use religion for our comfort and convenience or for the glory of God? Do we expect to be made different, or do we expect to go on very much as we have been doing with maybe a slight improvement in matters that are not inconvenient? Do we expect to belong spiritually to the band that after the coming of Christ turned the world upside down? Do we, unlearned and ignorant though we are, expect that men will know by our boldness that we have been with Jesus?

2   EXPECTING THE GOOD

"Thou wilt keep him in perfect peace whose imagination is stayed on thee."

In Galworthy's play *Strife* one of the characters protests that he is a "humane man," and is answered scornfully, "There's nothing wrong with our *humanity*, it's our imaginations." In America today we might say the trouble is not with our humanity, but our imaginations. We know that people are starving in India, China, and Europe, that there is a great increase in juvenile delinquency, but we do not have any realization of what these facts mean. We do not have any image of them.

Moreover our images of evil are much more definite and concrete than our images of good. A mother sending her son away from home imagines the dangers he will encounter much more vividly than she does the opportunities for good he will have. In the United Nations we see the difficulties, the faults, and the petty jealousies much better than we do the amazing possibilities for future peace and unity.

How different would the world be if we Christians used our imaginations to picture the good.

3   **RELIGION TO ME**

I have tried to put down briefly what religion means to me. There are four points.

(1) *The certainty of power.* God is no longer a form or a fact, but a force. He is no longer a force which used to work in the time of the Bible or the time of my parents, not one which might work at some vague time in the future, but a force which is active today and now.

(2) *The assurance of guidance.* I am not left alone, but I can tap the great power of God in the conduct of my life, just as certainly as I can use the force of gravity.

(3) *The availability of peace.* I am not always at peace because I do not always follow the laws of God, but I know that I can find peace in God, and that I will find it if I am willing to pay the price, which is simply that I put God before myself.

(4) *Confidence in an overruling destiny.* This point is strictly contained in the first three, for what is true of one individual is true of the universe. This power covers and controls not only me and my affairs but all the corners of the earth, and from it no little bit of space or time is independent. I do not believe that all is right with the world or that events are to be wrought out to my satisfaction. God has elected to give man independence and power to make his own decisions, but God is still in control.

4   **THE HEAD OF CHRIST**

Rouault's painting, *The Head of Christ*, seemed at first glance to be merely a series of scratches. The class looked

344

at it and said, "Whew! Call that a painting! Anybody could have done that!" But as they studied them, the seemingly careless lines began to look like a face, a face torn and suffering. There are scratches from the thorns on the brow and on the face great welts as from a whip. Some of the wounds have bled, and the face is streaked and smeared with blood. The picture would be horrible were it not for the eyes which shine out clear and bright. When the question was asked, "What is the most prominent feature of the face?" the answer came as a chorus, "The eyes!"

"And what is the expression of those eyes?"

"Sorrow," "sadness," "suffering," the words came from all over the room.

"Why is he sad? Is he sorry for himself?"

And it was a Jewish boy who said, "No, he's sorry for the people who are doing it to him!"

5   DICTATORS

In the early days of the Hitler regime when enthusiasm for the new leader was at its height, a German widow was trying to calm her daughters, who were upset by the rumor that their pension was to be discontinued. "Have no fear," she said: " 'unser führer' will take care of us."

In much that we say about dictators nowadays we tend to forget that dictatorships rest upon a very human tendency, the desire to avoid responsibility, to trust someone else to do our thinking for us, to have someone to whom we can appeal if things go wrong, with the assurance that they will be set right. Our "führer" may be the president, the senator, the political boss, the news analyst, or a relative—husband, father, son. Whoever he is, we turn to him for guidance and rest satisfied in what he has to say, instead of thinking things through for ourselves.

Traditionally women are more guilty of this type of irresponsibility than men, or at any rate their dependence is more frankly assumed and openly recognized. "Now my husband says . . ." "Don't give this another thought, Mrs. Blank, I will attend to it for you."

Are we as women accepting our responsibility as members of our families, our communities, and our nation, or are we trusting some "führer" to look after us?

6   THE HARDEST WORK

If we are not to accept blindly the opinions of our "führers," we must form our own opinions; and we must accept responsibility for our conclusions and actions.

This is not easy; thinking is the hardest work in the world; and most of us will go to great lengths to avoid it. We will sharpen pencils and clean our desks. As mothers we will bake pies and wear ourselves out keeping the house clean rather than admit the problems of our adolescent children and try to answer them. As teachers we give long quizzes and spend countless hours grading papers rather than think about the subject to be taught, how it relates the student to her world or promotes her mental and spiritual growth. In short, we will do all kinds of busy work rather than sit down and face a problem, separate fact from opinion, habit, and prejudice, distinguish future from immediate, real from superficial value, and then come to the best conclusion we can reach at that time. But this is just what we must do if are to be responsible citizens in our democracy.

We shall not all reach sound conclusions every time. We shall not know enough; and we shall not judge relations accurately; but we shall be alive; we shall be going forward; and we shall be learning how to play our part.

7   ROOMS

There are, roughly speaking, three kinds of rooms. There is the room that is ugly. And there is the room that is beautiful. Then there is another type of room for which there is no name, for this too is beautiful though with a different type of beauty. Of the second room, we say it is beautiful and stop; but this third room rises up and does something to us; and we feel we are different. In this room we breathe more easily; we want to sit down and relax. We know that in this environment we can think our best thoughts and talk about them honestly and openly. It is a room where we can talk to the washerwoman just as freely as we can to the boss's wife, and it is a room in which she feels just as much at home.

There are also three classes of people. There are those who make no pretentions of goodness. And there are those who are good; they live honest, "good" lives, but that is all. And there are those others who make us want to be different; there is something about them that makes us know they have something for which we are hungry.

How is the third type attained? Of rooms we say with certainty the third room cannot be bought. The paid dec-

347

orator can make a room that is beautiful, but he can go no further. For the third room, two things are necessary. First we must know what we want. And second, we must be willing to work for it. And the same is true of people; there is no short cut to the ideal we have; we must know what we want and work to get it.

8   VALUES

A distinguished architect said recently that it was a comparatively simple task to design a house in which a woman could live the kind of life she wanted, if she knew what she wanted, but that most women did not know what they wanted.

An intelligent widow of forty, when asked what is the chief problem women need to face, replied, "It's the question of what to do with their lives. Women should plan what they want from life, and not just let life happen to them and make of them what it will, as I did."

A recent poll asked Americans, men and women both this time, what they wanted most, and the results were:

1. New car
2. New house
3. Clothes
4. Permanent peace
5. House furnishings

Do we as individuals know what we want? Have we rather vaguely accepted as desirable the goals of the crowd or the ends advertised on the radio and in the paper?

Fundamentally our ideas are sound. We do not really

think that world peace is less important than cars or clothes or houses. But we need to stop and consider on what we are spending our time, whether we really want the things we are working for, what kinds of lives we want to live, what values we intend to put first.

9　　　　　　　WHAT JESUS SAYS

Agnes, aged ten, and Charles, aged six, were playing hide-and-seek; Charles was rushing through the living room to escape Agnes who was hot on the trail, when he ran into the French door and broke half the panes of glass. Both parents were away from home, and at first the children could only weep at the enormity of their guilt. But they had been taught to turn to God in any time of crisis, and soon Agnes suggested that Charles ask Jesus what he was to do. "No, you go, Agnes, you go." So Agnes walked upstairs by herself, to return after a short time with the message that Jesus said Charles had not intended to break the door, and Father and Mother would understand that it was an accident. But all the time Agnes was gone, Charles sat on the bottom step weeping loudly and calling out every few minutes, "What does Jesus say, Agnes? What does Jesus say?"

How often have we all sat down and wept over some misfortune, while crying out to our pastor or counselor, "What is right? What am I to do?"

10　　　　　PSYCHOLOGY VS. RELIGION

The modern study of psychology has revealed to us much about the thoughts and habits of the human mind.

Through it we have learned to know ourselves and to control our instincts so that we are free and independent. And some would say, "Do we any longer need God?" For the modern, intelligent man or woman does not psychology do away with the necessity for religion?"

This argument, which is fairly common today, has two fallacies. The first is that there is any antagonism between religion and science, in this case psychology. All knowledge is of God. It is not knowledge against God, knowledge that shows us how to do away with God; it is knowledge God has given us about ourselves, which we can use as we wish.

The second fallacy is that if we know the laws of our own minds, we have all that we need for the governance of ourselves. In other words, it would assume that religion can go no farther than psychology. But religion does go farther. In God are power and wisdom. And God is not neutral or hostile; he is actively working for the right. In psychology you may be emptied of your faults; in religion God fills your mind with active energy to reach a new level of achievement. In psychology you rely on yourself; in religion you rely on God and join all the forces of the universe.

11   FREEDOM IN SERVICE

The first time I became aware of the great prayer which is used as the second collect in the order for Morning Prayer. I was a very green young teacher in an Anglican convent. Day after day I heard the priest read the prayer, "O God, who art the author of peace and lover of concord, . . . whose service is perfect freedom . . . ," while all before me were the nuns kneeling in their black robes. The phrase seemed incongruous, even nonsensical. These women were living under a most exacting rule, and their actions were regulated almost hour by hour. Where was the freedom? Pah!

As I grew older, I learned that freedom, far from being opposed to rule, can be found only in following rule. A child playing with ball and tennis racket is free to hit at any time and in any direction he wishes; the skilled tennis player accepts the rules of the game and finds a greater freedom. The man who wants to be absolutely free to eat and drink all he wants when he wants it soon finds that he is not free; if he wants to have free use of his body, he must follow the laws of health. The man who wants to be free of any restrictions in the moral and spiritual world learns that the badges of his freedom become the chains that keep him from doing the things he most wants to do. The man who is free to tamper with the truth is bound by his lie. Freedom is only freedom to discipline oneself, to find the law which makes for one's best growth, the law of God, whose service is perfect freedom.

12   GROUPS

One day Miss Markham came home to find Elizabeth very much distressed. Mrs. Jones had telephoned to ask some question and then had continued, "Who are you?"

"The maid."

"Are you a Negro?"

"Yes."

"Well, I never would have guessed it. You have such a nice voice. It's as refined as a white person's."

There is a story of a high government official who had a long conference with a Chinese general about matters of grave importance to both the United States and China. When the conference was over, he put his arm around the Chinese and said, "Don't worry, General. We'll get the affairs of these Chinks settled."

Neither of these people meant to be unkind, much less insulting. Each was feeling very friendly; but he was so firmly intrenched in the group he belonged to that he saw other groups as different and therefore inferior. North—South; Harvard—Yale; black—white; American—foreign; army—navy; capital—labor; Baptists—Methodists; Jew—Gentile; we live too much in narrow groups and forget that people are just people, no matter what group they belong to.

13   DIRECTIONS

The theologians of the mediaeval church listed seven deadly sins—pride, anger, envy, avarice, gluttony, lust, and sloth. There is a clear connection between them in the order in which they are listed. If our pride is hurt, there is a tendency for us to hit out at others in anger or envy, or both. When that does not bring satisfaction, we try self-indulgence. We reach out for more money than we need, more food than is good for us, more satisfaction of physical hunger. The end result is an inevitable sloth—the sense that nothing matters.

The way to treat hurt pride is not to indulge ourselves,

but to face ourselves, to see where we have been wrong, and then move out to help others. The sequence then becomes humbled pride, appreciation of others, service to the needy, self-denial, and a deep sense of inner peace and the rich significance of living.

14   IN SIMPLE TRUST

Matthew tells that two young fishermen were mending their nets one day in the boat with their father when a new teacher passed by and called them. "And they immediately left the ship and their father, and followed him."

Centuries later another young man saw slaves being sold in New Orleans; and resolved that if he ever got a chance to fight slavery, he would hit it and hit it hard.

In the light of history and legend these decisions seem simple and clear. We see the results and know the choices were wise. James and John were two of the disciples closet to Jesus. Abraham Lincoln freed the slaves of America. In his case we can learn details of his life, the changes in and strengthening of his resolve. In the case of James and John we are told nothing of the fears and misgivings they may have had, the taunts and jeers from friends and neighbors and relatives. But in all three instances they kept to the road they had marked for themselves in simple faith, with single-minded integrity, knowing that the thing they had seen was true and right.

In simple trust like theirs who heard,
    Beside the Syrian sea,
The gracious calling of the Lord,

353

Let us, like them, without a word,
Rise up and follow Thee.[1]

15   **THIS IS THE WAY**

Yet he your Teacher never leaves you now;
you see your Teacher for yourselves,
and when you swerve to right or left,
you hear a Voice behind you whispering,
"This is the way, walk here." [2]

But, one objects, how can one know? History and legend have approved the faith of James and John, and of Abraham Lincoln. But there have been many others who have gone forth just as honestly and just as sincerely of whom history has not approved. What of them? We are faced with definite situations in which we must act or refuse to act; how can we know whether the voice we hear is of God or not?

There are certain checks which will occur to anyone.

Does the decision in question conform to my own highest standards? Does it follow the teachings of Jesus? Is it honest? Is it selfish? Am I profiting by it? How does it affect other people? Does it help or hurt them? Is it kind? loving?

Does it conform to accepted law, custom, authority? These usually have good reasons for their existence, and one should know and reckon with them. Often God's will is to go in the face of custom and authority; it was so with

[1] John Greenleaf Whittier.
[2] Isa. 30:20-21. From *The Bible: A New Translation* by James Moffatt. Used by permission of Harper & Brothers.

James and John, and Abraham Lincoln. But just the same we should know what these forces are and how we are going against them?

What do our friends say? It is good to get advice both from those who are in sympathy with the decision and those who are not. Best of all is the friend who will let us talk and by asking us questions help us to clarify our own motives and decisions.

Discussion with friends, consideration of law and custom, testing of our own highest standards help us to clarify our ideas. They help us to see a decision for itself and in all its implications, but no one of them nor any combination of them can take the place of the inner light. If there is any question, any doubt, we should wait. If we try to push a decision, we may cause disturbances that will take years to straighten out. We must wait for God's time.

In affairs of the spirit, the only sureness is the inner conviction, the inner certainty that what we propose is right, the Voice that whispers, "This is the way, walk here."

16   OF PROOF

We believe in God, but we wish we could have proof. We look back on the stories of direct divine intervention in the affairs of men with a certain longing. We almost wish we did believe that God would strike a man dead if he told a lie, or save an innocent women if she were thrown into the fire. We would like proof. But what is proof? Seriously and reverently, what proof can we expect?

The proof of God is interior, of the heart and soul. In this respect, knowledge of God is like knowledge of all the other great things of earth—love, wisdom, beauty. No one can prove that the music of Bach or Beethoven is beautiful, but we know. There is no external standard by which we can measure the wisdom of Shakespeare or of Socrates, but we know they are wise, and we learn from them. No one can prove love between husband and wife or even between mother and child, but we know that it is the greatest force in the world. We know without external proof. In the same way we know the truth of religion, not by external proof but by an inner certitude.

Furthermore, proof in any area of knowledge comes from patient following of the laws of that type of knowledge. If we want proof of the laws of chemistry, we must follow the laws of chemistry. If we want proof of the greatness of Bach or Shakespeare, we must follow the laws of art. In the teachings of Jesus we have the laws of religion, and if we will study and follow them, we shall have proof of God.

17   HAPPINESS

"I am come that they might have life, and that they might have it more abundantly."

In the preface to *Man and Superman* Bernard Shaw says, "This is the true joy in life, the being used for a purpose recognized by yourself as a mighty one; the being thoroughly worn out before you are thrown on the scrap heap; the being a force of Nature instead of a feverish selfish little clod of ailments and grievances complaining the world will not devote itself to making you happy."

This definition of happiness cuts across the average

young person's hopes of a white house by a stream, remote from any outside disturbing force. The average girl wants the novel to end, "And they married and lived happily ever after." The movie version almost invariably ends that way. American women have come to think of marriage as an institution which is aimed to give them happiness. If it doesn't, they complain before the judge and try another marriage, and our divorce courts reveal us as "feverish little clods of ailments." What would happen if women were determined to be used for purposes they recognized as mighty?

What would happen if nations gave up their feverish selfishness and stopped demanding that they be made safe and rich? What would happen if we demanded of our statesmen a foreign policy which commits these United States to a policy of being "thoroughly worn out" in a purpose recognized as a mighty one? Real, deep joy never seems to go with preserving the *status quo* and watching to see where our little life is hampered in its little pursuits.

18   AS IT IS

Ned was a very devout old man, but he loved to eat, and once when hog-killing time came, he ate too much of the fresh sausage, pork tenderloin, and headcheese. When he was suffering from indigestion in consequence, he began to fear there was something wrong with his spiritual development, and he prayed long and earnestly about the state of his soul. His wife looked at him quizzically and said, "I hate to see Ned worrying the Lord so long when all he needs is a little saleratus."

Anyone who attempts to grow in the spiritual life is bound to meet setbacks from time to time. The first step is to be realistic about the situation, to see the trouble as honestly and as fairly as we can. It may have a physical cause—we ate too much; we sat up too late; we are nervous. Underneath these physical symptons which need temporary treatment there are usually spiritual causes which must be diagnosed and cured. Why did we sit up too late? Where was the demand in that self-indulgence? It is essential to face such very real spiritual failures and recognize them—our feelings were hurt; our position was challenged; our prejudices were aroused.

Accurate diagnosis is not a cure, and it is painfully difficult—but it is a necessary step in allowing God to work a cure.

19   VIRTUOUS VICES

Mrs. Smith is one of the finest people I know—sincere, honest, loyal. She would never consciously compromise with any of her ideals. Moreover, she is willing to fight for what she knows is right, as she has proved many times. The most conspicuous case was that of her husband. He was a drunkard; but she would not let him go; she worked with him until she brought him back to a life of decency and sobriety. From these experiences she carried away very naturally a fear of the evils of drinking and a hatred of them. There grew up also a sense of satisfaction in what she had done, of conscious probity. By degrees, however, her hatred of drinking and her self-conscious virtue have formed a wall round her until outsiders can hardly get at the real woman inside the fence, if indeed she is still alive.

Our greatest vices are often very close to our greatest virtues. We are intelligent; we have brains and education; we stand for the best in the community; soon we begin to feel superior, to be proud that we are different. We love our children; and we want them to have the best; then we try to shield them from the dangers of the world; and we end by wanting to keep them for our pleasure and our comfort only. We may be proud that we are good housekeepers and the house is always clean; or we may be proud that we are not finicky about the house and people can be at home with us without fear of making a little dirt.

If we want to grow, we may well start examining the unpleasant aspects of our most cherished virtues.

20   HATRED

A French woman of distinction lost her husband and son at the time of the German invasion. As she and her daughter moved to the comparative safety of southern France, she discovered that she could no longer pray— her hatred of the Germans who had done this to her and to her family was too great. She tried to think of Christ's praying, "Father forgive them, for they know not what they do"; but she said that she couldn't believe that they did not know what they were doing.

One morning when she was trying to recapture her faith and the sureness of God's purposes, an idea startled her into new life. Like a direct command from God came

359

these words, "Stop hating the evil and hate the good
which was not strong enough to defeat the evil." From that
point on she and her daughter, who had been good women of a privileged class, moved on to a new level of action and thought. They assumed responsibility for building
up the morale of the people they were with and for giving
them a sense of destiny in the creation of a France strong
enough to withstand evil.

How many of us are good women who are not effective?
How many of us busy ourselves with good works but do
not know how to come to grips with forces of evil? Is
it because we never consciously come to grips with evil
in our own lives, see it for what it is, and see its relation to a
moral laxness in our nation? To the little boy's prayer,
"God, make the bad people good, the good people nice,"
we may add, "and make the good women effective in
their united action."

21   THE SINGLE EYE

An Oxford don was trying to explain to an American
friend the secret of the extraordinary effectiveness of one
of our great religious leaders, "He gets in his own way less
than any person I know."

Most of us get in our own way; we want to do a certain
kind of work or to be a certain type of person; and we
fail, not because of other people or outside circumstances,
but because of something within ourselves. We are divided; we are not unified; our eyes are not single; we are
not free.

Sometimes we get in our way because we have not made

a clear cut decision as to where we want to go, and like
the man in the story we try to go in all directions at
once. Sometimes we get in our own way because we are
not willing to subordinate, or if need be to eliminate, other
interests. We know our destination lies due east, but we
carry too much baggage, or else we stop with a friend on
the way.

Here again there may be a serious conflict, as when our
baggage represents material security or old, established
prejudices. The rich young ruler could not give up his
wealth. A young labor leader had a terrific fight with his
prejudice against capitalists before he could bring himself to put on a dress suit. Or it may be just a matter of
attention, like the man in Luke who wanted to follow
Jesus, but who saw no harm in stopping to say good-by
to the folks at home.

My only enemy is myself.

22   COME AND SEE

A young Norwegian physician wanted certain qualities
of mind and spirit which she saw in her friends. They
had peace while she was confused and divided in mind
and upset; they had purpose in contrast to her own sense
of futility; and they had joy in their work. On inquiry she
learned that they ascribed all these characteristics to God,
but that gave her little help because she did not herself believe in God. But they were so sure of their belief that
after a time she set out to experiment, to find out for herself if there is any God.

Being trained in science she set up a hypothesis: If there

is a God, he would have these characteristics; and I would expect him to make himself known to me in these ways; and if he spoke to me, he would expect me to obey. In order that she might be exact, she kept a notebook of her experiment.

The first message which seemed as though it might be from God had to do with her brother. She had wronged him; and she should apologize. His response seemed more than human, even God-inspired, but she wanted to be sure, "This may be only a coincidence; I will try further." Evidence piled up as to the reality of God; whenever she obeyed, God seemed to be at work at the other end. No scientist belives in a succession of coincidences, and before long she came to her friends with her eyes shining, "This is not a coincidence; I know God."

Philip's answer to Nathaniel's skepticism about the Messiah was "Come, and see," and it is still the answer. It is foolish to accept hearsay when we can know.

23   DEPENDENCE

A teacher in the Middle West was left alone when she about thirty years old. Her sisters were all married with families of their own, and her sense of loneliness took the form of dread of being dependent on them. So she scrimped and saved, studied investments and securities, annuities and pensions. "At least," she said to herself, "if I ever have to go live with any of them, I can pay my way!"

Then God became a reality to her, and religion a force, not just a form. And she began to change her point of view. "Where is your security?" she asked herself. "Is it

in God or your bonds?" And again, "What if you have
only money to give? Peter and John had no gold or silver,
but they did give health and life. . . . Your sisters are
kind; and they love you; is it only pride that is in your
way?"

At last she gave up her dread of being dependent. But
the acceptance of the idea that she might go to live with
her sisters as a pauper if need be was one of her most
costly decisions. And since that decision she has not been
a slave to money. Money has become a servant, not a master.

One of the hardest lessons many of us have to learn is
just to give up, to learn to take. We may be missing a
chance for peculiar blessedness by our unwillingness to be
dependent.

24   ON SOVEREIGN RIGHTS

"Unto us a child is born, . . . and the government shall
be upon his shoulder."

> Our sovereign rights with crown and scepter gleam
> In irony beside a crib, a babe,
> And wise men guided by a star's clear gleam
> As they bring gifts of gold, their hearts not weighed
> With leaden fear. Our chosen rulers dread surprise
> From weapons we have forged—we who are wise—
> So wonderful in seeing just as far
> As shines a crown! Come measure in light-years
> The wisdom of that babe beneath the star.
> He lived to show us that our fears
> Are not from God, a God of power, a God

Who sets us free from narrow selves. Release
Us, Lord, to think with Thee of neighbor's sod.
Thy sovereign love we bow to, Prince of Peace.[1]

25   CHRISTMAS DAY

"And it came to pass in those days, that there went out
a decree from Caesar Augustus, that all the world should
be taxed. (And this taxing was first made when Cyrenius
was governor of Syria.) And all went to be taxed, every
one into his own city. And Joseph also went up from Galilee, out of the city of Nazareth, into Judaea, unto the
city of David, which is called Bethlehem; (because he was
of the house and lineage of David;) to be taxed with
Mary his espoused wife, being great with child. And so
it was, that, while they were there, the days were accomplished that she should be delivered. And she brought
forth her firstborn son, and wrapped him in swaddling
clothes, and laid him in a manger; because there was no
room for them in the inn."

"I salute you. . . . There is nothing I can give you which
you have not got; but there is much, that, while I cannot
give it, you can take.

"No heaven can come to us unless our hearts find rest in
it today. Take heaven. . . . No peace lies in the future
which is not hidden in this present little instant. Take
peace.

"The gloom of the world is but a shadow; behind it, yet
within our reach, is joy. There is radiance and glory in

[1] Marjorie Carpenter.

the darkness, could we but see—and to see, we have only to look. I beseech you to look.

"And so, at this time, I greet you . . . with the prayer that for you, now and forever, the day breaks and the shadows flee away." [2]

26   THE REALIST

"Because he knew all men, and needed not that any should testify of man: for he knew what was in man."

Two of the favorite words of today are "real" and "realistic." Young people especially want to be hard and practical, to know the world as it is, not to be deceived. And the phrase, "Now to be realistic," is usually preface to some remark about the frailties and imperfections of human nature.

Jesus was the greatest realist the world has ever seen. There is no instance on record where he was disappointed in a person or disillusioned. When the rich young ruler came to him, he saw at once the weak spot and sent him away. He knew that Peter could not be trusted to stand by him at the crucifixion and told him so. *He knew what was in man.*

And yet because he was a true realist he did not despair of man. He saw good as well as evil, and he was no more deceived in the real good than in the appearance of good. He knew that Matthew, the tax collector, would arise at once and follow him, and that Zaccheous, though rich and a publican, would not love his wealth at the expense of his

[2] Ernest Hargrove. Copyright, Quarterly Book Department. Published by the Yale University Press.

service. And he trusted Peter with the last command, "Feed my sheep."

Jesus does not expect us to be sentimental idealists or disillusioned cynics, but realists.

27   PROVING ONESELF RIGHT

Did you ever try to imagine the expression on the face of Jesus when he straightened up and found himself alone with the woman taken in adultery? You remember that the scribes and Pharisees brought her to him, citing the law of Moses which said she should be stoned; and that Jesus had said, "He that is without sin among you, let him first cast a stone at her," and had stooped over and written on the ground.

Certainly there was no surprise on the face of Jesus as he raised himself up. He knew the men there would not be able to stand the accusation of their own conscience. Nor was there any self-congratulation. He knew they had brought her to him only to test him, and he had outwitted them again. Most of us would have been pleased with ourselves and a bit cynical about these great upholders of the law! But Jesus was not interested in proving he was right. He was only interested in the human being before him.

"Where are those thine accusers? hath no man condemned thee?"

"No man, Lord."

"Neither do I condemn thee: go, and sin no more."

The person who is sure has no need for self-congratulation. It is only when we have been doubtful that we want to prove we were right. And if we get interested in proving we were right, we may win the argument and lose the sinner. It does not matter how clever we are in outwitting our enemies, the only thing of importance is the human need.

28   RESISTANCE TO THE NEW

More important than good resolutions in these days of dramatic and basic world change is our consideration of our resistance to change. Such resistance is natural, for we have to adjust to the unfamiliar. We feel secure with the familiar. We look at a contemporary piece of art and say, "How silly!"; years later the same work will be easily understood because it has become familiar. It takes real effort of the will to work at trying to understand the new. It takes a desire to change to say quite simply, "I do not understand that now; but I should like to."

If we are to have more than a scientifically new world, people must learn how to be open to new truths and strange facts and unfamiliar groups of people. New people make a new world; that means that we, too, may have to become quite new. Watching for resistance to change in ourselves is a daily necessity if we are to accept the greatest of all promises: "A new heart also will I give you and a new spirit will I put within you."

Rigid examination of the points of view we hold, the virtues we cling to in ourselves, the little "indulgences"— "sins" in others—we grant ourselves is essential if we are to become new. Above all, there has to be an allegiance to a new purpose which is big enough to give us the moral energy to open our hearts and minds to new people, new ideas, and a new self which will be adequate for the demands of the scientific and physical forces newly let loose in the world.

29   NEW IDEAS

"Be renewed in the spirit of your mind."

Ideas which we resist may be of the type which stretch our credulity. The man who stood in front of the giraffe and said, "I don't believe it; there is no such animal" is very understandable in the light of our increasingly common experience with such phenomena as radio, atomic energy, and rocket planes. Only exposure to evidence which we cannot deny can make us accept such wonders.

Ideas which we resist may be of the type which irritates our inherited points of view. Most of us assert most loudly and underline most vigorously the statements of belief which we have not thought out for ourselves but which we repeat polly-parrot fashion. If we watch for one day the number of remarks which we make with no real conviction of experience behind them, we can begin to realize that it may be stimulating to listen to others' opinions and then sift for ourselves the evidence that will bring us to a genuine conclusion. Acting on the best we see at the moment brings clearer thinking than arguments which bandy about angry remarks unbacked by any living. Most of us talk in half-truths; and we need to add the other half of the truth on to our own corner of insight. Then we need to act on the combination. We can act our way to new levels of understanding—either about Russia or peace in our own family; we can seldom do more than rational-

ize our way to a selfish fragment of truth if we sit down
for so-called thinking which intends no step of action.

30   NEW PEOPLE

People seem strange to us if they come from a group
whose political, religious, sectional, or economic backgrounds have given them different points of view. The first
reaction in most of us is to bounce back like a rubber ball
from the antagonistic or opposite type, and to cling like
a sponge to the people like ourselves. There is a third relationship which God's purposes make imperative. Christ
dramatically exemplified it. The electric current that
charges the atmosphere whenever some people are near us
is the best analogy for a relationship which is really creative.

Electric currents work best when opposites meet. Somewhere in the process the best emerges with a force which
surprises us with the possibilities in ourselves and the other
people. This could happen when manager and workman
meet together to see what new and positive purposes
could be intended in God's world for any single business
or industry.

The current is short-circuited when we begin to lump
people into little labeled piles of "management" and "industry." The spark for new ideas and new productivity is
set off when two individuals are intent on tapping God's
power for the greatest good to others. The man and woman who care deeply about the future of a child can
change from the waste action in the "rubber ball" rebound
to the "electric charge" of energy which sets free the best

in each person to plan for a third good more important
than the selfish demand of either husband or wife.

31   **OF THE FUTURE**

As Christians we believe in God and in our redemption
through Christ. We know that we have received much
from God, not just physical possessions, but peace, the
power to find good in evil, the power to face life bravely
and courageously. This we have found in the past, what
do we expect of the future?

Do we expect from God more than he has ever given
us before? Are we looking forward to what God can do
with and through us, or are we holding back? Can we
honestly say that God is more important to us than anything else in the world? Do we reach every day on tiptoe
wondering what God will have for us on that day, and
ready to take the next step, whatever that may be? Do we
expect God to show us our part in the work of our town,
our nation, our world? Do we expect him to show us what
to do about juvenile delinquency, racial prejudice, education, housing, care of the sick, the starving peoples of the
world, the United Nations? Do we expect that the God of
peace will make us "perfect in every good work to do his
will, working in [us] that which is wellpleasing in his
sight"?

WHAT CONSTITUTES A YEAR THAT'S NEW?

Not just spiced punch, gay cards, and a din of noisy bells,
But close-felt sharing of the problems that unite
The men of every race, a plan, a pact that tells

Just where and how we mean to hold each other up,
To split the ego, release energy, the power
Pent up in every man and needed in this hour
Of panic and despair. First, we must drain the cup
Of truth, a bitter draught, this knowledge of ourselves.
With it we pledge the charter for a world that's new.
Inspired by crib and star, we move to sound the bells
That promise joy, real joy. We pledge to join the fight
Along with those who care to build a year that's new.[8]

[8] Marjorie Carpenter.

ABERNETHY, JEAN BEAVEN: Born in Rochester, New York, in 1912, Mrs. Abernethy is the daughter of the late Dr. A. W. Beaven, president of the Colgate-Rochester Divinity School. Her husband, Bradford S. Abernethy, is Chaplain and professor of the English Bible at Rutgers University in New Brunswick, New Jersey.

Mrs. Abernethy graduated Phi Beta Kappa from Mount Holyoke College in 1933 and has also studied at Oxford and Edinburgh. She received her Master of Arts degree and completed residence for work on her Doctor of Philosophy degree from the University of Missouri. She has taught, written, and lectured widely, and is at present a member of the Commission on the Home and Marriage of the Federal Council of Churches of Christ in America.

The Abernethys have three children—David, Billy, and Barbara. Their house in the middle of Rutgers University campus is the scene of constant student gatherings.

DOW, BLANCHE HINMAN: Dr. Dow—poet, author, translator—is a member of a teaching family. Her father, a New Englander, alternated between Baptist parsonages in Massachusetts and the presidency of Baptist colleges in Missouri; her mother retired in 1944 after twenty-six years as teacher of English in the Liberty, Missouri, high school. Blanche Dow did her undergraduate work at Smith College, her graduate work at the Sorbonne and at Columbia University, from which she holds the degree of Doctor of Philosophy in French. Between schooling periods she received a diploma from the School of Expression, Boston, and played for a year with the Garrick Players, Washington, D.C.

She is the author of a published study on the *French Attitude Toward Women in the Fifteenth Century* and has just made an English translation for Professor Gustave Cohen of the Sorbonne of his recent book, *La Grande Clarté du Moyen Age.*

Her articles and informal essays have appeared in many magazines. Since 1931 she has contributed verse to *The Catholic World.* She is at present chairman of the department of romance languages at Northwest Missouri State Teachers College.

DUDLEY, LOUISE: Dr. Dudley, a native of Kentucky, is now teaching in Stephens College, Columbia, Missouri. Her father was a Baptist minister and, for twelve years before his death, president of Georgetown College in Georgetown, Kentucky.

After receiving her Bachelor of Arts degree from Georgetown College, she took her Doctor of Philosophy degree from Bryn Mawr College in 1910. She taught at several colleges and served one year with the Y.W.C.A., working in the French munitions factories during the first world war, before joining the Stephens College faculty.

Dr. Dudley has published *The Study of Literature* and, with Austin Faricy as coauthor, *The Humanities.*

JOHNSON, JOSEPHINE: Miss Johnson was born in Kirkwood, Missouri, in 1910 and attended Washington University in St. Louis. She has written many short stories and articles, and painted pictures and murals. Several of her stories were included in the O'Brien and O. Henry short story annuals. She is also the author of several novels—*Now in November, Jordanstown, Year's End, Winter Orchard, Paulina Pot,* and *Wildwood. Now in November* was a Pulitzer Prize winner in 1934.

She is married to Grant G. Cannon, field examiner for the National Labor Relations Board. They have two children, four and seven years old, and they live at present in Covington, Kentucky.

OVERSTREET, BONARO W.: Mrs. Overstreet, an authority in the fields of adult education and psychology, is a native of California, and after attending the University of California, taught in the Kern County Junior College. Since her marriage to Harry Overstreet in 1932 she has worked with him in adult education all over the country—teaching, conducting workshops, carrying on various researches, and lecturing.

She is a member of Town Hall Club, Pen and Brush, the Authors' Guild, the American Association for Adult Education, and Phi Beta Kappa. She is also on the advisory editorial staff of the *National Parent-Teacher* magazine.

Her latest published works are *Freedom's People* and *American Reasons.*

PIERCE, EDITH LOVEJOY: Mrs. Pierce, who was born in Oxford, England, in 1904 of Canadian and American parents, spent most of her life before marriage studying and traveling. In 1928 on the way home from a summer visit to Canada, she met the Chicago lawyer whom she married in Oxford the following year. They came to Evanston, Illinois, to live. Their daughter, Mary, was born in 1931. Later Mrs. Pierce became an American citizen.

Her poems have appeared widely in magazines and newspapers, and she has recently brought out two volumes of poetry—*In This Our Day* and *Therefore Choose Life.* She has also done a translation from the French of Philippe Vernier's devotional book *With the Master.*

ROHLFS, RUTH SWANBERG: Mrs. Rohlfs has lived in Seattle, Washington, all her life except for a few years in Southern California. She attended the University of Washington and Union Seminary, and did both office and religious group work until her marriage to Marcus Rohlfs ten years ago. Since that time she has served as president of the National Business and Professional Council and Assembly of the Y.W.C.A. and as dean and faculty member of numerous youth assemblies and conferences, attending two world youth conferences.

She is at present working as a member of the National Board of the Y.W.C.A., president of the University of Washington Y.W.C.A., advisor of the Chinese Baptist Youth Fellowship, and as a member of numerous committees and boards related to religion, social work, and community welfare.

SHAW, MAUDE ROYDEN: Dr. Shaw is a native of England and received her education at Lady Margaret Hall, Oxford. She edited the official paper of the National Union of Women's Suffrage Society, *The Common Cause;* served as assistant pastor at the City Temple, London; and has traveled around the world lecturing in the cause of international peace.

She has received numerous honorary degrees, among them the honorary degree of Doctor of Divinity from the University of Glasgow—an honor only once before given to a woman.

Dr. Shaw is the widow of the Rev. Hudson Shaw and is now living at Sevenoaks, Kent, England.

TAYLOR, ELIZABETH WRAY: Mrs. Taylor, who was born in Rochester, New York, in 1904, graduated from Mount

Holyoke College in 1925. She received her Master of Arts degree from the Union Seminary and Teacher's College and soon after married Thomas Madison Taylor. She has done work as a student Y.W.C.A. secretary at the University of Rochester and lived for three "intensely exciting" years at Oak Ridge, Tennessee.

The Taylors are now living at Kingsport, Tennessee. Their three high-school-age children are Connie, Tom, and Julie.

TERLIN, ROSE: Miss Terlin—who is executive editor of the Woman's Press, the publishing house of the National Board of the Y.W.C.A.—graduated from the University of California, where she did both undergraduate and graduate work in the fields of economics and literary criticism. She was Secretary for Economic Education of the National Board of the Y.W.C.A. and for more than two years was a member of the staff of the World's Student Federation. In connection with this work she attended the Oxford Conference on the Life and Work of the Churches and the World Conference of Christian Youth at Amsterdam.

She has traveled extensively in Europe and the Far East. Her writings include many articles for magazines and a number of important monographs.

THURMAN, SUE BAILEY: Born in Pine Bluff, Arkansas, Mrs. Thurman took degrees from both the college and conservatory departments in Oberlin College. She served for four years as national student secretary of the Y.W.C.A., before her marriage to Howard Thurman.

She is the founder and honorary editor of the *Aframerican Women's Journal*. She also established—through the profits of her lectures on India, where she has traveled extensively—the Juliette Derricotte Memorial Foundation.

At present she is chairman of the World Fellowship Committee San Francisco Y.W.C.A. and a member of the board of directors of the San Francisco International Institute. Her husband is minister of the Church for the Fellowship of All Peoples in San Francisco.

WHITE, HELEN CHAPPELL: Mrs. White is the daughter of Dr. E. B. Chappell, for many years Sunday School Editor of the Methodist Episcopal Church, South, and the wife of President Goodrich C. White of Emory University.

Her older son, Goodrich, Jr., a young musician of promise, was a combat aviator in World War II and was killed in action late in 1944. The younger son, Chappell, also a former combat flyer, is at present a student in the graduate school of Princeton University.